The Long Schoolroom

POETS ON POETRY

DAVID LEHMAN, GENERAL EDITOR

Allen Grossman *The Long Schoolroom*
Jonathan Holden
  Guns and Boyhood in America
Andrew Hudgins *The Glass Anvil*
Carol Muske *Women and Poetry*

A. R. Ammons *Set in Motion*
Douglas Crase *AMERIFIL.TXT*
Suzanne Gardinier
  A World That Will Hold All the People
Kenneth Koch *The Art of Poetry*

DONALD HALL, FOUNDING EDITOR

Martin Lammon, Editor
  Written in Water, Written in Stone
Philip Booth *Trying to Say It*
Joy Harjo *The Spiral of Memory*
Richard Tillinghast
  Robert Lowell's Life and Work
Marianne Boruch *Poetry's Old Air*
Alan Williamson *Eloquence and Mere Life*
Mary Kinzie *The Judge Is Fury*
Thom Gunn *Shelf Life*
Robert Creeley *Tales Out of School*
Fred Chappell *Plow Naked*
Gregory Orr *Richer Entanglements*
Daniel Hoffman *Words to Create a World*
David Lehman *The Line Forms Here*
  · The Big Question
Jane Miller *Working Time*
Amy Clampitt *Predecessors, Et Cetera*
Peter Davison
  One of the Dangerous Trades
William Meredith
  Poems Are Hard to Read
Tom Clark *The Poetry Beat*
William Matthews *Curiosities*
Charles Wright *Halflife · Quarter Notes*
Weldon Kees
  Reviews and Essays, 1936–55
Tess Gallagher *A Concert of Tenses*
Charles Simic *The Uncertain Certainty*
  · Wonderful Words, Silent Truth
  · The Unemployed Fortune-Teller
Anne Sexton *No Evil Star*
John Frederick Nims *A Local Habitation*

Donald Justice *Platonic Scripts*
Robert Hayden *Collected Prose*
Hayden Carruth *Effluences from the*
  Sacred Caves · Suicides and Jazzers
John Logan *A Ballet for the Ear*
Alicia Ostriker
  Writing Like a Woman
Marvin Bell *Old Snow Just Melting*
James Wright *Collected Prose*
Marge Piercy
  Parti-Colored Blocks for a Quilt
John Haines *Living Off the Country*
Philip Levine *Don't Ask*
Louis Simpson *A Company of Poets*
  · The Character of the Poet
  · Ships Going into the Blue
Richard Kostelanetz
  The Old Poetries and the New
David Ignatow *Open Between Us*
Robert Francis *Pot Shots at Poetry*
Robert Bly *Talking All Morning*
Diane Wakoski *Toward a New Poetry*
Maxine Kumin *To Make a Prairie*
Donald Davie *Trying to Explain*
William Stafford
  Writing the Australian Crawl ·
  You Must Revise Your Life
Galway Kinnell
  Walking Down the Stairs
Donald Hall *Goatfoot Milktongue ·*
  Twinbird · The Weather for Poetry ·
  Poetry and Ambition · Death to the
  Death of Poetry

Allen Grossman

The Long Schoolroom

LESSONS IN
THE BITTER LOGIC OF
THE POETIC PRINCIPLE

Ann Arbor

THE UNIVERSITY OF MICHIGAN PRESS

A CIP catalog record for this book is available from the British Library.

Library of Congress Cataloging-in-Publication Data

Grossman, Allen R., 1932–
      The long schoolroom : lessons in the bitter logic of the poetic
      principle / Allen Grossman.
            p.   cm.
      Includes bibliographical references (p.   ).
      ISBN 0-472-09637-0 (cloth). — ISBN 0-472-06637-4 (paper)
      1. Grossman, Allen, 1932–   —Aesthetics.   2. American poetry—
      History and criticism—Theory, etc.   3. English poetry—History and
      criticism—Theory, etc.   4. Poetics.   5. Poetry.   I. Title.
      PS3557.R67Z47   1997
      811.009—dc21   96-29634
                                                                    CIP

ACKNOWLEDGMENTS

"The Language of the Present Moment" originally appeared in James
Wright's "The Language of the Present Moment" from *Above the River*
Copyright © 1990 Wesleyan University Press by permission of Univer-
sity Press of New England.

"Skeleton Fixer's Story" originally appeared as Copyright © 1986 by
Leslie Marmon Silko, from *The Delicacy and Strength of Lace,* reprinted
with the permission of the Wylie Agency Inc.

Contents

My *Caedmon:* Thinking about Poetic Vocation   1

Orpheus/Philomela: Subjection and Mastery in the
Founding Stories of Poetic Production   18

Milton's Sonnet "On the Late Massacre in
Piemont": The Vulnerability of Persons in a
Revolutionary Situation   39

The Poetics of Union in Whitman and Lincoln: An
Inquiry toward the Relationship of Art and Policy   58

Hart Crane and Poetry: A Consideration of Crane's
Intense Poetics with Reference to "The Return"   85

The Poetry of Robert Lowell   130

The Jew as an American Poet: The Instance
of Ginsberg   150

Jewish Poetry Considered as a Theophoric Project   159

Nuclear Violence, Institutions of Holiness, and the
Structures of Poetry   168

Holiness   179

Fragment of an Autumn Conversation between
Allen Grossman and Daniel Morris on the
Question of Another Logic   189

My *Caedmon*
Thinking about Poetic Vocation

There stood beside him a certain man in a dream and bade him
God speed, and calling him by his name said to him: "Caedmon,
sing me something!"

Bede

I walk through the long schoolroom questioning

W. B. Yeats

I

I first put myself to school, in "the long schoolroom" of the
poetic principle, when I began reading with the intention of
making poems—in 1951 (I was nineteen), on a hot August
morning (in my memory, it is always 11 A.M.), in a rural public
library in Colorado: bright, cleanly smelling of wax. The essays
that follow (selected from thirty years of writing about poetry)
are some account of the lesson I learned there. I learned the
lesson; it determined my way of work as a poet. But, today, it
seems to me that these various writings of mine had when writ-
ten, and have now, no other purpose than to inquire whether or
not that first lesson was also the last, whether there are more
ways of work by poetic means than only this one.

Derived in part from "The Calling of Poetry: The Constitution of Poetic
Vocation and the Recognition of the Maker in the Twentieth Century,"
which originally appeared in *TriQuarterly* 79, (fall 1990), a publication
of Northwestern University.

But firstness is not, in any case, a characteristic of experience. What I speak of as "first" experience is very likely the supply of terms for many experiences that came before the "first" one: in fact, a sequence of first experiences collapsing backward toward the beginning of conscious life; and, then, backward again to the beginning of the world; and then, at last, to the great receptacle of all there is—the figure of no beginning.

Every signifier of "first experience," such as "creation" or "vocation," is also a figure of the forgetfulness of no beginning (as in "bright," "cleanly," "smelling of wax"). In these essays, I read the experience of vocation backward from subsequent recurrences of that "first" lesson in the bitter logic of poetic practice, toward these questionings of that bright morning in the long schoolroom.

I have never—for whatever reason—made a distinction between the schoolroom of the poetic principle and the schoolroom of the life-forms of the civilization in general. They are the same workplace and I have worked in them the same and do still.

I entered the schoolroom as a student (in the late '40s and early '50s, after World War II) thinking that violence had erupted into the schoolroom and the civilization it maintained *from the outside,* and ruined its fully known right form. I returned to the schoolroom as a teacher (in the '60s) to discover that the violence we deplored was not from the outside, but *from within* the civilization, and indeed very likely from within representation itself. And that there is no outside to representation.

In what light, then, have I read and still do read poetic vocation (*my* Caedmon)? I do so in the light of the discovery that the main thing I had been taught in the schoolroom was untrue. By a schoolmaster who nonetheless made an impossible demand: "Sing me something," he said. But I knew no songs.

The only response to an impossible demand ("say something," "sing me something," "sing") must be a false response, an evasion (there is, after all, no doing the impossible). The only logical compliance to a demand for a text that does not exist is to fail (one way or another—there are lots of ways to fail) to produce the required song; but, then, by intricate strategies of resistance and flight, to succeed in producing something else—the only response that is really wanted, the text that is not a text—the poetic text.

All life is thinking about vocation. Vocation is not merely a "first" instance, a beginning of the appointed work. Vocation is all there is. But whether the first lesson is the final lesson is, still and always, the question.

The public library I speak of supplied me with standard histories of English literature, including English poetry. All accounts of English poetry began with Bede's story about Caedmon, the first poet in English who has a name ("Caedmon"), and a poem (his "hymn"), and a story (his life story that begins with his vocation, in old age, and ends with his death). I was reading that morning to see how poetry comes to be.

My intuition was then, as it is now, that valid poetry comes to be only when the man or woman with work to do has exhausted all means other than poetic for doing the work that needs to be done. As if poetic work always remembered a state of affairs in which the necessity of social appearance (life or death) could be obtained by this means and no other. And among exhausted means it is always poetry itself that must be mastered, changed— and overcome.

Fortuitously, then, that library moment of which I speak—my first entrance into "the long schoolroom"—presented me with the Venerable Bede's account (in all its particularity) of the making of the first poet: Caedmon, a sceptical peasant, illiterate (throughout his life), and hitherto ignorant of songs in any language, who began Christian poetry in English—that is to say, began in fact British *and American* poetry—by singing, in a dream, a praise poem to the maker of the human world, strictly the impossible text: an account of an action that cannot be witnessed, creation—an exploit also that cannot in any practical sense occur.[1]

This is how *The Oxford Anthology of English Literature,* these days, translates Caedmon's seventh-century poem, itself a translation, on its first page of text:

> Now must we praise of heaven's kingdom the Keeper
> of the Lord the power and his Wisdom
> The work of the Glory-Father, as he of marvels each,
> The eternal Lord, the beginning established,
> he first created of earth for the sons
> heaven as a roof, the holy Creator.

> then the middle-enclosure of mankind the Protector
> the eternal Lord, thereafter made
> for men, earth, the Lord almighty.

And this is how Bede's Latin paraphrase of the same Caedmon poem was translated by the sixteenth-century Catholic translator of Bede's *Ecclesiastical History of the English Nation:*

> Now ought we to praise the Maker of the heavenly kingdom,
> the power of the Creator and His counsel, the acts of the
> Father of glory; how He being God eternal, was the author
> of all miracles; which first created unto the children of
> men heaven for the top of their dwelling places, and
> thereafter the almighty Keeper of mankind created the earth.

But this is how (except for my use of modern letters) the Anglo-Saxon scribes of Bede's *History* heard the poem, and wrote it in their vernacular, beside Bede's Latin paraphrase in the margin or at the end of their manuscripts of Bede's Latin text.

> Nu sculon herigean heofonrices weard,
> metodes meahte and his modge thanc,
> weorc wuldorfaeder, swa he wundra gehwaes,
> ece drihten, or onstealde.
> He aerest sceop ielda bearnum
> heofon to hrofe, halig scyppend;
> tha middangeard moncynnes weard,
> ece drihten, aefter teode
> firum foldan, frea aelmihtig.

II

Caedmon, a seventh-century peasant, as the story tells us, ran away from the social firelight when a song was demanded of him, a song of the kind men sang at their ease, in the language (Anglo-Saxon) of their nation. Caedmon ran away because *he had no such song and had never had a song of any kind.* But later that night he began (impossibly) to sing in a dream.

He composed his precisely impossible poem, the precise work of which he knew himself incapable, asleep, in response to a second, mysterious demand by an unnamed (male) person *(quidem)* of indeterminate cosmic status—angel? demon? muse? pagan? Christian?—"Caedmon, sing me something" *(canta mihi aliquid)*.

Caedmon was commanded by someone in a dream to sing something. Confessing himself unable to think what or how to sing, he was directed to sing, in his dream, "the beginning of the creatures." And he did so. Upon awaking, in the presence of persons of authority in the monastery (Whitby) where he worked, Caedmon *remade,* again on demand, his poetic text. Then the abbess (Hild) of the monastery and her elders took council; and (after the fact) they authorized Caedmon's vocation. And they claimed it. That is to say, they abolished by decree the indeterminacy of Caedmon's calling, identified the unidentifiability of Caedmon's vocational master (demon? angel?). Suppressed, in Caedmon's exemplary case, the inherently indeterminate ideological destination (demonic? angelic?) of the imperative to do poetry.

In its kind or genre, Caedmon's hymn is a "praise poem" ("Now must we praise"/"Nu sculon herigeon"). In that respect, it is like Genesis 1, which recounts as praise the characterizing action ("creation") of the hero whose name is covered over by the expression "my lord" *(adoni).*

Caedmon's "hymn" is sung, impossibly, by a singer who knew no songs and could not sing, about a (likewise) unknown Lord, master of first making who did the prototypal impossible thing (that is why he is remembered and praised)—which was not however, as in Judeo-Christian text (Caedmon, of course, would have known the Creeds), precisely to make something out of nothing. Rather, Caedmon's "Wuldorfaeder" is praise-worthy because he constructs out of existing materials a house for human beings, and donates it to their keeping.

III

The translation of Bede's *Ecclesiastical History,* as I found it in Colorado in 1951, was a 1930s revision of a translation (from Bede's Latin into sixteenth-century English) made in 1565 by Thomas Stapleton at Louvain. Stapleton presented it to Queen

Elizabeth, daughter of Henry VIII, for the purpose of summoning her back to the true Catholic religion of the nation. Here is some of it.

> For as long time as [Caedmon] was settled in secular life, until he was well stricken in age, he had not learned any songs. And so it was that sometimes at the table, when the company was set to be merry and had agreed that each man should sing in his turn, he, when he saw the harp to be coming near him, would rise up in the middle of supper and, going out, get him back to his own house.
>
> And as he did so on a certain time, and leaving the house of feasting had gone out to the stable of the beasts which had been appointed him to look to that night, and at the fitting hour had bestowed his limbs to rest, there stood beside him a certain man in a dream *[adstitit ei quidem per somnium]* and bade him God speed, and calling him by his name said to him: "Caedmon, sing me something!" ["Caedmon, . . . canta mihi aliquid."] Whereupon [Caedmon] answering him said: "I know not how to sing; for that is the reason why I came out from the table to this place apart, because I could not sing." "But yet," quoth he again that spake with him, "you must sing to me." "What," quoth he, "should I sing?"
>
> Whereupon the other said: "Sing the beginning of the creatures!" At which answer [Caedmon] began immediately to sing in praise of God the Creator *[Dei Conditoris]*, verses which he had never heard before, of which the sense is this: "Now ought we to praise the Maker of the heavenly kingdom, the power of the Creator and His counsel, the acts of the Father of glory; how He, being God eternal, was the author of all miracles; which first created unto the children of men heaven for the top of their dwelling place, and thereafter the almighty Keeper of mankind created the earth." This is the sense but not the selfsame order of the words which he sang in his sleep: for songs, be they never so well made, cannot be turned of one tongue into another, word for word, without loss to their grace and worthiness *[decoris ac dignitatis]*. Now on rising from slumber he remembered still all the things that he had sung in his sleep, and did by and by join thereto in the same measure more words of the song worthy of God.
>
> And coming on the morrow to the town administrator under whom he was, he shewed him what gift he had received; and being brought to the Abbess, Hild, he was commanded in the

presence of many learned men to tell his dream and rehearse his song, that might by the judgement of them all be tried what or whence the thing was that he reported. And it seemed to them all that a heavenly grace was granted to him by the Lord [*caelestem ei a Domino concessam esse gratiam*].

Bede's narration continues until Caedmon's death in old age, which Caedmon foresees. He was made a monk, declared "a clean beast," and sang the Christian story, as it was taught him, in Anglo-Saxon language and prosody.[2]

The work of poetry, whatever else it may get done—to whatever other purposes it may be directed—intends to bring the world to mind as a depiction, and then to give it away to an institution (Hild's church is an example) that regulates its powers, that is to say, assigns meanings, reasons for credence. But the discourse of poetry is not ever identical, nor is the depiction it affords, with the ideology of the institution that supplies its grounding. The master in Caedmon's dream (a certain man) is neither a muse nor is he an angel, and Caedmon's Lord is not the Judeo-Christian God.

The poetic principle requires institutions (*religious* poetry is normative in our civilization), but also by its nature always escapes or exceeds them. In this sense, the poetic principle is more like sanctity, which is prior to all institutions that mediate it, than it is like civil order, which is inscribed upon order of another kind. (Cf. chap. 9 below, "Holiness.") Caedmon's hymn is, as Bede professes, not precisely translatable "without loss to [its] grace and worthiness."[3]

IV

The story about vocation is one part of a whole master-story: the story of the maintenance of the intelligibility of the human world by symbols—the "long schoolroom." In the story, the symbols that effect the maintenance of intelligibility obtain their stability in history because they are grounded in an axiomatically nonhuman "first" reality. The master-story about vocation says that nonhuman reality continually calls certain persons, alienating them to its purposes, burdening the world with the recognition (poetic knowledge) that identity requires memory of transcendental relationship. Vocation is—as Yeats put it—the story of a civilization's struggle for self-control, or a person's. That is why poems are always found in the school of the secular nation, promulgating poetry's bitter lessons (Horace's "Regulus" ode is, perhaps, the archetype), and why also within the poem there is another school and another schoolmaster that supplies the truth of the lesson.

Let us express this structure of *the whole story*, of which the story of the vocation of Caedmon is an instance, as a quadrature of stations or callings, all *four* of which—the whole story—are always present whenever there is a valid poem. The story is roughly speaking a double story, told once as a story about the relation of the person to the transcendent other (e.g., Caedmon's dream), and then told a second time about the relation of the person, thus alienated by transcendence, to the immanent or social other (e.g., Caedmon's presentation of his powers upon demand to Hild).

1. The *first calling* narrates the summoning of the self by deep, unconscious memory (however named) of the human world, including memory of its making "as from the above"—which means (at very least) from the outside of history considered as life consciously remembered by individuals. At the first calling (the story about Caedmon's genesis-type "hymn" is, of course, our example), the voice that is not the voice of a person, not human, constitutes the person as a singer or poet, invents the human voice. "Singing" theatricalizes speaking, the action by which the person is acknowledged as such in the social world. "Singing" displays as social performance the origination from outside the social world of the recognitional action by which we know one another. Thus, a singer (i.e., the constituted person) mediates between the collective and the individual—that is, figured, let us say, as the divine and the human.

The singer, the poet, is authorized to repeat, as I have said, the founding of the collective as it is grounded outside the social. In this sense, poetry is always theologic, where the *theos* (the god term) is the principle of that necessary generality of discourse on the grounds of which social relation is based. As such, however, poetry effects a claim on the person that reinvents a person or culture at the expense of the legitimacy of an alternative claim, which may be precisely the claim of the (psychological) self. In Caedmon's example it is of course the native culture that shines through the Judeo-Christian appropriation. This separation of the self and its desire (at best, desire is the other of poetic work) from poetic work and its destinations is written over and over again, both as a civilizational inevitability, and at the same time as violence against excluded alternative discourses or outcomes of discourse. (Cf. the scribal marginalization that I have noticed of the Anglo-Saxon text of Caedmon's hymn.)

Discourse, like consciousness, is built—and made strong—by distinction. Such is the "bitter logic" of poetic practice actualized as violence—the violence of religion, race, class, and gender all driven by the engine of distinction—which representation, nonetheless, requires.

Vocation brings to mind the structure of poetic identity. What is a poet? *The poet is the person who, by reason of the calling, is committed to do his or her human work within the logic of the calling, that is, the logic of representation of the poetic kind.* And everyone is a poet. There is only vocation where there is significance. And that is what I meant when I said that "vocation is all there is."

Poetry means, to put it crudely, the context-independence of the person, whose right of presence is not a contingency of history alone, and is in many respects inimical to life itself. This strangely guarded and endangering empowerment, this "bitter logic" of which life and death are weak signifiers, is the principle subject of this book.

The logic of vocation, especially evident in the first calling, is analyzed in the familiar founding stories of Western poetic practice, and I study it as such (chapter 1, "Orpheus/Philomela"). And it is the disfiguring theme of the American lyric. (Cf. chapter 4, "Hart Crane and Poetry" and also chapter 5, "The Poetry of Robert Lowell.")

2. The first calling is structurally external to the poem. By contrast, the *second calling* is structurally internal to all genres of

poem except lyric. Conventionally, we speak of the second calling as "invocation," always a calling back toward the source of the first calling ("Sing, muse . . .").

The stream of poetic speaking arises, as I have indicated, from a source outside of speaking, in the first calling from the above and the outside: "Caedmon, sing me something." When the poet thus called begins to speak, his speaking, like all speaking, is always an answering back in the stream of speaking—because the beginning with speaking is not a power of speaking.

Why, then, does the speaker in the poem begin speaking? The speaker in the poem begins speaking with the *intention of reconstituting* the validity of speaking—in which consists the intelligibility of the world—by calling back to the origin of his speaking. More specifically, the motive of speaking in the poem often appears as the question of the justice of God (the "theodician" question). Speaking in the poem is driven by consciousness of the inadequacy to experience of the received (institutional) account of the world. In short, the speaker in the poem is moved to begin speaking by the failure of God to make sense. The poem is the last recourse before despair. This state of affairs is studied in chapter 2, "Milton's Sonnet, 'On the Late Massacre in Piemont.' "

Milton's sonnet is programmatically the enraged counterpoem to Caedmon's hymn of praise to the God who built a world that protects human beings. Milton's poem commands the God (on pain of not being God—for being God requires the praise of the poet) to remain worthy of praise, that is, to protect worthy persons and thereby to make sense once again.

> Avenge O Lord thy slaughtered saints, whose bones
>   Lie scatter'd on the Alpine mountains cold,
>   Ev'n them who kept thy truth so pure of old
>   When all our father's worshipp't stocks and stones
> Forget not: in thy book record their groane
>   Who were they Sheep and in their ancient Fold
>   Slayn by the bloody Piemontese that roll's
>   Mother with Infant down the Rocks. Their moans
> The Vales redoubl'd to the Hills, and they

> To Heav'n. Their martyr'd blood and ashes sow
> O're all the Italian fields where still doth sway
> The triple Tyrant: that from these may grow
> A hundred-fold, who having learnt thy way
> Early may fly the *Babylonian* woe.

Milton's poem demands justice from God not obtainable in history. This I take to be in general the reason in any poem for the speaker to begin speaking. But the bitter logic of representation is prior even to God.

It works, as I will show at some length, like this: the requirements of justice—for example, the Reformation (Cromwellian) extension of representational privilege—are paradoxically obtained by disabling the symbolic ground of the intelligibility of experience, that is, by killing the king. This state of affairs produces Babylon, which only divine violence can obliterate—thus restoring intelligibility but destroying also the newly acquired (scarcely realized) visibility of large regions of the human world.

3. The third and fourth versions of the fourfold narrative of vocation repeat the first and second. But "transcendence" now discriminates (in the secular repetition of the vertical dialogue of vocation and invocation just discussed), not the above and the beneath, but, in the horizontality of the secular world, the social self and the social other.

The *third* vocational moment is the address by the poet speaker to the human world, which hears or overhears the poem. This is the schoolroom moment, the moment of dissemination and instruction, of the paideia. As I have observed, the poetic principle requires institutions and is claimed by institutions. But also exceeds and escapes them.

My premise in these essays is a commonplace: the manifest world (the only one there is) is subject to the logic of representation because it comes to mind only as representation. And representation, our only access to world, reproduces its hierarchical and exclusionary structures as social formations. The poem is the site on which originality is expressed as the attempt to discover alternative structures of intelligibility that do the work of representation in another way. The central paper in this book (chapter 3, "The Poetics of Union in Whitman and Lincoln") undertakes to examine the question that the Caedmonian vocation raises and represses, "whether there are more ways to work than only this one." Whether there is a closed Lincolnian way of work, or system of order: tragic, Aristotelian, and rational. And *also,* by contrast, an open liberational Whitmanian way of work that escapes the bitter logic of hierarchy and exclusion that accompanies difference-based, thick representations of tragedy and can deliver actual social formations capable of comic, integrated outcomes.

My conclusion is that, on the evidence of actual poems (Whitman's being the example), there is in fact only one strucure of representation. In any case, talk about style (largely binary in character; open/closed, informal/formal, proprietary/communitarian, extensive/intensive, etc.) does not reach to the bottom of the matter.

4. The *fourth calling* is the calling by persons in history back to the poetic principle that magnetizes attention, filled both with *hope* and *recrimination.* This is the impossible demand addressed to the poet, not by the god this time but by the "children of earth." Such is the interrogative "stare" of the schoolchildren in Yeats's "long schoolroom," which unendurable look says to the poet: Old man, sing me something that makes a difference. Hence, "I walk through the long schoolroom questioning."

This final recourse by persons to poetry will keep on forever whether there are any new poems (or likelihood of poems) in the world, or not. The interest in "poetry"—that is, the poetic principle, precisely, of course, nonidentical with poems—is riveting because of the the implicit promise (which my analysis may be seen to revoke or turn) of secular techniques of negotiating the violence within discourse, which means renegotiation of the relation between the individual and the collective. But this is, in short, the essential "impossible" demand: "Sing me a new song."

Paradoxically, there is a disposition to appeal to the poetic principle, when it is thought that the regulation of violence posed by new access to force (for example, nuclear) requires redemptive cultural discontinuities, such as can produce the final counterforce of mind to mind and be the residual other to all ideologies.[4] Chapter 8 below, "Nuclear Violence, Institutions of Holiness, and the Structures of Poetry," addresses the likelihood of a good outcome to this enormous requirement.

"Exemplarity"—the example of examples—is one way of talking about how the poem, as failed response by its nature, accomplishes social work. A poem is like an example. Why? Because an example is always other than what it explains, as a poem is always other than the impossible work that it replaces but shows what such work will be like. In Caedmon's subjected pagan world, the Christian account of the Jewish God, of which Caedmon's hymn is a parodic repetition, offers a logically higher abstraction and therefore a more general model of social formation than native Anglo-Saxon narrative. Yahweh governs by reason of greater abstractness a larger domain. Greater, however, than the abstractness of the God is the poet who tells of it.

Or the poem is like a translation, because translations are always bad translations. The Caedmon "hymn" is a bad translation of the founding text, Genesis, of the Christian institution that it is claimed by Hild to serve. Indeed, Bede observes, as we have seen, that "songs, be they never so well made, cannot be turned from one tongue into another without loss." The margin of aberration that translation of the poetic text always introduces into the account of omnipotence is an instance of the regulative inadequacy of which I speak. In chapter 9 ("Holiness") I argue that the text of the Jewish God (fundamentally inimical to representation) is perhaps the most persuasive model of a solution to the fatality of representation that civilization in the West presents. Therefore, I conclude with an analysis of the category of which God is a member.

V

Before the inevitable journey no man
shall grow more discerning of thought
than his need is, which is to contemplate before
his going hence what good or evil will
be adjudged to his soul after his death-day.

Bede's "Death Song"

Tradition assigns the Venerable Bede a "Death Song," in Anglo-Saxon. The doctrine that this song promulgates is "religious ignorance," ignorance that is religious because it restricts valid knowledge to the distinction between the good person and the bad person. The value of a life depends on action. And there is no action acknowledged as significant by God other than person-making, in accord with institutionally sanctioned criteria (good or bad). In this sense, the religious vocation and the poetic vocation are regulated to the same end. Both constrain mind to the discipline of presenting the well-formed image of the person. Poetic vocation, however, presents the calling of the person to the poetic kind of this making as inherently interrogative (subject to question) because the criteria of the goodness of poetic making are never fully instituted—subject to claim, and never fully claimed.

Stories are told, Caedmon reminds us, about how the world was made. "In the beginning, God created heaven and earth . . ." But how "God" was made is not part of the story in Judeo-Christian culture—indeed, is not a story. It is this secret of God that the poet knows.

In Judeo-Christianity there is no story about the making of the world-maker. It is a secret that even the professional possessors of secrets—sages, priests—do not know. In the Creeds of the Christian Church the hiddenness of the making of God is doubled upon the unknowness (or holiness) of sexual reproduction: Christ is *begotten* like a person, not *made* like a world. By contrast, the making of the (poetic) maker is rendered mysterious, but it is told—as in Hesiod's *Theogony,* or Whitman's "Out of the Cradle" ("Now I know what I am for"), or in the story about Caedmon. First he is not a singer and then, as a result of a dream, he becomes a singer.

The story about "poetic vocation" contributes the significance of the person whose business is, subsequently, significance. It is always a story about the calling of—the assignment of significance to—a person who has previously been without it (Whitman, "My tongue sleeping" or Caedmon, "I know not how to sing"). Thus the story about poetic vocation remembers the moment before the signficance of the person and requires, as a principle entailment of the idea of making, or poiesis, wakeful encounter with the inevitability of unmaking.

Poetic vocation always remembers the moment before the calling, before the making of the maker, but not I think before the making of the maker's discourse, which is the condition of the knowability even of making. There is, I am sure, a valid sense in which everybody makes herself or himself—but subject, surely, to the radical outsideness of meaning to the human world, and subject also to the resistance of materials. For that reason, inquiry into the making of the poet is like the inquiry into the making, impossibly, of every woman or man, and discloses something about the making of the person altogether. The making of persons, like the making of the worlds persons know, refers in any case to a possible state of affairs. There are both persons and worlds, though there once was not.

But the analogy of world making and person making depends on the likeness of the two actions, and that likeness rests in the *impossibility* of producing in either case the difference between the not-being and the being of the world as an act of the autonomous will. *Creativity* (since the eighteenth century) names precisely the production *per impossibile* by persons of persons or worlds or poems. In what schoolroom is the doing of that thing taught? No one has been present at the doing of it. Most gods, in fact, cannot accomplish the making of either persons or worlds. For example, Zeus cannot, nor any member of his family. Yahweh can make worlds (but only this one) and persons (but just those), only by reason of the Semitic theologic of absolute difference (and therefore perpetual exile) from the world he makes.

As I understand poetic vocation (*my* Caedmon), poetic vocation is like world making and person making in that it is both possible and impossible: possible in fact—there are, as I say, both persons and poems—but strictly, logically, materially, as a matter of deliberation, *impossible*—destined to fail. The poet is the artisan (the skilled worker) whose work it is to tell of this state of affairs. Poetics accordingly (in which the story of vocation is a theoretical moment) is the science of the weight and implications of the resistance that produces not any world but just this one.

Much effort is directed at the present time toward the construction of some account of a valid human world without the socially divisive principle of transcendental difference. The story about Caedmon's vocation, which I take as normative, asserts that there is no strictly secular poiesis. Among "the lessons in the bitter logic of the poetic principle" that amplify but do not contradict the first lesson in the sunny library is a particular sense of the word *bitter*. *Bitter* is the sentiment of undecidable conflict, between the will to (re)build the human world, and the resistance to alternative (heterocosmic) making inherent in the materials of which any world must be composed.

In this matter, poetics is the bitter (not the gay) science—the science of the resistance of materials to the will that intends other making. The truth may be contrary to our liking, especially when it is poetic. But, in the long schoolroom of the poetic principle, the only question put, worth the inevitability of failure, is: Why are things as they are, and not another way?

NOTES

1. It appears to be the empirical case that "praise" is the prior kind of all Western poetries. The *Iliad* is the praise poem (epideictic) of Achilleus, as Genesis is of Yahweh. Cf. Gregory Nagy, *Pindar's Homer* (Baltimore: Johns Hopkins University Press, 1984).

2. What in fact the dream supplied Caedmon was not a story (he would have known the story) but a prosody—more precisely, the imagination of the application of Anglo-Saxon prosody to the Roman Christian subject. Angels understand prosody. Cf. "According to Fuller, some say a dunce-monk, being to make [Bede's] epitaph, was nonplussed to make that dactyl which is only of the quorum in the hexameter [i.e., to find an appropriate Latin word to supply the dactyl in the fifth foot without which you don't have a dactylic hexameter], and therefore at night left the verse gaping, 'hic sunt in fossa Bedae . . . ossa,' till he consulted his pillow, to fill up the hiatus; but returning in the morning, an angel (we have often heard of their singing, see now of their poetry) had filled the *chasma* with *venerabilis*." Quoted in Bede, *Historical Works* (Cambridge, Mass.: Harvard University Press, 1994), 1:xxi–xxii.

3. See Jeff Opland, *Anglo-Saxon Oral Poetry: A Study of the Traditions* (New Haven: Yale University Press, 1980), pp. 117–18: "One might argue simply that Caedmon's poems were didactic and leave it at that; or one might care to argue that in attempting to arouse action in his audience . . . Caedmon is performing one of the functions of the hypothetical tribal poet . . . and note that Caedmon's inspirational poetry is produced in praise of God, exhorting his hearers to loyalty and obedience to him just as the tribal poet serves to arouse in his audience loyalty for the chief or king he serves. . . . The dream inspiration to produce poetry, as has frequently been noted, is hardly unusual, but is

common to poetic traditions throughout the world. To the analogues of the Caedmon story—stories of Mahomed, the Helian poet, Hesiod and many others—I could add more from the Xhosa and Zulu speaking peoples in South Africa. . . . In other words, it may well be that in Caedmon we have the first Anglo-Saxon to extend a native tradition of eulogistic poetry in praise of chiefs and kings to poetry in praise of God." Cf. G. A. Lester, "The Caedmon Story and Its Analogues," *Neophilologus* 48 (1974): 225–37.

4. Cf. Wallace Stevens in *Adagia:* "If the mind is the most terrible force in the world, it is also the only force that defends us against terror. Or, the mind is the most terrible only force in the world principally in this, that it is the only force which can defend us from itself. The modern world is based on this *pensee*. . . . The poet represents the mind in the act of defending us against itself."

Orpheus/Philomela

Subjection and Mastery in the Founding Stories of
Poetic Production

First of all, I am going to discuss two ancient Greek stories of the
founding of poetic practice, as if any occasion of making (each
moment when we write poems, or construct ourselves as per-
sons) were already foretold. By contrast to the story about
Caedmon, the logic of which these stories repeat, the stories of
Orpheus and Philomela disclose the structure of history without
being themselves "historical" as Bede intended the story about
Caedmon to be. This is what we mean when we speak of the
Orpheus and the Philomela stories as myths. I choose to talk
about the founding myths (or stories) inside which poetic prac-
tice is enacted in order to contribute to our power as poetic
makers, which I take to be our power also as moral persons.
Power flows from knowledge of the prophecy—from the ability
to hear the story as it is known in the source, and having heard
the story to work with it out of knowledge of it, and by working
with it, out of knowledge of it, to turn subjection (the state of
being in which our writing is already written and our lives al-
ready lived) into such mastery as the resistance of materials
allows (all that we can call "originality"), that is, writing both
from knowledge of the origins and against it.

Western civilization (our given set of life-forms) is singularly
discontinuous. Gentile religion in the West, for example, was
interrupted and then overpowered and changed by Judeo-
Christianity as Caedmon found it. It is, therefore, a split tra-

From *TriQuarterly* 78 (spring 1989), a publication of Northwestern
University.

dition with a dominant, manifest aspect or face and also a suppressed, unmanifest, darker, and older countenance always below, bespeaking another source and another world (pagan, for example, rather than Christian).

But the founding stories, in accord with which we construct our management of representation in general (our poetic practice), are, by contrast to the founding stories of our dominant religious institutions, continuous and ride through time the same as, are patient and structured like, perception, that is to say, the knowability of all else. The story about Orpheus and the story about Philomela (the nightingale) are paradigms of such knowledge, poetic knowledge. They precede, are maintained within, and follow after (survive beyond, as some think) the split life-forms of Western religion—in the same way and for the same reason that representation as such is ubiquitous and prior to all particular figurations of the world. The poetic maker is both the beneficiary and the judge of the logic of the practice.

I

Consider the fifth poem of the first sequence of Rilke's *Sonnets for Orpheus* in Leishman's translation:

> Set up no stone to his memory.
> Let the rose bloom each year for his sake.
> For it is Orpheus. His metamorphosis
> In this one and in this. We should not trouble
> about other names. Once and for all
> It's Orpheus when there's singing. He comes and goes.
> Is it not much already if at times
> He overstays for a few days the bowl of roses?
>
> O how he has to vanish for you to grasp it!
> Though he himself take fright at vanishing.
> Even while his word transcends the being-here,
>
> He's there already where you do not follow.
> The lyre's lattice does not snare his hands.
> And he obeys, while yet he oversteps.

For the West the name (Orpheus) signifies the person who signifies by poetic making, *poesis;* and all speaking about Orpheus is speaking about the origin and logic of speaking in the poetic way.

> Once and for all
> It's Orpheus when there's singing.

The story about Orpheus is a story that founds the poetic work as a human work (an origin story of poetic practice), not because it is, as it were, a boundless subject for poems, but because it is the story that is always enacted when poetry becomes the action of the person—"it's Orpheus when there's singing." The Orpheus story encodes a powerful logic, both of the civilizational effect of the artistic form of words (the structure of the human world that the structures of poetry reproduce), and also of the form of life that poetic power produces in the person, subject of that logic.

My word "logic" points to the invariant entailments in the world of materials (and there is no other) such that, for example, this must be before that, or such that this be because of that, or *such that this be and not that*. The unmistakable trace of the narrative logic of the story about the poetic maker—(Hart Crane calls it the "bright logic")—who is always present in the making of civilization (and who is therefore *always present,* as Rilke says) is the name Orpheus itself, which is etymologically derived from Greek *orphanos.* "Orpheus" signifies the person who is set the task of constructing a human world by singing, *because* the givenness of the world (the inevitability of any relationship of persons or terms) is lost.

> Orpheus with his Lute made Trees,
> And the Mountaine tops that freeze,
> Bow themselves when he did sing.
> To his Musicke, Plants and Flowers
> Ever sprung; as Sunne and Showers,
> There had made a lasting Spring.
> Everything that heard him play,
> Even the Billowes of the Sea,
> Hung their heads, and then lay by.
> In sweet Musicke is such art,
> Killing care, and griefe of heart,
> Fall asleep, or hearing die.

> (John Fletcher)

The Orpheus story that the Jacobean singer sings about the orphaned singer (who by singing makes a world out of nature) is unmistakably gendered male. But the subjection of nature that we hear at the beginning of this poem ("Trees . . . And the Mountaine tops . . . Bow themselves"), and the exclusion of care and grief that we hear in the killing and death at the end, become the other story: the woman's story of the nightingale Philomela, whose song Orpheus, wandering in his bereavement after the loss of Eurydice (as Virgil tells us), hears and is not consoled.

> Month in, month out, seven whole months, men say beneath a lofty cliff by lonely Strymon's shore [Orpheus] wept, and deep in icy caverns, unfolding this his tale, charming tigers, and making the oaks attend his strain; even as the nightingale, mourning beneath the poplar's shade, bewails the loss of her brood, that a churlish ploughman hath espied and torn unfledged from the nest: but she weeps all night long and, perched on a spray, renews her piteous strain, filling the region with sad laments. (*Georgics* IV, ll. 507–14, trans. Fairchurch)

Philomela's song (the nightingale's song) is omnipresent in history in the same way that pain is omnipresent in history and therefore mythographically older than Orpheus's narrative, because always already there, even as witness to Orpheus in his pain.

Philomela's song is the female-gendered predecessor to the Orpheus song, reminding of the limits of the mastery of Orpheus's song and defining, by her story of rape and infanticide, the reality Orpheus's song subjects. We hear Philomela's song in the seventh stanza of Keats's "Ode to a Nightingale" as the high requiem that constitutes the unity of history:

> Thou wast not born for death, immortal Bird!
>   No hungry generations tread thee down;
> The voice I hear this passing night was heard
>   In ancient days by emperor and clown:
> Perhaps the self-same song that found a path
>   Through the sad heart of Ruth, when sick for home,
>   She stood in tears amid the alien corn;
>   The same that oft-times hath
> Charmed magic casements, opening on the foam
>   Of perilous seas, in faery lands forlorn.

This invariable song ("self-same," "The same that oft-times") produced as a single word "forlorn" is the *other* song counter to the Orpheus song. It is Medea's song, Antigone's song, Sappho's song, Ophelia's song, Dickinson's song, Plath's song; but its word "forlorn" is kindred (in the strange kinship of interrupted kinship) to that of Orpheus/*orphanos*—for both these originary stories of poetic practice are about blocked communication— communication blocked in the social world, the overcoming of which blockage generates the poetry that completes relationship another way, insofar as poetry can.

Thus far I have spoken of the Orpheus story, gendered male, as displaying the general logic of civilizational order in the West on the basis of a story about singing (representation); and I have spoken of the Philomela story, gendered female, as constituting the general logic of pain, the entailment of representation in the sense that representation *precedes* all of its cultural applications. I have observed that these two stories constitute (also) the originary narratives of the production of poetry (indeed of literary production in general), and I have also observed that each story (each logic, if there are two) seems both prior to and derived from the other. I will explain and amplify these matters.

I wish, however, to dwell for a moment on the fact (as I understand the matter, and have already suggested) that these two stories or story systems function as *paradigm stories,* or ideal narrative patterns. By "paradigm stories" I mean stories that are transmitted across time and reproduced *invariably* by reason of their self-sameness, inside which self-sameness there are deeply encoded features of the story that make it recognizable and reproducible across time and that bear upon civilizational practice—of all kinds. Orpheus is always a civilizational hero who *therefore* loses Eurydice and as a consequence sings with greater power. ("Once and for all / It's Orpheus when there's singing.") Philomela is always violated, infanticidal and in pain, as a result of which her song becomes, as Keats reminds us, a principle of universality in history.

As I pointed out with respect to the vocational summoning of the poet, my story about Caedmon and myself, we are committed to the poetic principle. The reason for my presentation of the myths and paradigms of poetic construction is to articulate its logic and to give an account of the implication of that logic for the vocational person and the social order that receives him or her.

II

I want, now, to frame these stories by a large structure of concern that contains them and is stated by them. What concerns me is the following: all the founding stories of poetic discourse, the originary myths of the generation of song, are violent. This violence—indeed atrocity—so deeply encoded in the poetic logic of Western civilization arises within a life-and-death struggle (as Hegel predicted), generally gods on one side and humankind on the other, between sponsors of competing descriptions of the person who is the subject of poiesis.

Thus, the practice of art is urgent and dangerous. What is at stake in the competition for the power of description of human being is the value and status of the person in the cosmos and social order. In the gentile world as we now receive it, the champion on the human part is the poet. For this reason, all poetic practice because of its function is situated *in crisis, at the edge or boundary of human being altogether*. Representation in general, and poetic representation in particular, as the story about Caedmon exemplifies, requires reference to the nonhuman—divine, or transcendent. But the nonhuman resists the human image, or competes with it. This paradox, which commits the maker both to solicit and to resist the transcendental term, frames the bitter logic of which I speak. Poetics is the science of the management of the resistance of the nonhuman (both inside and outside the person) to the human, in the interest of the self-representation of the person. And the poet-singer, master of that voice of wonder which presents the whole beauty of human kind, is nonetheless a dependency of, subjected to, what opposes.

In this matter there are many stories. For example, at *Iliad*, book II, line 594, we read in the "catalogue of ships," in the course of the account of the cities whose warriors were under the leadership of Nestor, particularly of a place called Dorion and a poet called Thamyrus:

Encountering Thamyrus the Thracian stopped him from
  singing
As he came from Oichalia and Oichalian Eurytos;
For he boasted that he would surpass, if the very Muses,
Daughters of Zeus who holds the Aegis, were singing against
  him
And these in their anger struck him maimed, and the voice of
  wonder
They took away, and made him a singer without memory.

(Trans. R. Lattimore)

In the case of Thamyrus, the human challenge (Thamyrus's boast) to the description of the human state of affairs sponsored by the high god (the Muses are daughters of Zeus) is punished by the violent taking away of the poet's voice, the voice of wonder. This disabling of the poet is effected by the canceling of poetic mind, *the taking back of deep memory*. For the Muses (daughters of Memory on their mother's side) are Memory itself, conformed (later) to the various genres of the poetic art. Thamyrus is an experimenter with the freedom—the "free verse," as it were—of human self-description. Thamyrus claims freedom from the narrative tyranny of Zeus—the freedom of the self-constructed, self-witnessing description by humanity of humanity. This Thamyrus does by turning poetic remembering against its source (the Muses, daughters of Memory). The effort to produce a dominant description sponsored by poetic humanity—a free song—results in the withdrawing of all song, the taking away of the voice of wonder, the poetic voice. This is the violence, structured as warfare between describers, of which I speak.

A further example: you will remember that Marsyas, a musician who invented a new form of music for the oboe, challenged Apollo and was horribly skinned—lost his human image, his manifest outside. And Linus, another ancient singer about whom stories were told, was a brother of Orpheus. Herakles, whom Linus was tutoring, killed him with a blow of the lyre, but was exonerated on a plea of self-defense. Again, we see how dangerous in our civilization the practice of poetic art is, and how it is implicitly and inevitably a challenge—apparently the extreme challenge, on the knife edge of existence, or nonexistence—to the hierarchies that maintain the universe.

Further, the example of Marsyas, who lost the skin of his *physical body*, which constituted his recognizability as human, his body as the "best picture" of the self, requires that we note how the same atrocious sanctions against human self-construction bear upon, both the symbolic production, and also the material reproduction of the body—the authorship of the woman's sexuality and the mother's glance. Although the male paradigmatic singer most like Orpheus is Amphion, who by his singing built the walls of Thebes, the violence that is required by the logic of the paradigm is, in Amphion's case, displaced—for he is said to have become husband of Niobe, in whose story as told by Homer (*Iliad*, book IX) we find the genderically feminine—the woman's, the Philomelan—boast on behalf of human making in its profoundest material form, the reproduction of the human image as a function of the physical body. Not the male Orpheus version (Thamyrus; Linus, Orpheus's brother; Amphion; Musaeus, Orpheus's son), but the woman's version, the nightingale version:

For even Niobe, she of the lovely tresses, remembered
To eat, whose twelve children were destroyed in the palace
Six daughters and six sons in the pride of their youth whom
    Apollo
Killed with arrows from his silver bow, being angered
With Niobe, and Artemis killed the daughters
Because Niobe likened herself to Leto of the fair coloring
And said Leto had borne only two, she herself had borne many;
But the two, though they were only two, destroyed all those.
Nine days long they lay in their blood, nor was there anyone
To buy them, for the son of Kronos made stone out of
the people; but on the tenth day the Uranian gods buried them.
But she remembered to eat when she was worn out with
    weeping
And now somewhere among the rocks in the lonely mountains
In Sipylos, where they say is the resting place of the goddesses
Who are nymphs, and dance beside the waters of Acheloios,
There, stone still, she broods on the sorrows the gods gave her.
                                                (Trans. R. Lattimore)

The image of Niobe—her statue that is her body, "stone still," image of the greatest pain endurable *without the loss of human form, the pain of the image*—is the atrocious outcome of the challenge by the woman, on behalf of the beauty of the person as mortal, to the immortal form of the person as it is instituted by the gods.

You will note that there are *two intricated systems characterized by violence* that the originary stories of poetic production and its logic seem to present: (1) the intrinsic violence of image making patterned in the stories of Orpheus and Philomela— violence that belongs primarily to the representational logic of *this instead of that,* for example, symbolic instead of organic life; and (2) the extrinsic (human/divine) violence patterned in the stories of Marsyas and Niobe, which extends the bitter economies of scarcity deep into the life of the universe itself and enforces consciousness of the paradoxes of division internal to the constituting alliances by which reality is composed.

III

Orpheus was either the son of Memory itself, Mnemosyne as mother of the Muses and therefore the divine form of the poetic mind, or the son of one of Memory's daughters, Calliope ("beautiful voice"), who presides over the epic, the genre that constructs the cosmos and state—whether Hesiod's, or Virgil's, or Milton's, or Hart Crane's. Calliope, as mother of a genre, commits her son to a genre—and therefore to a constrained kind of freedom produced but also qualified by the (heroic) requirements of service to social order. Orpheus, the mortal hero, belongs to the generation of the fathers of the heroes who fought the Trojan War. The epic project of which he is part is recorded in the *Argonautika* of Apollonius Rhodius (circa 250 B.C.)—the story of the quest for the Golden Fleece. Orpheus is taken aboard the Argo, Jason's ship, as a technician. He has no self. He neither acts nor suffers, but rather performs the tasks his powers *as a poet* enable him to perform.

As poet he is master of rhythm in service of meaning. Therefore he sets and regulates the rhythmical activity of the working sailors and the rowers. As the child of cosmic Memory, he knows the order of the universe, and therefore can resolve quarrels that arise on shipboard by singing of the harmonious order of things—a song that conforms the order of the human world to the order of the divine. As poet, Orpheus also is master of the music that has mastery over the demonic (divine) countersong to the human song—the song of the sirens that bereaves humanity of its image, interrupts the prophetically driven enterprise of the human community, and kills men (*Argonautika,* book IV, ll. 900ff.):

> And ever on watch from their place of prospect with its fair haven, often from many had [the sirens] taken away their sweet return, consuming them with wasting desire; and suddenly to these heroes too they sent forth from their lips a lily-like voice. And [the argonauts] were already about to cast from the ship the hawsers to the shore, had not ... Orpheus ... stringing in his hands his Bistonian [Thracian] lyre rung forth a hasty snatch of rippling melody, so that their ears might be filled with the sound of his twanging; and the song overcame the [siren's] voice.

Orpheus, technician of the artifact of the human image, also assures the harmony of marriage by marriage song, brings invisible springs into visibility by materializing the nymphs of the springs, assigns names to places, and inducts into mysteries. But all that he does flows from his poetic function as the cosmic male who regulates the human world by supplying order and destination to the energies and powers of mind and nature, in accord with the Great Memory that is his by right of birth and in service of the world that acknowledges Zeus (the principle of things as they are) as Lord. Indeed, Orpheus becomes associated in historical times with a religion (Orphism)—an ascetic pagan Protestantism. A prominent contribution of Orphism was an account of the origin of human beings that represents human beings as reconciling an archaic guilty nature (Titanic) with a modern rational nature (Apollinian). This Viconian aspect of Orphean tradition (Orpheus as *priscus theologus*) is father of the world-constructive mysticisms of the modern poet (Yeats, Eliot, Crane, Merrill, Olson). Orpheus, then, is omnipresent in the history of poetic making as the archetype of the regulator, the perfect servant of his mother, daughter of Zeus. Orpheus is memory as language, and specifically language in service of the order of the world (Cf. Horace in the *Ars Poetica*).

But the most commonly invoked story about Orpheus tells of his marriage, and the loss (before the marrriage was consummated) of his wife Eurydice to the underworld, where she still rules, in accord with her name as "a wide judging" power, because Orpheus violated a law promulgated by Hera that permitted him to fetch her from the underworld, but prohibited him from looking back at his lost bride as he conducted her upward to the world of life. Hera's rule made reunion with the beloved, in effect, a contingency of deferral of ocular assurance, which Orpheus could not endure. In the myth, this story *follows* the history of Orpheus's service to the Argonauts, and finds Orpheus imprisoned in the bitter logic of the paradigm of his discourse at the point of personal relationship. Though Orpheus saved the heroes of the Argonautic expedition from wasting desire by the power of his song, he was unable to consummate his own marriage—he who was the master of the marriage song.

As the paradigm of the Orphic myth is transmitted from Apollonius to Ovid and Virgil, and through innumerable medieval and Renaissance versions to Milton, Hölderlin, Whitman, Yeats, Rilke, and Blanchot, it becomes increasingly an inquiry into the impotence of the master—his subjection to the violent logic of a story in which he redeems the world, but not himself. The order that Orpheus serves is not an order in which he can participate because he enacts the logic of his art (if presence, then not image; if image, then not presence) and suffers its violence. He bears the burden of the generality of the song (the function of poetic language), and sacrifices as the cost to himself of his vicarious powers for others the destination of his own desire (the function of natural language).

The voice of the poet in the West is orphaned (Orpheus is an *orphanos*) in the same sense that the persona who speaks the poem is not (cannot be) the same *person* who writes but rather is a *general order of speaking* that serves the human world as Orpheus served the Argonauts but for that reason cannot serve the self. Orpheus is admitted to the underworld by reason of his song, which knows the structure of all things as they are in the Great Mother Memory (Mnemosyne). He may dwell in all the regions of his song and move from mansion to mansion in it (from the world of life to the world of death), but he is forbidden to look back, for *to gaze* in Orpheus's case is to (re)construct experience on his own behalf, and that is a violation of the decorum of the persona.

By the bitter logic of the poetic principle, Eurydice must be lost.

> And now as he retraced his steps he had escaped every mischance, and the regained Eurydike was nearing the upper world, followed behind—for that condition had Proserpine ordained—when a sudden frenzy seized Orpheus unwary in his love. . . . He stopped, and on the very verge of light, unmindful, alas! and vanquished in his purpose, on Eurydike, *now his own,* looked back! In that moment all his toil was spent, the ruthless tyrant's pact was broken.
>
> (*Georgics,* book IV, ll. 485ff.)

The motive to look back—memory not being enough—engages Orpheus against the paradigm, like a character in a story who seeks to evade the logic of the narration of which he is a part, seeks to become "real" (actual) and therefore to cease signifying on behalf of the other. It is in this sense that Christianity identified Orpheus with the crucified Christ, another *orphanos.* In accord with this dialectic, much discussion of how poems ought to be written takes place within a binary logic of representation that sets (cosmic) Memory against (individual) experience, the general (formal) against the personal (undetermined), "form super-induced" (in Coleridge's language) against "form self-witnessing," freedom as service (Orphic freedom) against freedom as autonomy.

But Orpheus's wordless, illegal, particularizing backward-looking gaze is an appeal directed toward the outside of language, as to the outside of narrative (or of art itself), back into which he is drawn by the divinely appointed logic of his nature as discourse. The cultural preoccupation, never at an end, with Orpheus's pain, reflects the weariness of the masters of language with the paradox of poetic language reproduced as the structure of poetic life, presence through absence that requires the subjection of language's servants, the poets. "Does the imagination dwell the most," Yeats's poet asks, "On a woman won or a woman lost?"

Orpheus's lamentations, after Eurydice is lost, are the most powerful poems of his making. It is through them (the poems of precisely uncompensated pain) that he charms the animals, builds walls of cities, commands trees to constellate orchards, produces the space of the (collective) human world in which—as orphaned desire—he has no power to dwell. Orpheus is mortal. As "vocation" itself he models a mortal predicament, and serves to compensate as poetry does scarce economies imaginable only within the consciousness of *finite* life. In the end he is torn to pieces by Thracian women—aroused by his beauty—in the inevitable (systemic) violence that befalls the maker—the sponsor of a general discourse. (And no one is entirely exempt from the action of making.) His individual form is destroyed, a form inconsistent with his function. He becomes, like the written word or a published poem that constructs the world, a talking head that is slow to die.

IV

When Orpheus in Virgil's account wanders lamenting the loss of Eurydice, he is compared (as we have already observed) in his inconsolability to the *philomela* that is the nightingale, the ever desolate lover not of the signified but of the sign.

> Month in, month out, seven whole months, men say beneath a lofty cliff of lonely Strymon's cave he wept, and deep in icy caverns unfolding this his tale, charming the tigers, and making the oaks attend his strain; even as the nightingale mourning beneath the poplar's shade, bewails the loss of her brood, that a churlish plowman *[durus arator]* hath espied and torn unfledged from the nest: but she weeps all night long and perched upon a spray renews her piteous strain, filling the region round with sad laments.

The moment of Orpheus's grief—his lament for desire's dead child, the mortal beloved—is the crossing point of the two paradigm stories of artistic production that I am retelling: Orpheus and Philomela. *Orpheus* is omnipresent in history (with us especially when we write) as the power of order contributed by *Memory (mother of the Muses) without experience,* order that in fact expels experience (the always-lost Eurydice) and by doing so, paradoxically, reproduces the harmony of the universe through poetry as the productive rhythm of social work. *Philomela,* on the other hand, is omnipresent in history (the "self-same song," Keats says) as the pain contributed by *experience without Memory* (the sign of it is the "churlish plowman," *durus arator*)—the eruption into the proper body that is figured as rape, infanticide, and final metamorphosis in which the human image is lost. In Virgil's simile the *philomela* functions as the always-at-hand representational vehicle of the grief of the (male) maker.

What is the Philomela story? There were two sisters, daughters of the Athenian king, Pandion. In accord with decorum between sisters, the elder is given in marriage first—to a barbarian king to whom the father is indebted. The husband's name is Tereus. The elder sister, the married one, in her loneliness sends Tereus to fetch her younger sister for a visit. Tereus is aroused by the beauty of the younger sister, imprisons her among his slaves in a dark wood, rapes her, and cuts out her tongue so she cannot tell her story. At this moment of violation and atrociously blocked communication there arises a founding instance of woman's text. The violated girl weaves a textile epistle addressed, in the older versions of the story, by Procne to the wife (Philomela) of her rapist: "Procne is among the slaves." (In the later versions of the story the beautiful name is assigned to the mutilated girl and *she* is called Philomela, thus condensing pain upon the beautiful word.) The wife of Tereus (let us call her Procne) receives the message, and liberates her sister.

Together they avenge themselves upon Tereus by killing Tereus's child, the child of the elder sister, and feeding the corpse to the brutal husband and father. In his rage, Tereus pursues the women and all three are turned into birds, Philomela into a nightingale. The fitness of rape as a founding story of poetic discourse (and also of the novel, Richardson's *Clarissa*, for instance, being both a rape story and a generic exemplar, as Frances Fergusson has pointed out) is widely attested. The woman's counterstory of loss to the male story—(the Orpheus story)—founds poetry, not only at the point of pain, but precisely pain resulting from the overwhelming of the personal will (the power that maintains human form) by the inhuman desire that the human form arouses, but cannot regulate. "Philomela is among the slaves."

Orpheus is a captive of the *above* (memory prior to experience); Philomela is captive to the *beneath* (experience prior to memory). In each case, song arises punctually at the moment after loss has become inconsolable, and the destination of the self irretrievable by other means, at the moment when there is no recourse other than song.

In Orpheus's case, as I have indicated, "form" is a captivity—Orpheus's bitterly paradoxical transcendent power of representation. In Philomela's case, the captivity is formlessness, Philomela's bitterly paradoxical power of experience without memory. Indeed, in many medieval and Renaissance texts Philomela must remind herself (so memory-less is she) of the cause of her pain by leaning upon a thorn as she sings beautifully in the night. It was thus that Keats's poet found her. Memory of her personal history is abolished in the metamorphosis by which she becomes a general power in the human world.

I will draw my example of Philomela's story from Shakespeare. In *A Midsummer Night's Dream,* Philomela is invoked to guard the body. The domain of her peculiar care is the night-body of the lover (act II, scene ii):

> Philomel with melody,
> Sing in our sweet lullaby;
> Lulla, lulla, lullaby; lulla, lulla, lullaby.
>
> Never harm, nor spell, nor charm
> Come our lovely lady nigh.
> So good night, with lullaby.

While Philomela, the raped and mutilated girl, is heard to sing, lovers have permission of their bodies—as when Juliet awakes in bed with Romeo (act III, scene v):

> *Juliet.* Wilt thou be gone? It is not yet near day.
> It was the nightingale, and not the lark
> That pierced the fearful hollow of thine ear.
> Nightly she sings on yon pomegranate tree.
> Believe me, love, it was the nightingale.

In both these cases the Philomela song is invoked in order to obtain its mastery (its survival as voice) in the contest for the description of the world (against the demonic magician, against the social lark). As in the Orpheus paradigm, the logic of the material real as manifest is mediated by vicarious suffering put in service of the care of the vulnerable body of the other. The subjection of Philomela becomes the mastery of disorder on behalf of general humanity (the audience of song) through the poem of which her metamorphosis is the sign.

As we have seen, the paradigmatic story supplies mastery of disorder in history by interposing the vicarious suffering (the subjection) of the first masters, their master-piece—Orpheus and Philomela. *But when the violence of history exceeds the violence of the paradigm, what then?*

When the stories of first poets, which anticipate on the world's behalf and vicariously displace the atrocious logic of poetic representation, fail to include the pain of history, then history, what does occur, no longer within the paradigm of representation, ceases to be a theme of representation, ceases to be representable, memorable, lamentable. Whatever Adorno may have meant when he wrote that there can be no poetry after the Holocaust, there is a sense in which there can be no poetry *about* the Holocaust. This state of affairs, which finds the violence of history in excess of any violence already written, was the concern of Shakespeare in his earliest analysis of the Philomela story.[1] We see already in the speech of Juliet the fading of the vicarious power of the paradigm—for the day that will bring death *has really dawned.* But the most radical case in Shakespeare of the invocation and overwhelming of the paradigm occurs in his first tragedy, *Titus Andronicus.* (Act IV, scene 1)

Lavinia, daughter of Titus, is raped and mutilated in the course of a dynastic struggle. Her assailants cut out her tongue; but also (because they have read Philomela's story in Ovid) cut off her hands as well, so that Lavinia (unlike Ovid's heroine) cannot weave the textile letter that betrays the barbarity of Tereus. The man who discovers her says:

> Fair Philomel, why she but lost her tongue
> And in a tedious sampler sewed her mind.
> But, lovely niece, that means is cut from thee.
> A craftier Tereus, cousin, hast thou met,
> And he hath cut those pretty fingers off
> That could have better sewed than Philomel.

But Lavinia with her stumps discovers an edition of Ovid.

Titus.	Lucius, what book is that she tosseth so?
Boy.	Grandsire, 'tis Ovid's *Metamorphoses*.
	My mother gave it me.
Marcus.	For love of her that's gone
	Perhaps, she culled it from the rest.
Titus.	Soft, so busily she turns the leaves.
	Help her. What would she find: Lavinia,
	shall I read?
	Ravished and wronged as Philomela was,
	Forced in the ruthless, vast, and gloomy woods?
	See, see. Ay, such a place there is where we did
	hunt—
	O, had we never, never hunted there!—
	Patterned by that the poet here describes,
	By nature made for murders and for rapes.

Shakespeare represents his characters in a world in which the "patterns" (the paradigm stories) are received by reading.

But there is bad reading and there is good reading. Bad reading is exemplified by the rapists' reading: the rapists read to find the "pattern" of the crime they intend so they can repeat it. They read not to do otherwise but to do the same, and to learn how to escape doing's consequences. This disposition to reproduce a state of affairs in art as history and thus to render history identical with representation, no longer its other and beneficiary, turns the violence of representation back into history and destroys the regulative difference betweeen image and fact. Hence, Lavinia enacts—is compelled to become—the paradigm, ravished and mutilated. She identifies her narrative by means of its already writtenness, which however has ceased in her case to be a general, mythic, and therefore a virtual, state of affairs. Poetic representation has failed of its regulative function by reason of the atrocious violation of constraining actual life to the virtual image.

The story Lavinia suffers in her own person functions as a founding story of representation. In her story action is, it would appear, the agony of insufficient difference—which reproduces as story, and does not defend against, the violence of representation in history. Rape founds poetry because it is the radical challenge to the woman's self-characterization as human—as the Orphic bereavement is the man's. In her paradigm, it is the precisely obliterative assault by the violence of the alien describer that drives into existence the counterpower on behalf of the woman's body and name: Philomela's letter and Philomela's song. Philomelan poetry (its consolatory magic) is driven into existence by the body's pain, pain indicating the fundamental indescribability of the body, its finally undefendable vulnerability. The poetry that solicits the peace of the body (poetry of the open kind, free, the counter-Orphic kind) is not, as I shall show (chap. 3, below, on Whitman), poetry without violence and alienation; but it is a poetry that by reason of the productive powers of alienation keeps the human image by keeping the difference to history of the counterstory, which difference is one of our few great allies against the force that would reduce us to the ash of its indifference—"so rudely forced."

When the themes of art reproduce crime (the rapists' reading) rather than prevent it (as might have occurred had the story taught the father not to hunt in the "ruthless, vast and gloomy woods")—when, in short, the pattern ceases to regulate force and becomes the fact—then the pain of the paradigm becomes the pain of history and the competition for the description of the human world is lost to the energies that do not know human form (the *durus arator*). It is the bitter fact (and the subject of this book) that the energies that do not know the human form are among the energies (barbarism both of the divine and natural) that also construct the human form, as the pain of Philomela produces consolatory song and the grief of Orpheus elegiac possibility. But the logic of representation is unendurable by the natural person. The function of poetic practice is to defer the implosion of the poetic principle into the actual world.

When the difference, then, between representation and reality is lost, we are all with Philomela among the slaves.

V

Anglo-American poetry since Keats and Emily Dickinson tends toward the female model—the lyric, the Philomelan kind, the painstory—which engages the contest of describers at the point of threat to individual self-invention. Orpheus, by contrast, the cosmic singer, the male epic-master *alienated to the above,* the technician of the social order, has become the implicit enemy of our project, especially in his high-modern exemplars (for example, Yeats).

The moment in English poetic history that projects the (post-modern) crisis of the Orpheus paradigm (the turning toward poetry of another kind, Philomelan) is Milton's account, in "Lycidas," of the last segment of Orpheus's story. Here we find Orpheus expelled from personal life (and finally from life itself) after the loss of Eurydice, and become the greater singer, the builder of walls, gatherer of orchards, tamer of animals—in effect, not a person but a persona. Orpheus has become the true poetic voice who arouses feeling but cannot reciprocate the feeling he arouses, and so is torn to pieces by the inflamed women of Thrace, who ratify his death as an individual subject by making of him a singing head.

In "Lycidas," Milton's speaker concerns himself with the fact that his drowned friend, a poet, served the institution of poetry but was not rescued by it from the sea, which defeats the image of the person that Orphic poetry promises to conserve—as if the mistake of the Thracian women who cannot distinguish between persona and person were a mistake also of the elegist himself.

> Ay me, I fondly dream,
> Had ye been there!—for what could that have done?
> What could the Muse herself that Orpheus bore,
> The Muse herself, for her enchanting son
> Whom universal nature did lament,
> When by the rout that made the hideous roar
> His gory visage down the stream was sent,
> Down the swift Hebrus to the Lesbian shore?

Here the master, himself, is seen to be subjected; and the subjection of the master must be understood to demonstrate the impotence of the mastery (the divine sponsors of the art and the institutional order it constructs including church and university)—the impotence of *poetry* to overcome the violence of the obliterative counterdescription (the "hideous roar") that has defeated the paradigmatic agent of representation. There is in Milton's poem a strong sense of a poetic culture that produces more violence than it pacifies, as if the logic of representation *were* the logic of history, as indeed might seem to have become the case when Milton's early imagination of revolution passes into the fact of the Commonwealth. This state of affairs, both theoretical and practical, is discussed at length in context of Milton's text and world, in the next chapter.

Here our concern is that the elegiac hero (the drowned friend, Henry King) is seen in "Lycidas" to embody the fate of the structure of poetic representation, and thus to entail upon the elegiac speaker *the search for a culture of representation that is neither vulnerable to, nor complicit with, the violence of history.* This is the reason why the speaker in "Lycidas" begins speaking. And this search seems to be the fundamental motive of poetic originality. Milton's solution to the enigma of Orphic logic, which fails at the point of the destruction of the agent of representation in history (Henry King, the individual person), is to appeal to an even deeper abstraction of source and order, not Mnemosyne but the "heavenly Muse" Urania—as at the end of "Lycidas," or in book VII of *Paradise Lost* (the invocation):

> Still govern thou my song,
> Urania, and fit audience find, though few.
> But drive far off the barbarous dissonance
> Of Bacchus and his revelers, the race
> Of that wild rout that tore the Thracian bard
> In Rhodope, where woods and rocks had ears
> To rapture, till the savage clamor drowned
> Both harp and voice; nor could the Muse defend
> Her son. So fail not thou who thee implores;
> For thou art heav'nly, she an empty dream.

The poet intends the reconstruction of the sufficient conditions of the representation of persons against the dissonant clamor ("barbarous" and "savage") of the demonic counterpowers who do not know the person. Therefore Milton summons by invocation another source, more powerful for persons, Urania (the Christian by contrast to the gentile muse). The action of such invocation or "calling back" to the archaic source of discourse is fundamental to (indeed, the normative cultural practice of) British poetic work in the Christian tradition. As we have seen it was precisely this higher abstraction for which Hild claimed Caedmon's vision.

The Miltonic question (as we shall see) is whether representation as such—the voice of the poet—is effectively prior to all other terms and therefore our destiny, though weighted with the bitter instability that I have pointed to in my analysis of the founding stories of poetic practice. Or whether there is an alternative that is prior, historically and in the cosmos, as the Bible says God is.

We live between the productive violence of representation as poetry and the destructive violence of representation as history. Only vigilant practice can keep them apart. But the culture in which we live, including poetic culture, has grown weary of the productive violence (the work) of representation and has tended to *identify* it for reasons that are not trivial with the violence of history. Such is the postmodern crisis of confidence in the validity of representation—in its power to defer the violence that it also requires—a crisis of the generality of intelligibility that we shall confront in several forms beginning with Milton's example.

NOTE

1. Cf. the theological problem posed the Jew when the story about the sacrifice of Isaac (Gen. 22) is seen to be an insufficient account of the actual sufferering of the Jew in history (chap. 7, below).

Milton's Sonnet "On the Late Massacre in Piemont"

The Vulnerability of Persons in a Revolutionary Situation

Si non vales, non valeo

Milton's most famous sonnet, when seen in its historical situation, compels us to discuss the nature of poetry in relation to history, and particularly those moments in history when important social changes are taking place that we are now accustomed to refer to as crises of representation. At such moments, it becomes apparent, as I think, that the ironic complexity of the relation between the formal imperative to justice, on the one hand, and the equally urgent substantial imperative that demands the maintenance of such transcendental recognitions as constitute the value of justice to the human world, on the other, are in fundamental conflict. And that this enigma is a poetic concern.

The particular situation that impelled me to produce this analysis (first published in 1972) was the great difficulty encountered by myself and others in the matter of obtaining (in the sixties) a useful theoretical account of conflict that appeared to be social and economic in character but that, then as now, seemed also to demand an analysis of another kind. Perhaps, I thought, the economics relevant to the situation require terms eidetic rather than monetary—terms that reach beyond questions of relationships mediated by money to those that touch upon the value of money and therefore lie within the domain of poetic analysis.

From *TriQuarterly* 23–24, (winter–spring 1972), a publication of Northwestern University.

The trial and judicial killing of a king in 1649 was a unique event in the political life of Europe, and created unique legal problems, such as the question of the competence of the court to try the person upon whom its authority was based. The hierarchical civility in which the social value of persons was previously identified had been destroyed at its root in response, as it were, to the Baptist's revolutionary slogan, in Matthew 3:10, "And now also the ax is laid to the root of the trees." The killing of the king and the establishment of the Commonwealth was, like revolutionary acts in general, an initiative in the interest of new and more desirable relationships among men. What I shall point to in Milton's sonnet is the clear sense that the effort to establish the new dispensation, the *novus ordo,* entailed a corresponding devaluation of personal identity such as to suggest that the means of revolution and its ends are in conflict one with the other.

Further, I wish to propose that most of Milton's poetry is, like this particular poem, an effort to restore meaning to experience, which his very deep, indeed inveterate imagination of revolution, as reflected for instance in the early "On the Morning of Christ's Nativity," tended to place outside previous categories of meaning; and for which his imagination of revolution or for that matter reformation provided in the end no sufficient categories of intelligibility.

Marvell's image of the author of *Paradise Lost* destroying the world to avenge his sight seems to me a substantially true statement about Milton's motive as a poet. Milton's sense of history (and consequently of moral *experience*) is always in advance of his sense of the intelligibility of that experience; and his poetry is an attempt to restore the sightedness that the ability to understand experience confers. Milton's poetry is part of the unfinished history of the secularization process that by destroying old servitudes created new freedom, without, it seems, at the same time creating viable conditions for the practice of that freedom.

If politics has as its goal the reduction of violence, and religion the conservation of value, then the Waldensian massacre was a case of politics and religion at the breaking point. Milton's poem comes at the end of a long series of political addresses written by Milton on behalf of Cromwell's government, aimed at redress for, or at least influence over, an ongoing atrocity committed in enforcement of a territorial settlement by Carlo Emmanuele II, duke of Savoy and prince of Piedmont, against the Vaudois (or Valdenses, an ancient Protestant sect excommunicated by the Church in 1215), some of whom lived in certain valleys of the Pellice and Agrogna Rivers, tributaries of the Po. On April 24, 1655, a plan to root out these heretics completely was put in action by the marquis of Pianezza, commanding a force of Piedmontese, French, and Irish. That this attempt at genocide was a matter of religious concern as well as political—if the two are separable in this period—was apparent from the shocked response of the Protestant English nation as news reports of which Milton's poem makes use made their way back out of the desolate valleys of the Italian Alps.

First of all, God's providence with respect to his elect (his "seed") was called in question; secondly, God's ability to avenge visibly assaults on those under his care was being tested before the audience of a nation whose leader got his early education from Dr. Beard, author of *The Theater of God's Judgement Displayed;* thirdly, the ability of the Lord Protector of the international Protestant community to protect was called in question. The purpose of the revolution was to establish a new premise of relationship within the Protestant community (as in the biblical phrase "we are all members of one another"); correlatively, each member of the extended body of the Protestant community became in a new way vulnerable and in a new way obligated by reason of participation in the new autonomy of the communal person.

Genocidal atrocity turns sectarian religious identity into a fatal stigma unless some redeeming meaning can be attached to the lethal consequences of belonging to the persecuted party. The purpose of Milton's poem seems to be to summon meaning from God as the origin of meaning to redress an imbalance between experience on the one hand and value on the other. The text of "On the Late Massacre in Piemont" follows:

> Avenge O Lord thy slaughter'd Saints, whose bones
> Lie scatter'd on the Alpine mountains cold,
> Ev'n them who kept thy truth so pure of old

When all our Fathers worship't Stocks and Stones,
Forget not: in thy book record their groanes
    Who were thy Sheep and in their antient Fold
    Slayn by the bloody *Piemontese* that roll'd
    Mother with Infant down the Rocks. Their moans
The Vales redoubl'd to the Hills, and they
    To Heav'n. Their martyr'd blood and ashes sow
    O're all th' *Italian* fields where still doth sway
The triple Tyrant: that from these may grow
    A hunderd-fold, who having learnt thy way
    Early may fly the *Babylonian* wo.

God is summoned (a gesture that if it is not redundant must be evidence of its own futility) to transform meaningless death (slaughter) into meaningful death (martyrdom). The pastoral landscape appropriate to the world of sheep and shepherds has been transformed (and this emphasis is already contained in contemporary accounts prior to Milton's poem) into that desolate unfulfilling realm, that world from which meaning has been withdrawn, with which we are familiar from Sidney's double sestina in the *Arcadia* or Blake's mythology of the fallen Tharmas.

That the violence the Waldensians suffered was genocidal in character is emphasized by the stress, also derived from contemporary accounts, on the destruction of women and children. The genetic immortality of this community is threatened; and this community is the acknowledged parent of the Protestant community in Europe. Morland, in his *History of the Evangelical Churches of the Valleys of the Piemont,* reports that Cromwell was "often heard to say that it lay as near or rather nearer his heart than if it had concerned his nearest and dearest Relations in the World." Echo in English pastoralism is the sign of a fulfilling universe, but in this poem about ultimate scarcity the succoring vales are filled with cries that they amplify toward heaven or God upon whom in direct, unmediated relationship the independent Protestant must depend. The poetic speaker commands that God turn slaughter into martyrdom by "sowing" (that is, turning into instruction, for "the seed is the word of God," Luke 8:11) the "blood and ashes" of the Waldensians, who, not in their own persons but in this indirect manner, will create consciousness of oppression in Catholic Italians.

The divine rememberer is commanded by the poet to conserve, in the face of the inability of the human community to identify the slain and to compensate their incomparable pain, the memory of his primitive servants. The asymmetry between conspicuous merit and atrocious destiny, between value and experience, has been further exacerbated by the assault upon the generative persons in the community, mother and infant, so that collective immortality, the life of the community, is threatened; this as a consequence of the religious self-identification of its individuals. By turning passive suffering into intelligible sacrifice the Lord will promulgate sufficient knowledge so that captives of tyrannical religion in still unconverted Italy (which Cromwell had vowed to liberate) may become conscious of their subjection and turn away in a revolutionary gesture from the destruction that the inevitable historical process directed by God has in store for that nation. In the transformation of pain into consciousness the individuality of the martyrs is lost, but their consequence, "redoubled" like their groans, has become a hundredfold.

Violence has been turned into consciousness of oppression, which in turn rescues a part of the human community from the counterviolence of God, masked in the typological shadow of the "Babylonian wo." The grammatical hiatus, the withheld substantive ("hunderd-fold, who") in the last line but one, calls attention to the sacrifice of individuality that creates an unconcealed pathos in the conclusion of the poem, not unrelated to the peculiar posture of the speaker, who in the face of the unredeemed event commands God to act, as he has not yet done, in a way consistent with the rationality of his nature. The bond between the speaker of the poem and the Waldenses is that of spiritual filiation. The speaker derives assurance of his religious identity from the ancient faith of the Waldensian saints, as from a spiritual by contrast to a natural family ("*our* Fathers"), whose slaughter consequently threatens the roots of his spiritual being. *They* have borne the cost of *his* identity, *and their vulnerability portends the extinction of his party "root and branch."*

We may imagine (with Masson) the circulation of Milton's sonnet in Cromwell's government at the time when all but the last of an extensive series of diplomatic remonstrances over the Piedmont massacre had been composed and dispatched. Milton had written on Cromwell's behalf to the duke of Savoy, to the heads of state of Transylvania, Sweden, the United Provinces, the Swiss cantons, Denmark, to Cardinal Mazarin, and others in part to assert the hegemony of Cromwell as the Protestant power in Europe, in part because not to do so would be a breach of communal solidarity with the Protestant kinship. But the Piedmont massacre shared the singular character of all atrocity; it was an occasion demanding redress in excess of anybody's (even a Lord Protector's) ability to effect redress. The details of the Piedmont event were unusually arresting to the England of the day. The newsletters *(The Perfect Diurnal, The Weekly Post, The Faithful Scout, Mercurius Politicus)* recounted week after week the ingenuities of torment (impalement, evisceration, cannibalism) inflicted on the Waldenses, who were the most deserving because the most ancient of God's Protestants.

As in the case of some modern atrocities, the event seemed perverse evidence of human creativity, not only in the extraordinary ingenuity (a kind of inspiration) with which millennial strategies of barbarism were explored and executed (and later illustrated, like important experiments in science, by Morland in his *History*); but also in the sentiment, which pervades the event, of enormous, almost superhuman labor accomplished. The discrediting of the immortality of the other is a great labor that from the time of the early martyrs of the Roman amphitheaters possessed that quasi-theatrical character conserved in a title such as *The Theater of God's Judgement*. This aspect of atrocious event (its discontinuity with ordinary experience, its traditionality, and its quasi-aesthetic character) renders all the more difficult the discrimination of the personhood of the victim, and all the more exigent the restoration of one's own mastery over the fascination of the spectacle by the devising of a response.

The problem is additionally complicated by two considerations at least: in the first place no civil society can deliberately respond to an atrocity in kind, and in the second place (as the Christian knows better perhaps than any other religionist) no man's pain is equivalent to anyone else's. In which case, response in kind is merely random reprisal. The Christian God was himself a victim of an atrocious death (we are reminded of Herbert's Christ "The Sacrifice": "Never was grief like mine") that, despite the irreducible singularity of all pain, lays a perpetual claim upon every man's capacity for feeling, an obligation to imitate the Passion, by its nature inimitable.

The Piedmont massacre was an occasion not merely for the practice of the science of the justice of God, but also for the justification of man's will to be real against the fact of the isolation of the psychic locus of pain, and therefore the person in pain, from all access of participation. Pain (or its unverifiable and undeniable evidences in others) disintegrates community by centering personhood upon its irreducible psychic incommunicability. In addition, the vulnerability of one part of a community is equivalent to the vulnerability of the whole ("We are all members of one another"). The Piedmont atrocity involved aggression against the genetic continuity of the people, as is clearly indicated from the emphasis in contemporary accounts on the rape and evisceration of women and the cannibalism of children. Since the Low Church depends centrally on the holiness of individual interiority and the redemptive character of sectarian distinctness, pain may be seen as a socially disintegrative parody of inner light, and genocide as the annihilation rather than the creation of the self in communal identification.

Under these circumstances participation in a community with characterizing marks results not in the immortality that communities confer upon the individual but, by a radical irony, in that oblivion from which the community was designed to rescue the singular person. These considerations are some part of the situation that lies inferentially in the background of Milton's sonnet.

Eschatology (reliance on final, posthistorical remedies) is the contrary of politics, and indeed Milton's poem exhibits no allusion to that reliance on the eschatological justification of the individual (the perfecting in the flames) that characterizes primitive Christian attitudes towards martyrdom. By contrast to other sonnets of Milton that are meditations on the meaning of names in a fame culture, there is also a total absence of singular identity in the report of the Waldensian event. Milton's poem exhibits these persons as they were known to their executioners, as anonymous members (unidentifiable amputated limbs, as it were) of a fatally identified community. Martyrdom is traditionally an adjunct of the epistemologies of faith. Only the will to die is sufficient to assure a community of the nonduplicitous character of man's hopefulness. As Professor Boime reminds us, men must, traditionally, die in order to be trusted. But victimage and martyrdom are not identical, and Milton wishes to deal with victimage in terms of martyrdom, a chancy and in itself potentially duplicitous gesture toward meaning.

Above all, Milton's poem-opening (the strong conjunction of the imperative and vocative, "Avenge O Lord") is a command to God that he behave in a manner consistent with his predicates (his biblically assured qualities), that he give meaning to an event that threatened the whole of life with meaninglessness. The prayer gesture commands the continuity of moral reality by a volition of the human will as exhibited in language. The God addressed is the God of history, vengeance being the abhorrent but rational evidence of a compensating intelligence in history.

> And when he had opened the fifth seal, I saw under the altar the souls of them that were slain for the word of God, and for the testimony which they held: And they cried with a loud voice saying, How long, O Lord, holy and true, dost thou not judge and avenge our blood on them that dwell on earth. (Rev. 6:9–10)

The speaker in Milton's poem declares that vengeance (the application of meaning to experience, central meaning to central experience) has not occurred. An abyss has opened up between fact and value that threatens to discredit retrospectively the revolutionary initiative. Milton's speaker, driven to the boundaries of the autonomy of the will, both moral and political, demands that the book of history be opened at the fifth seal, that victimage become martyrdom and that martyrdom exhibit its epistemological, its inherently gnostic essence.

The poem, like the journalistic accounts on which much of its language is based, contains iconic representation of dehumanized speech, "their moans," the hidden soul of harmony untuned. The incorporation of prayer in poetry, which is the effect of Milton's sonnet, repeats the motive of the will toward the reconstitution of the threatened continuities of vital relationship, speech being the culture of human intercourse with God. The sealing of man from God by the dehumanization of speech or the destruction of its agent, the poet, was already a subject of

Milton's imagination in "Lydicas" and is the awesome eventuality aversion to which compels the *Areopagitica*.

We may recall that a characterizing mark of Milton's shorter poems is the pastoral topos of the resonant, compensated, responsiveness of mind and world, the *echo*. Plenitude of sanctioned experience is affirmed when as in Spenser, "The woods shall to me answer and my echo ring." In the poem before us human utterance is not confirmed but rather distorted, amplified, and expelled by the landscape. As in Sidney's double sestina, the subject of which is the disappearance of the central symbol (origin of meaning) from experience, the Italian vales have become barren mountains and are filled with cries instead of music. This more than infernal landscape of existential degradation is the true Miltonic Hell. The "vale" is the generative fold in which English poetry displays man's life as justified under the figure of audible speech and within the ordered set of stations discriminated by the diurnal cycle from the hour before dawn to the hour after sunset. In the world of this poem the ample vale has been transformed into a strait place, a place of anguish; tortured outcries (the true voice of feeling) are redoubled without becoming intelligible, forced up out of the human universe by the impossibility of social response, toward God whose equally unresponsive hiddenness is the occasion of the poem.

Milton's sonnet incorporates a prayer form that itself incorporates the wordless outcry of total violation. *Prayer supervenes when the secular will has reached the boundary of its autonomy. Poem incorporates prayer when religion also reaches the limits of its singular authenticity.* At the bottom of this poem is a wordless cry (voice separated from meaning) upon the interpretation of which, through God to the human community, the speaker in the poem must by the logic of his situation stake his authority both as a poet and as a religious man.

There is in Milton a constant competition between the immortality that the poet facilitates by means of his privileged access to the collective continuity of the human community across time, and the alternative immortality ("eternity") of which God is agent as the perfect rememberer. Milton's central subject in "Lycidas," for example, is the supersession of an art-mediated fame culture by a God-mediated culture of redemption, and such in effect is the subject also of the early "Ode on the Morning of

Christ's Nativity." But the Piedmont sonnet represents the point of crisis of a successor culture (Protestant) in the interest of which the feudal hierarchies of king and episcopacy were overthrown. The Waldensian massacre is the test as to whether the revolution effected an instauration of the value of existence or an irreparable devaluation leading to hopeless vulnerability in the extended body of the Protestant community.

Milton is the poet of a crisis in the intelligibility of experience, which experience in the form of history *(The Theater of God's Judgement)* must resolve, if resolution there is to be. Milton's major poems are placed at flawed moments in the nexus of value and experience (of which the creation itself is always potentially one, as indeed it has become in *Paradise Lost*) when consciousness requires and is ready for new explanations. In the absence of divine manifestation the moral person is thrown back on secular resources for the sustaining of value, and speaks as a poet—the agent of memory in history—to the God who is the agent of memory beyond history. This epic-in-little and *Paradise Lost* in its vastness are evidence of the exhaustion of the human will in the labor of value, the poet at the end of his authority.

The elegiac topos, ubi sunt? ("Where were ye, nymphs, when the remorseless deep. . . ?") corresponds to the situation of the speaker in our sonnet. The pains of the laboring mother in the "Nativity Ode" (the predecessor of the mother of Orpheus in "Lycidas" and the mother slaughtered with her children in sonnet 18) are rendered meaningful by the birth, from the marriage of divinity and history, of the miraculous child. "Lycidas" deals in terms of individual life with the same moment that, as a crisis of collective life, is the subject of the "Ode." In the "Ode" the pains of the suffering mother are expressed as the shrieks of the dying gods of the older dispensation. In this way an intact hypothesis about the meaning of history makes possible the principal business of religion, the transforming of pain into value or, more specifically in the case of the "Ode," an absolute disseveration of the dying part from the theologically substantial ego. In the Piedmont sonnet this has become impossible. In "Lycidas" the intervention of redemptive transformation ("Weep no more, woeful shepherd, weep no more") against all hope and without explanation solved the problem of the loss of intelligibility through the transformation of its agent. But in the poem before us the Providential Solution has itself become a "false surmise." "Vengeance" in this poem could not be a form of counter-knowledge to empirical knowledge about history, since the revolution, like all revolutions, has given itself as a hostage to history. Sonnet 18, like most religious poems in this period, is an appeal from a fame culture that has failed toward a transcendental rememberer (God as the successor form of Mnemosyne) who, however, does not, as in "Lycidas," remember. In the Piedmont sonnet there is no hand that wipes the tears forever from their eyes. The gnostic component of martyrdom has been lost or is unmanifest, and the body of the new community of the revolution cannot amputate the being in pain, for that being is itself.

Milton as a theocratic revolutionary was the apologist of an antiepiscopal church in which individual identity was to be sustained by a direct relationship to God, and in which the sect or community of men was totally present in all of its parts as in a brotherhood. Feudal ecclesiastical hierarchies substantiate identity and mediate authority from above so that the community has a symbolic identity that transcends and at critical moments supersedes its parts. The revolutionary (the regicide) has the task of authenticating identity from below in the mysterious and yet to be defined totality of the new fraternity. Indeed, the revolutionary looks into the abyss between realms of value where value has lost one set of symbols and has not yet acquired another. Further, the fragility of the new regime of value once established may be shattered at any moment, for it is the hostage of its all-too-falsifiable hypotheses, as Cromwell with his obsession with the simplicities of military success knew very well. Beyond the military trial of God's preference lies the much more risky and unexplored enterprise of building Jerusalem. The Piedmont massacre was an occasion when the abyss was once again opened. A fast day was decreed by the same government that had sanctioned the atrocities of Wexford and Drogheda (which Tory historians such as Maurice Ashley still justify), a subscription for the Waldensians was taken in the whole of England, diplomatic letters were dispatched, documents gathered, a history written, as was this sonnet that summons the Author of being to avenge, remember, and make efficacious as meaningful event the pain of the victims.

Milton's imagination of revolution, as the supersession of one ground of value by another, preceded (as the "Ode" and "Lycidas" make apparent) the historical revolution in which he took part. Milton was throughout his career the apologist of the new alliances with meaning that are the condition of the coming to pass of new value and that at the same time imperil all value: the Fall of man, the birth of Christ, the Cromwellian revolution are central and cognate instances, with the difference that the last-named gave truth as a hostage to history—as an inescapable present. Defense, apology, justification are Milton's characteristic gestures. "Lycidas," for example, works in the personalistic elegiac topoi with the fundamental predicament of the death of meaning, of which the metaphor is the morally inexplicable bodily disappearance of the archetypal singer-priest whose culture is discredited by its proved inability to conserve its central practitioner. Milton is always the apologist, never the philosopher. Freedom depends on the moral autonomy of the reasoning individual, but reason in Milton is bound up in the intensely personal gesture of the gigantic rhetorician who, by mingling his will with his discourse, summons a meaningful state of affairs rather than defines its conditions. Milton's prose functions as a preemption of reality rather than a description of it, and in this reflects the limits also of the kind of poetry that he practices. His thematic gigantism in poetry and hypotactic comprehensiveness in prose suggest that for Milton psychic totalism is manipulated as an argument against cosmic nihilism. Milton's early life and education were in effect a gathering of authority toward the crisis that the proem of *Paradise Lost* seeks to master. The limits of his poetic style, which Eliot saw very clearly, and the limits of his rational apologetic are seen in the effort Marvell intuited in him, to exchange mind (as language) for world, rather than submit to the evidences of final complexity in historical experience.

II

Milton's sonnet, which is our subject, is an occasional poem, the occasion being the absence of any compensating event by which the Waldensian atrocity could be rendered consistent with a

Providential view of history. Either history is evidence of the congruence of God's rationality and man's, or it is not. If it is not, then there is nothing more to be said, since tragedy is not a possible alternative interpretation of history within the Miltonic frame, for it does not conserve the central value of the marriage of mind and world. There can be only one aesthetic (comedy) in *The Theater of God's Judgement*. Overshadowed by a possible cognitive dysfunction between God and man (which would make idiocy of all speaking), the speaker in the poem turns to prayer of the spontaneous or ejaculatory sort (as defined in, for example, Taylor's *Holy Living*). Such prayer depends on the prior readiness of the praying person, and explores the heart as given, since there is no time for the heuristic self-recollection of the meditative tradition. Milton's sonnet is therefore a prayer-like poem that, like all prayers (and all lyric poems, the characterizing mark of which is always the solitude of the speaker), is a strategy toward solving the problems that arise when the speaking person recognizes the final one-sidedness of cognitive experience. Prayers and poems also resemble one another in that they come at the end of a sequence of verbal strategies of another sort, as Milton's sonnet comes at the end of a sequence of diplomatic documents seeking political redress for the Waldensians. The exhaustion of social means, the abandonment of the historical fraternity that cannot protect though ruled by a Protector; and also of the languages of society that are imperfectly defended against duplicity, lead to the assertion (a kind of palinodial despair) of a prior filiation (God) toward whom language is directed in another way, since the Christian God, unlike the social other, knows the heart of the speaker directly (we might say intuitively).

Milton's prayerlike poem, unlike earlier such poems on the ejaculatory model, which are frequent in the canon of English poetry in the period (e.g., Donne's "Batter my heart . . ."), is only indirectly on behalf of the speaker. Milton is singular in his acknowledgment of history as part of the self. The massive grammatical tropes (imperative, vocative) that mark all prayers of petition are administered on behalf of a separated limb of the brotherhood of true Christians. The revolution broke down the sacramental narcissism that governed the earlier tradition of English religious poetry, which had as its subject the redemptive predicament of the Christian individual. The supranational fraternity of God's children has become the body on behalf of whose pain the speaker in the poem petitions God as the origin of the meaning of experience.

In the earlier poetry there is a scarcity of pain, the capacity to feel one's humanity as God experienced it, and a superabundance of meaning that shames and accuses the laboring soul (see, for example, Donne's "Good Friday, Riding Westward"). In this poem of Milton there is a superabundance of pain and a waning of existential certitude. The Miltonic-Cromwellian revolution having tampered, in the interest of the perfection of relationship, with the canons of civility (regicide, divorce), having destroyed the king's Englishmen and invented God's Englishmen, is consequently dependent directly at every moment, as Cromwell declared himself to be, on the rationality of Providence.

Illacrimabilis is the term Horace, in *Carmina* 4, 9, applies to those who lack representation because they lack a bard. Horace called "unweepable" those who, like the victims of atrocity, have no just or compensating images of themselves. Such a state overwhelms the heart, also, when the social world (the world in which men must be visible to one another) is disrupted, because the sufficient conditions of representability have been destroyed, often, as is the case in the killing of a king or the repudiation of a God, in the interest of liberation, or when new classes of persons (hitherto unrepresented politically and artistically) claim a stake in the scarce resources of manifest presence that are the treasure of a polity. (See, for example, John Philip's translation of Las Casas's *The Tears of the Indians, Being an Historical and True Account of the Cruel Massacre and Slaughter of above Twenty Millions of Innocent People*, which was dedicated to the Protector in 1656.)

Milton's speaker is pitched, not toward prayer but toward the prayerlike poem, by the mimetic desolation of persons who represent the annihilation of the self (as in "Lycidas," "He must not float upon his watery bier / Unwept"), which is a possible destiny deeply understood by all men, and not the least by Milton. God is the recognizer (redeemer, rememberer) of the inward self-recognition of all persons. The Puritan independent, like the Jew, seeks affiliation with and justification before that God, rather than in lesser human communities, and is therefore dependent for self-recognition on the complex epistemologies of the transcendental Deity, and ironically also on the historical world to which the Puritan has given himself as God's hostage.

Christopher Hill touches on Milton's subject when he says:

> Things were always going wrong, but it was the duty of the godly to make them go right, to snatch impossible victory to the greater glory of God. It was *in defeat* that Milton set about justifying the ways of God to man. Both the sense of sin, and the feeling of justification, came, ultimately, from readiness to break with the tradition, to obey the internal voice of God even when it revealed new tasks, suggested untraditional courses of action. (*God's Englishman,* p. 243)

As I have indicated, Milton's poems both before and after the Commonwealth take as their subject the rational continuity of value and experience expressed as the relationship between God and man. Both the human individual and the human community are intact when that relationship is expressible in intelligible speech. When it is not, man lies scattered as on the Alpine mountains cold. The forces in Milton's work early and late pitted against the survival of the human image ("the blind fury"), and the counterforces that conserve that image, are in a relationship of critical tension, uncertain combat. Everywhere the birth and continued visibility of the human image is threatened, the diurnal cycle invoked, both as a promise and as a peril to "the human face divine," since only through divine intervention is the hour before dawn turned into providential day.

The continuity of the human image in the culture of fame is a contingency of the continuity of the human community. But Milton's poetic subject up to *Paradise Lost* is in general the inadequacy of historical communities to remember and thereby conserve the human image, and the consequent necessity of turning away from society in the apostrophic or palinodial gesture toward a new regrounding of the human image in its remote and absolute origin, God. Politically this means regicide, and psychologically a turning away from secondary relationships, from self-realization in the social world, toward symbolic versions of primary relationship, that is to say, religion. Hence *Paradise Lost* is an attempt to reconstruct the human community from its origins in the primordial parental world of the generic first parents, in which disobedience becomes once again the fundamental prohibited act. The Waldensian sonnet lies in a midregion between stages of this process, and is in effect an example of the historical predicament without which the apologetic substance of *Paradise Lost* would be unintelligible. That the rejection of the social origin of the substantiating symbols of human identity ("What could the Muse herself, that Orpheus bore?") in favor of a prior transcendental account of symbolic origin (the Uranian muse) in effect pits the existential desire for intelligible existence directly against the evidence of historical experience is a paradox exemplificatory of the bitter logic of poetic functioning in its extended sense. It is this paradox that links Miltonic religious independence with secular states of mind.

In Milton's sonnet 18 "vengeance" would be a justification of the human will toward a human version of existence, and the sonnet finds that will at the outermost limits of its autonomy. The palinodial turning away from a tyrannic society in which only parodic versions of the human form are possible, toward a new version of community that has no historical form, links the "Babylonian wo" with apocalyptic (antihistorical and antinatural) aspects of the Romantic imagination. The resolution of the conflict of the "sense of sin" and the "feeling of justification," of actual personal and political situations and the desire for perfect personal rectitude and social authenticity, is incomplete in Milton. The "gathered churches" of Cromwell's New Model cavalry, which descended on its enemies screaming psalms, is as final an image of the aberration of the attempt to actualize integral transcendentally substantiated human communities in history as is the awesome and terrible balance in Milton's style between the world-destroying and the world-actualizing powers of the word.

In the epic tradition of the West, in the *Iliad* and *Aeneid,* the "true" God sends down real weapons in the service of his favored warrior. By contrast to Blake, who interiorized the struggle, Milton is a nonvisionary, mythographic poet for whom God's presence in history will be manifested in some real and visible order of the human community, or not at all. There is in Milton no sentiment such as the Blakean "mental fight," which seems in fact to have been derived as an imaginal response to the failure of the historical Commonwealth. The critical and defining predicaments of value seem in Milton to move from inward and symbolic to outward and historic. For example, the relationship between Milton's representation of the Waldensian massacre and the Miltonic theme of the world's threat to discourse and therefore to the continuity of the human image through representation in the historical community can be seen in the *Areopagitica* (1644):

> We should be wary therefore what persecution we raise against the living labours of public men, how we spill that season'd life of man preserv'd and stor'd up in Books: since we see a kind of homicide may be thus committed, sometimes a martyrdome, and if it extend to the whole impression, a kind of massacre, whereof the execution ends not in the slaying of an elemental life, but strikes at the ethereall and fifth essence, the breath of reason itself, slaies an immortality rather than a life.

The Waldensian massacre was just that "slaying of an elemental life" which threatened the "breath of reason itself." For Milton an oppressive society is a continuous assault on the human image, and immortality itself, so long as it is contingent upon the right order of society, is vulnerable. In the Piedmontese atrocity Milton's metaphor of the books reverses itself. The slaying of "an immortality rather than a life" becomes genocide, and the vulnerability of immortality becomes unendurable but not unimaginable. In Morland's *History* the depiction of the assault on the generativity of "The ancient Stock and seed of the Primitive and Purer Church" extends to the disemboweling of praying women and the hanging of men by the genitals. The immortality of a community in history, as it admits of no boundaries in historical time, admits also of no boundaries in social space.

Religious wars are conflicts over competing and mutually exclusive claims to occupy the same real existential universe that in Western civilization is represented by the negation of mortality. The price of communal authenticity that is the condition of individual immortality is the destruction of "meaningless" social mediations. The result is the vulnerability (unless God prevent it) of men who are all members of one another, and who by reason of their redemptive claims and affiliations occupy too much space in the world, as did the Waldensians in the valleys of the Pellice and Agrogna Rivers.

The English Revolution conceived as a theological event was in fact a counterrevolution in the interest of the transcendental tyrant against his ministers, the king and the episcopacy. When history is placed thus directly under the hegemony of the prior tyrant, historical event becomes prima facie a test of the efficacy of Providence. Milton's polemical career including *Paradise Lost* is in effect an argument with the human community on behalf of the intelligibility of experience conceived as a direct exchange of recognition between the sect and its divine master. The initiative of *Paradise Lost* to justify the ways not of man to God, but of God to man, confirms our sense that God has failed his test (history being the unendurable and perverted theophany), and that poetry must intervene as the instrument of the human will toward meaning *per impossibile.* In young Milton's confident ode, "On the Morning of Christ's Nativity," the birth of the divine surrogate of the self, the child God, compensates history for the agony of revolution. The aging revolutionary by contrast finds that the successor culture no longer sustains the cost of its establishment, which was detected first in the moans of the dying gods of antiquity but later in the mortal cries of the slaughtered mother and infant, the primal human group, in the transmogrified pastoral landscape of the Italian Alps. Milton, by contrast to his immediate predecessors in the religious subject, is not merely a lay poet but a secular poet. The function of poetry, in Milton and after, is not to register the agon of man in response to the demands of God, but to reconstitute the "false surmise" of a sacramental universe. The pervasive theme of temptation in Milton incorporates the conflict between experience and value. The Miltonic sentiment of this conflict bears out Marvell's fear

> That he would ruine (for I saw him strong)
> The sacred Truths to Fable and old Song,
> (So *Sampson* groaped the Temples Posts in spight)
> The World o'rewhelming to revenge his Sight.

The bourgeois revolution was the occasion of a trial of God. The Waldensian massacre was an episode in that crisis of the relationship between value and experience which the revolution precipitated. The bourgeoisification of literature was and still is an incomplete task. *The mimetic privilege (the privilege of image) that is the secular correlative of divine remembering has by no means been accorded to all the members of any society. In our time the recognition of the human other as real, and by that person's very existence a prior value to all more abstract values, is the major social crisis to which poetry speaks.* The Waldensians are the image, such as it is, of the self driven beyond recognition and therefore outside of existence. Milton's prayerlike poem is in effect a secular version of the prayer that brings man before God, in his inner form as language, for acknowledgment. Poetry and prayer represent the will of man toward self-identification in the fundamental value of the person manifested in the ambiguous medium of language at the boundary and breaking point of the autonomy of the instrumental will whose forms are religion and politics. In post-revolutionary cultures the function of poetry is the reconstitution of human identity, so far as poetry can reach, in the face of the perhaps impossible deficit created by "liberation."

The Poetics of Union
in Whitman and Lincoln
An Inquiry toward the Relationship of
Art and Policy

The preceding paper proposed to show, from the example of Milton, how the turn to poetry is compelled when the central institutions of a postrevolutionary culture have reached the end of their capacity to shelter the value of the person. The motive of revolution that is the redistribution of the scarce resource of fundamental social value, the image of the person, insofar as revolution succeeds, produces a proportionately disabling problematization of the terms that ground those recognitions in the interest of which it was undertaken. Such is the bitter logic of the poetic principle that governs the construction of human recognition. "In postrevolutionary cultures the function of poetry is the reconstitution of human identity, so far as poetry can reach, in the face of the perhaps impossible deficit created by 'liberation.' " The question that the present inquiry addresses is, simply, *how far can poetry reach.*

In his "Second Annual Message" Lincoln recommmends his emancipation proclamation with these words: "It is not 'Can any of us *imagine* better?' but 'can we all *do* better.' . . . As our case is new, so we must think anew and act anew. We must disenthrall ourselves, and then we shall save our country." Thus Lincoln raises the issue of the difference between imaginable states of affairs (which can be thought but not brought to pass) and

From Walter Benn Michaels and Donald Pease, editors. *The American Renaissance: Selected Papers from the English Institute, 1982–83*. Reprinted by permission of the Johns Hopkins University Press.

actualizable states of affairs that can happen. The poem is a case of a state of affairs of the latter sort—a real order of terms—which can come to pass and is actual. But what kind of order is possible, what states of affairs can become actual? Whitman proposes that there are new possibilities of actual structure, unanticipated by the "feudal" past (both of poetry and polity), that escape the bitter logic of which I speak, and that the poet can discover and contribute to the social world. Did Whitman do so?

I

To begin with, I shall suppose that both policy and art are addressed to the solution of problems vital to the continuity of the social order, and, therefore, to the human world. In the period of America's Civil War (the "renaissance" moment both of America's literary and its constitutional authenticity) there arose two great and anomalous masters, the one of policy and the other of poetry: Abraham Lincoln and Walt Whitman. Both men addressed the problem of the reconstruction of their common human world—the Union as a just and stable polity—at a time when the elements necessary to the intelligibility of that world seemed fallen, in Seward's words, into "irrepressible conflict."[1]

The political and constitutional situation, as both men understood it, was clear. The Missouri Compromise of 1820, which had reconciled the equality requirement of the Declaration of Independence with the continuity requirements of the Constitution (among them slavery), was undone between 1846 and 1857 by the outcome of the Mexican War, the Fugitive Slave Law, the Kansas-Nebraska Act, and Dred Scott. In effect, competition between the claims of two incompatible systems of labor with their attendant social structures, precipitated by the acquisition of new territory in the Mexican War and the opening of the Northwest, required deliberated choices, as if in an "original position," among contradictory descriptions of the human world. By the accident of history, these choices involved the staggeringly primitive question as to which human beings were persons.[2] That deliberation was, in the end, condensed upon the figure and discourse of Lincoln, whose "mould-smashing mask" (as Henry James put it) was a bizarre picture of *concordia discors*, the imagination's conquest of irreconcilables; it was interrupted and restated by the cruel, integrative, and perhaps artificial catastrophe of the Civil War; and at last ironically inscribed in the Thirteenth, Fourteenth, and Fifteenth amendments.[3]

On the literary side, Emerson, Thoreau, Melville, and Whitman addressed the same problem of the union or connectedness of the human world, which they also saw by deliberated fictions as if for the first time in a new territory where the worth of persons was subject to the risk of finding a form. The long aftermath of the Revolution had destroyed the old America, a confederation of separately constituted religious communities, in which personhood was validated or canceled by reference to the eucharistic mystery of the hypostatic union. Whitman and others worked toward a reconstructive poetics appropriate to a modern political society, in which this same validating function was equivocally provided in the centerless rationality of the Constitution legislated by the secular decree of the people. Authentic American art, as well as true American constitutionality, awaited a solution to the crisis of the establishment of the person.[4]

In America at midcentury, both art and policy confronted a culture that lacked an effective structure (a meter, a genre, an epistemology, a law) to mediate between the pragmatic ideal of political unity—the unwritten poem of these states—and the mutually excluding legitimacies for which right and place were claimed in consciousness and the nation—Declaration and Constitution, equality and order, body and soul. Lincoln supplied that structure in the form of a conservative ideology of union based in ethical constitutionalism, promulgated by a rational style of discourse of unfailing adequacy and persuasiveness. He was a *novus homo,* a man impersonated by his language, the structure of whose tragic song of self-invention (a recapitulation of the significant past of America, as he understood it) came in the event to be repeated as America's present, the Civil War. The literary master of union was Whitman, for whom also the one justifiable order of the world was the order of the discourse by which he invented himself, his song. ("The United States themselves," he said, "are essentially the greatest poem.") Neither of these men could *appear,* except as a function of their language that bore upon them, and subsequently upon their world, as Emerson remarked of perception in general, not as a whim but as a fate.

The only social role that could make actual the enigmatic particularity of Lincoln's self-invention, speak out loud the pure language of individual personhood by which he discovered the tragic laws of social peace, was the citizen presidency. The only social role that could express the function of the person for Whitman—immanent, comedic, doxological, choral—was the poet-nurse, commissioned healer of the violence of language of another sort. At the end of the war, Whitman signified the inclusion of the tragedy of policy within the comedy of his art by receiving Lincoln into the night—"hiding, receiving"—of his elegy, as he had received in his arms so many of the dead of Lincoln's war.

Insofar as the actuality of both policy and poetry require sentences a man can speak, the material upon which poetry works and the material upon which policy works are identical because of the ubiquity of language, and present the same resistances. The reasons that one cannot make just any poem, or just any policy, good are the same. An entailment of any style a person speaks is the structure of a social world that can receive it—a political formation and its kind of conscious life. Whitman and Lincoln were autodidact masters. As such, they received the implications of acculturation without interposition of mediating social forms, and restated its structure directly as the structure of the worlds they intended.

Lincoln was born in the wilderness, whereas Thoreau deliberately chose to live there. Lincoln's literacy derived from personal labor. For Lincoln the crisis of union repeated the enigma of his own socialization. His legendary honesty specifies him as a man of his word, as Whitman's theatrical "nakedness" makes him a man whose self is his song. For Whitman as for Lincoln, the legitimation of personhood (the crisis of union) involves the justification of a mode of discourse, not merely a particular case of practice. But the autodidact self-invention of Whitman—his self-commissioning praxis—identified him with the ethos of poetry. In his understanding poetry is the leisure of receptivity, not the rational labor of the will—"I loafe and invite my soul." A poetry that authorizes a personhood reflexively validated by its own discourse can have no category of fictionality. (He who touches this book touches all the man there is.) A poetry that has no category of fictionality is a policy.[5] Correlatively, a policy that intends, as did Lincoln's, the same structure as its discourse is a poetry. In this sense, both Whitman and Lincoln are profoundly conservative figures. Both bind the world, with totalitarian immediacy, to the configurative implication of the central sentences of a cultural instrument.

Therefore, one may ask the question whether, as between Lincoln's politics and Whitman's poetry, there are two policies of union, or only one—insofar as they are representative of two distinct cultural modes. Does poetry know anything that policy does not? One may also ask, given the singular nature of these two figures, both of whom practice language that intends as a function of its structure a just order of the human world, whether there really is a nontragic, open-form, egalitarian version of the reconciliation of justice and order, or only the brilliant, closed, individualist, logic-based Lincolnian version so profoundly implicated with our world as it has come to pass.

II

The supposition with which I began, that art and policy are addressed to the same problems, assumes that prior to both art and policy is the common intention of an order of the human world, and that the world has a stake in knowing (and criticism a means of inquiring) what art and policy cannot do.

Lincoln's strategy of order was an amplification of a legal grammar (Blackstonian) adapted to political use, the structure of which was based in the Aristotelian laws of thought—identity, noncontradiction, the excluded middle. He judged the world that he constructed by a hermeneutic criterion of intelligibility, modeled on Euclid. A house divided against itself, like a sentence that asserts contradictories, cannot stand because it makes no sense and accords with no possible state of affairs.[6] He judged the substantial moral world similarly, according to the criterion of simplicity. Lincoln accepted as self-evident the distinction between good and evil, implied as a restriction on choice by the Declaration of Independence (all men are created equal), and assumed that there was a state of fact in accord with the criterion that the two authoritative documents of his reality (Declaration and Constitution) meant the same thing. Correspondingly, the meaning of the law, for Lincoln, was "the intention of the law-giver," and all the givers of authentic law, including God, intended the same thing.[7] "The will of God," he notes in 1862, "prevails. In great contests each party claims to act in accordance with the will of God. Both may be, and one must be, wrong. God cannot be for and against the same thing at the same time." Hence, Lincoln's speaking induced a sentiment of what Marianne Moore called his "intensified particularity," deriving first from a willed overcoming of complexity and consequent clarification of the world, and second from the indissociability of that clarification from his own person.[8] Thus, Lincoln's policy subordinated and conserved an ineradicable autochthony against a reality of immense complexity. In its severest form, the form given it in history by the hands of Grant and Sherman, his rhetoric was obliterative. "Both may be, and one must be, wrong."[9]

In the crossing of kinds of discourse in history, poetry situates itself where other instruments of mind find impossibility. Thus, Walt Whitman found his truth, and the unity of his world, precisely at the crisis of contradiction where Lincoln found disintegrative instability. Unlike Lincoln's God, who cannot be for and against the same thing at the same time, Whitman's "greatest poet" inferred from the traditional fame-powers of his art a fundamental principle of undifferentiated representation, which constituted a massive trope of inclusion. Representation (the class of all classes) was itself an implicit unification, the fame of the world; and the great bard, "by whom only can series of peoples and states be fused into the compact organism of a Nation," promulgated the goodness of simple presence as a human state of affairs. Of *his* legislator Whitman says in the "Poem of Many in One": "He judges not as the judge judges but as light falling round a helpless thing." Whitman's originality consisted in the discovery of a regulative principle that permitted an art based in the representative function itself, and organized in its ideal-typical moments (for example, the world inventories in #15 and #33 of "Song of Myself") as a taxonomy of which the sorting index is mere being-at-all. The argument that made the meter of

Whitman was the unification of the world in the one power of language, the secret authority of the poet (his "Santa Spirita"), the bestowal of presence across time. The theater of that presence is the poetic line; and the poetics of the line is the multiplicative logic of presence by which Whitman replaces, and contradicts, the world-dividing logic of Lincoln's rational sentence.

The English poetic line, as Whitman found it, was the synergetic outcome of the two orders of form: an abstract and irrational pattern of counted positions, on the one hand, and the natural stress characteristics of language heightened and articulated by the semantic concerns of the reader, on the other. But the repertory of abstract patterns (e.g., blank verse) that the reader received was, in his view, indelibly stained by the feudal contexts of its most prestigious instances, and in addition required the subordination of the natural stress characteristics of language, and therefore an abridgment of the freedom of the speaker. But Whitman was an end-stopped-line writer. And for him the abstract patterns (the "mechanical" aspects of structure) served, at the least, two indispensable functions: the provision, first of all, of the external and (by convention) timeless *locus communis* where the "I" and the "you" could meet, a principle of access; and, second, the establishment of a finite term that sealed utterance against silence and granted form. Whitman compensated this deletion of the metrical aspect of the line by revising the poetic mechanism of access of person to person on the basis of the "transparence," or reciprocal internality, of persons one to the other ("What I shall assume you shall assume"), and by the hypothesis of a world composed of a "limitless" series of brilliant finite events each of which imposed closure at the grammatical end of its account. It is, however, opposition to the meaning-intending will by the resistance of abstract form that produces, in the English poetic line, the sentiment of the presence of the person as a singular individual; and this Whitman could not restore.

We see, therefore, that the paradox that the logic of poetic construction posed to Whitman, the ideologist of union as happiness, is analogous to the paradox that the logic of clarification posed to Lincoln, the ideologist of union as "fairness." In Lincoln's case the unification of the world required the dissolution of one term of any set of contradictories in order to obtain thereby the inherent simplification required by truth—a totalitarianism of hypotaxis. In the poet's case, the abandonment of abstract pattern put in question the validity of the instrument of fame itself by dissolving its subject—a totalitarianism of parataxis. The problem for both Whitman and Lincoln was how to preserve the ends of the enterprise from the predation of the means.

III

When Matthiessen named Whitman "the central figure of our literature affirming the democratic faith," he did so because he saw Whitman as the champion, not only of liberty and equality, but also (unlike Emerson, Thoreau, and even Melville) of fraternity—the master of union as social love.[10] But Lincoln was the great speaker of the American Renaissance whose imagination empowered the democratic faith. Its way, he said, is "plain, peaceful, generous, just." In the 1850s, both Whitman and Lincoln held more or less the same politics, including the view that slavery *and also abolition* were barbarisms: abolition because it interrupted contract and exchange, without which there was no social world in which anyone *could* be free; slavery because, as an impermissible variation of the practice of liberty (you cannot choose to enslave), it destroyed the value both of labor and leisure, without which freedom was empty of praxis.[11] Lincoln's characteristic strategy for freeing slaves was *compensated* emancipation, the completion of the Revolution by the co-optation in its service of the constitutional principle of contract—the justification, in effect, of logical discourse. Whitman supposed that the same result could only be obtained by a more fundamental revision of the central nature of relationship—the establishment of a new basis of speaking in the counterlogic, and infinite distributability, of affectionate presence. Both Lincoln and Whitman intended the same thing. The two systems (the closed and the open) that they sponsored aspire each to specify the inclusion of the other as the best outcome of its own nature. The limits of each of these two systems in view of their common goal becomes plain in the two related issues of *hierarchy*, the constraints upon variation consistent with union as structure, and *equality,* the management of access of persons one to the other consistent with union as value.

In Lincoln's "First Inaugural," a performative utterance at the moment of oath-taking, which he described as an account of his own worthiness of credence, Lincoln identified secession as a transgressive practice of freedom—a disordering variation—inconsistent with the intactness of the organic law of the nation; and he defined by contrast the true democratic sovereign:

> Plainly, the central idea of secession is the essence of anarchy. A majority, held in restraint by constitutional checks, and limitations, and always changing easily, with deliberate changes of popular opinions and sentiments is the only true sovereign. Whoever rejects it does of necessity fly to anarchy or to despotism. Unanimity is impossible; the rule of the minority, as a permanent arrangement is wholly inadmissible; so that, rejecting the majority principle, anarchy or despotism is all that is left.[12]

Oath-taking is Lincoln's peculiar form of honesty. At the moment of the "First Inaugural" he identifies himself with the union, grown suddenly abstract with the secession of seven states, and establishes himself as its regulative presence by articulating the grammar of the one authentic sentence that expresses both equality and intelligible structure.[13] But the world the Constitution describes is organized around the conservation of the singular person by the concession of totalistic right—excluding despotism, anarchy, *and also unanimity.* By the principle of majority rule, equality is delegated and unanimity eternally postponed. This delegation takes the form of an exchange whereby autonomy is given up, and social life, the human scale of the person, received in return. Lincoln's true sovereign is a collectivity less than the whole, a "majority held in restraint" by a regulative principle external to itself that by its measure produces freedom in the form of resistances to the will structured to conserve its own nature.

At the heart of Lincoln's conception of constitution is a commutative process: life is given up for meaning, the significance of the whole sentence; and the interest of all persons (and, therefore, potentially the whole interest of each) is exchanged for a rational sociability based in a hierarchy of ends of which the highest term (union) is external to the person, and not within his power of choice. Paramount among these exchanges, and implied in all, is the exchange of life for meaning (the bitter sacrificial logic of the poetic principle), an idea that Lincoln repeated as a hermeneutic principle in his explanation of the war (e.g., "From these honored dead we take increased devotion to that cause for which they gave the last full measure of devotion"). Since secession was a transgressive exercise of choice (the repudiation of the social bond) on behalf of slavery, and slavery a perversion of the social contract intended to repudiate rather than affirm personhood, the urgency of restoring Union was doubly driven by the ethical motive, not only (and perhaps not primarily) to establish all human beings as persons, but also to revalidate the principle of the whole social world. Secession made inescapably apparent the inherently conflictual character of the legal understanding of the Constitution by making unmistakable the incompatibility of the freedom of the individual (the freedom, for instance, to enslave) with the order of the state—the inherently imperfect inclusion under rational auspices of the many in the one.

Whitman's motive, by contrast, was to get death out of sociability (and by implication, out of representaton), to devise "death's outlet song." The bard is the better president because he is the "perfect" agent of human presence—the voice's announcement, prior to all other messages, of the presence of the person prior to all other characteristics. As such, the bard distributes the value of personhood, which is the value commuted in all other economic transactions. The poem is of the same nature as central value, because the whole function of its discourse is acknowledgment. Consequently, universal access to the poem is a policy to overcome scarcity. To effect this, Whitman devised a "song" that would reconcile variety and order, equality and constitution, one and many without compromising either term. Once again Whitman situates his new American organic law and true sovereign precisely where Lincoln finds impossibility, at the zero point of unanimity.

The destruction of the constitutional settlement in the 1820s precipitated the crisis of the Union in the form of the scarcity of personhood. A characteristic recuperative episode of the 1850s is the Dred Scott decision, which solved the problem of such scarcity by ruling the African slave out of the human community by a distinction as severe and of the same effect as that between the redeemed and the unregenerate.[14] In the slave codes of the South the chattel slave must call every man "master." By his uncanny difference—a human being who is not a person—the slave precisely specifies and thereby generates and maintains (this is his work) the boundary between the nonperson and the person upon which the distinction of the person is established.[15] The refounding of personhood, the historical function of the poet, was the deferred business both of the American revolution and of American literature. But the perfect equality of all human beings requires, as Whitman understood, an infinite resource of fame.

Whitman's policy was to establish a new principle of access that would effect multiplication, or pluralization (the getting many into one), without the loss entailed by exchange—the glory of the perfect messenger. In the chronology of Whitman's work, the "open" line as formal principle appears simultaneously with the subject of liberation, and is the enabling condition of the appearance of that subject. That is to say, his first poems in the new style are also his first poems on the subject of slavery and freedom (specifically, "Resurgemus," "Blood-Money," "Wounded in the House of Friends"). His first lines in the new style altogether (so far as I can tell) are recorded in a notebook as follows:

> I am the poet of the slave, and of the masters of the slave
> . . . .
> I am the poet of the body
> And I am the poet of the soul
> I go with the slaves of the earth equally with the masters
> And I will stand between the masters and the slaves,
> Entering into both, so that both shall understand me alike.[16]

In another early notebook Whitman gives an account of what he calls "translation," the power he uses in place of the Coleridgean poetic "imagination." (He sometimes, as in the Lincoln elegy, calls it "tallying.")

> Every soul has its own individual language, often unspoken, or feebly spoken; but a true fit for that man and perfectly adapted for his use—The truths I tell to you or to any other may not be plain to you, because I do not translate them fully from my idiom

into yours.—If I could do so, and do it well, they would be as apparent to you as they are to me; for they are truths. No two have exactly the same language, and the great translator and joiner of the whole is the poet.[17]

Instead of a "poetic language" (always a mimetic version of the language of one class) Whitman has devised a universal "conjunctive principle" whose manifest structure is the sequence of end-stopped, nonequivalent, but equipollent lines. By it he intends the power of the God to whom (as in the "Collect for Purity" that introduces the Mass) "all hearts are open . . . desires known . . . from whom no secrets are hid." His poetic authority is J. S. Mill's "overheard" soliloquy of feeling, and his physicalist basis is the phrenological continuity between inner and outer mind. The drama of translation is enacted at the beginning of an early poem, "The Answerer":

> Now list to my morning's romanza, I tell the signs of the
>   Answerer.
> To the cities and farms I sing as they spread in the sunshine
>   before me.
>
> A young man comes to me bearing a message from his brother,
> How shall the young man know the whether and when of his
>   brother?
> Tell him to send me the signs.
> And I stand before the young man face to face, and take his
>   right hand
> in my left hand and his left hand in my right hand
> And I answer for his brother and for men.

By curing the human colloquy, the poet (the translator, answerer, perfect messenger, better president) intends to establish a boundless resource of the central acknowledgment-value, and to rid sociability of death by overcoming the scarcity of fame, a process that requires elision of the mechanical checks and balances (reifications of the competing will of the inaccessible other) that characterize the poetics of Lincoln's constitutionalism. But Whitman's new principle of access—his line—is not "organic" in Matthiessen's Coleridgean sense. It has the virtuality of a paradigm; and the negotiation of its actualization against the resistances of history and mind is Whitman's major subject.

The primal scene of that negotiation is the "transparent morning" of part 5 of "Song of Myself." It is the inaugural moment of Whitman's candor, and as such it recapitulates the first subject matter liberated by his line. The form is the confession of a creed:

> I believe in you my soul, the other I am must abase itself to you
> And you must not be abased to the other.

The rewriting of hierarchies—soul/body, collective/individual, nation/state—as equalities, and the rewriting of conventional dualities as identities, above all the self and the other, is the task of the "translator," whose goal is union conceived as the fraternalization of the community. In the Nicene Creed what follows is, of course, the hypostatic union. What follows in Whitman's creed is the greater mystery of the mortal union of two, the competent number of acknowledgment, and the archetype of all political relationship. For Lincoln, labor is prior to capital and is the praxis of the individual will by which all selfhood, and therefore all value, is produced.[18] It is indistinguishable from the act of clarification (the intention of the lawgiver) by which univocal meaning is derived, many made one. To loaf ("Loafe with me on the grass") is to exchange the posture of hermeneutic attention for the posture of receptivity, the unity of all things in the last sorting category of mere consciousness prior to interpretation ("the origin of all poems"), of which the voice is the "hum," the sound of the blood doing the cultural work of God (a further secularization of the "sound of many waters" of Revelation, repeated by Wordsworth as the mystically integrative speaking of the Leech Gatherer), the doggerel of life. What follows, then, is the sexual union reconstructed as a moment of primal communication, the tongue to the heart. The principle of the language of the soul is the deletion, as in Whitman's metricality as a whole, of centralizing hypotactic grammar, and the difference-making prosodies both of individual meaning-intention and abstractly patterned (stress/no stress) metricality. What is obtained is an unprecedented trope of inclusion—the sign, embodied in that revision of primary human relationship ("gently turned over upon me"), of which the greater inclusions of emancipation and union are the things signified:

And limitless are the leaves stiff and drooping in the fields
And brown ants in the little wells beneath them
And mossy scabs of the worm fence, heap'd stones, elder,
    mullein and poke-weed.

But what is created, paradoxically, is a new slave culture. The Whitmanian voice, like the slave, is uncanny—a servant of persons, but not itself personal—a case of delegated social death: "A generalized art language, a literary algebra" (Sapir). "Comradeship—part of the death process. The new Democracy—the brink of death. One identity—death itself" (Lawrence). "To put the paradox in a nutshell, he wrote poetry out of poetry writing" (Pavese).[19] There is truth in these judgments. The logic of presence, Whitman's "profound lesson of reception," has its own violence. The Whitmanian convulsion ("And parted the shirt from my bosom-bone, and plunged your tongue to my bare-stripped heart"), attendant upon the reduction of all things to appearance, is the counterviolence to that which flows from the logic of clarification, the reduction of all things to univocal meaning. The tongue of the soul is the principle of continuity figured as the "hum" of subvocal, absorbed, multitudinous, continuously regulated "valved voice," or "this soul," as Whitman elsewhere says, "its other name is Literature."[20] The tongue sacrifices the subject of justice in the interest of personal immediacy that overcomes the difference of the social body, but at the same time destroys (tongue to bare-stripped heart) the destiny of the secular person that the social body is.

In a tract Whitman wrote in 1856 on behalf of Fremont (whom Lincoln also supported), Whitman produces his model of "The Redeemer President" whose way will be "not exclusive, but inclusive."[21] Lincoln was not Whitman's redeemer president. Lincoln was the type of the "unknown original" (Sapir's expression) from which, as from the utterance of the hermit thrush of the elegy, Whitman translated his song. Whitman's taxonomic line runs "askant" history (the abstract pattern he deletes is precisely the element of the line that has a history).[22] That variation produces the infinite access he required for his "peace that passes the art and argument of earth." In Lincoln's terms such a variation is as transgressive (and of the same nature) as Douglas's "squatter sovereignty," or slavery itself.

Lincoln's sentence, by contrast, prolongs the history of each soul beyond mortality in a never-darkened theater of judgment. In the midst of an argument in his "Second Annual Address" (1862) in support of compensated emancipation, Lincoln inserts the following sentence: "In times like these men should utter nothing for which they would not be responsible through time and in eternity."[23] In the straitening of choice, Lincoln in his language grows thick with character, the pure case of tragic personhood enacting the indissolubility of a moral identity that persists across eschatological boundaries in continuous space and time (the cosmological expression of ethical contract)— unmistakable, eternally situated, judged. The peroration of the same speech begins: "Fellow citizens *we* cannot escape history. We of this Congress and this administration, will be remembered in spite of ourselves. No personal significance, or insignificance, can spare one or another of us. The fiery trial through which we pass, will light us down, in honor or dishonor, to the latest generation."[24] By deleting the abstract pattern of internal marks that closes the traditional line and carries it across time, Whitman deleted history, founded an infinite resource of acknowledgment, dissolved the moral praxis of the singular individual, and "launched forth" (as he says at the end of the "Song of the Answerer") into the desituate universe of transparent minds, generated by an open metrical contract, "to sweep through the ceaseless rings and never be quiet again." Lincoln's language, unlike Whitman's, is empowered because it is of the same nature as the institutions that invented him, and his space and time are institutional space and time. In such a world, judgment and acknowledgment are inseparable; and the economy of scarcity is reconstituted in the oldest economic terms of our civilization—honor or dishonor.

Both Whitman and Lincoln are captives of a system of representation, which they are commissioned to justify and put in place as an order of the human world—a policy for union. *Are there two policies, or only one?* On the one hand, a Whitmanian policy—open, egalitarian, in a sense socialist (as Matthiessen thought it to be), generalized from the fame-power of art, and darkly qualified by that abjection of the subject of value that is the other side of receptivity; and, on the other hand, a Lincolnian system—closed, republican, capitalist, a regulative policy driven by the logic of clarification, and darkly qualified in its turn by the obliterative implications both of moral exclusiveness and the delegatory economies of labor? We have seen that the centered, hierarchical, Lincolnian ethical rationality is precisely the enemy element from which Whitman is bent upon exempting his human world. We see also that the resonant, scale-finding, integrative vocality of Lincoln is the most severe criticism our literature affords of Whitman's indeterminate realization of the person— "You whoever you are." Whitman's "Word over all, beautiful as the sky" reconciles what Lincoln's ethical dualism drives into division, yet only at that distance; Lincoln's sentiment of ethical difference cruelly specifies the limit of variation in which regulative rationality can produce the actual life of all men. *But despite the reciprocally canceling nature of Whitman and Lincoln as liberators, the gravity of representation itself unites them in a common conservatism.*

In the "Preface of 1855" Whitman lays down his own regulative sentence: "Nothing out of its place is good and nothing in its place is bad."[25] For Whitman the final sorting category of presence, the place of good life, is (as I have said) mere existence, of which the dwelling is the open air, and the poetic structure the internally unmarked line manifesting "as amid light" the natural stress characteristics of langue in the natural order, determined at the end by the objectively finite plenitude of each of an infinite number of faces *caught in a brilliant virtuality from which it cannot depart:* "Passing the yellow-speared wheat, every grain from its shroud in / the dark-brown fields uprisen."[26] For Lincoln that same place of good life is "the national homestead"—a boundless, mastered autochthony specified, rendered continuously intelligible and therefore free, by the internal markings of superordinate measure. It is Lincoln who says: "There is no line, straight or crooked, on which to divide."

IV

One reason we turn to criticism of poetry is to bring to pass projects that become possible only when we make statements about poetic texts. We do criticism because we are busy about something else. In this sense, we do not intend the poem; we intend the intention that brought the poet to poetry, which is not the poem but the reason for taking poetry in hand. Our judgment upon the poem is an assessment of the likelihood of the coming to pass of what is intended. And our judgment, or the poet's, upon poetry itself is an assessment of its usefulness as an instrument of our urgent, common work.

In "a society waiting," as Whitman says of his America, "unformed . . . between things ended and things begun," Whitman intended a revision of all "conjunctive relations."[27] Of this revision the "great poet" was the sign, and also the incarnation of the regulative principle of his own signifier, the poem—man of his word. As the world over which Lincoln presided darkened through the Civil War, Whitman saw the defeat of fraternity that was the substance of his policy. The seal of that defeat, the murder of the president, he inscribed with his great reconstructive "Burial Hymn," "When Lilacs Last in the Dooryard Bloom'd." During that period, Lincoln in his speeches drew the world with justificatory intensity and comprehensiveness ever deeper into the system of representation whose structure was expressed in his political and strategic judgments, as in the "Second Inaugural": "Until every drop of blood drawn by the lash shall be paid by another drawn by the Sword." Whitman, on the other hand, tended more and more to modify his regulative principles to release the world from the overdetermination of all systems of representation, as in the consummatory cry of perfect translation: "I spring out of these pages into your arms—decease calls me forth."[28]

As is the case with pastoral elegy in general, "When Lilacs Last" is, first of all, a gesture of riddance of a prior representational dispensation unable to "keep" its children. (Whitmanian celebration by pluralization extinguishes all personhood that has *only* singular form ["Nor for you, for one alone / Blossoms and branches green to coffins all I bring"].)[29] Second, the elegy effects the reconstitution of the world on the basis of the new supersessory system (in "Lycidas" the "unexpressive nuptial song"; in Whitman's poem "yet varying ever-altering song"). Finally, Whitman's elegy investigates the implications of a "passing," or paratactic transcendence, of that new system of representation toward a right state of the world undeformed by any mediation of discourse. One reason for the fullness of articulation of Whitman's poem lies in the complexity of its judgment, not only on the failed predecessor system of which all that survives is love without an object, but also on itself as a policy toward the consummation of that love—a union not broken by the means of its accomplishment. In this judgment of the judge whose justice does not divide consists the final profundity of Whitman, his "delicacy," as the late James Wright called it.

"When Lilacs Last" repeats the millennial archetype of the death of the Beloved Companion whose *nostos* it completes ("Nothing out of its place is good; and nothing in its place is bad"). The elegy returns to the West Lincoln, who had departed four years earlier on his journey from West to East (displacing an autochthonous power in the service of an alien rationality) with the great sentences of farewell at Springfield, Illinois (11 February 1861), which begin with a double negative that seals, at the moment of deracination, untranslatable individuality into irreducible space and time: "Friends: no one not in my situation, can appreciate my sadness at this parting. . . . Here I have lived. . . , and have passed from a young to an old man. Here my children have been born, and one is buried."[30] By contrast, Whitman's correlative rehearsal of departure in the opposite direction, from East to West (his revision in 1862 of the opening stanza to "Starting from Paumanok") sets the self at large in the field of consciousness—at the other end from Lincoln on the truth table for the particle /or/:

> Aware of the fresh free giver the flowing Missouri, aware
> of the mighty Niagara,
> Aware of the buffalo herds grazing the plains, the hirsute
> and strong-breasted bull,
> Of earth, rocks, Fifth-month flowers experienced, stars, rain,
> Snow, my amaze,

released from the rational justice of situation, inclusive of many places at once (here and also there) not as seeing is but as light is. And yet "Solitary, singing in the West." The old situated world of unexchangeable Euclidean marks provided the object of love—the Beloved Companion—to Whitman as elegist; but the new world of the open principle provides the elegy. It springs forth at the death of the loved person, released from the hermeneutic bondage ("O the black murk that hides the star!") that invented that person and destroyed him—a supersessive culture of keeping as union of one and many ("each to keep and all"), by its nature requiring his loss. The loss of the companion precipitates the speaker in the poem upon a new autonomy—a searching of the boundaries of representation ("dusk and dim") for an instrument of sociability that does not produce the disappearance of its object.

At the heart of Whitman's elegy is the scene of the reading of the song of the hermit thrush named "Solitary," the "loud human song" of the unknown original, the singular person. This scene is a repetition of the inaugural action of translation (as pluralization) by which in "Out of the Cradle Endlessly Rocking" the poet received his commissioning ("Now in a moment I know what I am for.... / And already a thousand singers ... have started to life within me, never to die"). To accomplish this *katabasis* a refraternalization is required by which the poet becomes the conjunctive term between the "thought" of death and its "knowledge," general and particular, many and one—the "hand in hand" of union mediated only by the consciousness of continuous vitality. In this relationship, the poet becomes the "Answerer," who addresses the central question of freedom, which is suffering, as recognition itself, the signifier of nothing. From the renewal of his central originality Whitman receives the vision of things as they are with the living and the dead. He translates Lincoln's death without exchanging it for any term whatsoever, and the "slain soldiers of the war" without the sacrificial commutation of any rational value.

> I saw battle-corpses, myriads of them,
> And the white skeletons of young men, I saw them,
> I saw debris and debris of all the slain soldiers of the war,
> But I saw they were not as was thought,
> They themselves were fully at rest, they suffer'd not,
> The living remain'd and suffer'd, the mother suffer'd,
> And the wife and the child and the musing comrade suffer'd,
> and the armies that remain'd suffer'd.

Through the establishment of difference between the living and the dead—a laying of ghosts, including Lincoln and his meanings—the Whitmanian elegist recovers the perceptibility of his world, as Lincoln had established the difference between persons and things by the emancipation of the slaves, and thus restored the rationality of the polity. But the act of perceptual autonomy ("free sense") finds Whitman, at the moment of his greatest originality, at the greatest distance also from the social world in which alone his intention can have meaning. That one social world over which Lincoln presided as emancipator, accounting for the same facts of suffering (at Gettysburg, for example, or in the "Second Inaugural") according to the compensatory economies of theodicy, those of dedication, sacrifice, and the vengeance of God.

Both Whitman (poet citizen) and Lincoln (citizen president) intended a "*just* and *lasting* peace" in a polity that had lost regulative stability and consequently postponed the antimony of those two terms (the revolutionary term "just" and the Constitutional term "lasting"). Each took in hand a millennial instrument of representation the nature of which he articulated as policy with singular fidelity: in Lincoln's case, the political principle of sociability based in commutative justice, the logic of noncontradiction, singular identity, and the hierarchy of rational order—the language of tragic personhood; in Whitman's case, the poetic principle of sociability, based in an abstraction from the representational function of art, and organized in accord with a redistributive counterlogic of presence as pluralization and the transparence of affection—a comedy of justice without exchange. But the Whitmanian distributive politics of "transparence" fails to obtain unanimity because it has no natural standpoint (there is no transparence consistent with the social life of the person), and thus obtains only justice without constitution. Likewise the Lincolnian poetics of fairness does not obtain fairness, because the nature of the person on whose behalf it acts limits the systemic change possible to the institutions that represent the person—constitution without justice. Both men succeeded in mastering their instrument, *but not (as each so profoundly intended) in overcoming its nature*. The contradiction between equality and perpetuation—Declaration as justice, and Constitution as structure—was more powerful than the systems of representation that invented these men (and which they sponsored) could conciliate, because the contradiction is of the same nature as the system.

Thus, having made one out of many, the common work of policy and poetry, Lincoln and Whitman left behind the inherently unfinished, reconstructive task of making many, once again, of one—the creation of a real world consistent with its principles both of value and of order. Near the close of his "Second Annual Message" in which he promulgated the Emancipation, Lincoln distinguished, as I have noticed, between imagining and doing, and between the present and the past:

> It is not "Can any of us *imagine* better?" but "can we all *do* better?" . . . The dogmas of the quiet past, are inadequate to the stormy present. The occasion is piled high with difficulty, and we must rise with the occasion. As our case is new, so we must think anew and act anew. We must disenthrall ourselves, and then we shall save our country.[31]

Both men, together with most of their literary contemporaries, saw the historical moment as one requiring new structures of response; both deprecated the category of the imaginary, and both intended to "disenthrall" the self in the interest of national authenticity. In the end, however, the freedom conferred by Whitman and Lincoln remained, as I have suggested, virtual and paradoxical. The empowered master, Lincoln, was unable, by the very nature of his power, to legislate a social world in which his intention could become actual. Whitman, the master of social love (the better president as he understood it), was unable, by the nature of his fundamental revision of personhood, to enter the world by any act, except the deathwatch of the wounded in Lincoln's war.[32]

The fate of Whitmanian policy brings to mind the observation that words in poetry are only as effective as the institutions in which they have meaning. More particularly, "bad faith" attaches to open form in that it anticipates, by the radical nature of its truth, no institution in which its words can have effect, no world in which its text is transmitted, and yet no presence of the self-authorized person it liberates except the image or eidolon of the poem. Correlatively, we note from the fate of Lincolnian policy, which is our history, that the language of closed form is empowered because it is of the same structure as human institutions: but that such institutions, or for that matter such poems (Yeats's for example), are only as moral as the grammar of their construction, and powerless to mediate by secular means the irrepressible conflict of legitimacies that is the principle of their life.

And there then, as between Whitman and Lincoln, two policies of union or only one? There is, on the showing of this argument, only one—with this qualification: A faithful response to Whitman's originality will be a continual critique, in view of a policy toward institutions, of the structures of representation, in the light of the revelation of personhood unmistakably presented in Lincoln's language and countenance—the archetype of the doomed companion laboring in history, whom we now know and hope to love. The open road is the one line that is not imaginary.

NOTES

1. The argument of this paper is extensively indebted to James Buechler, "Abraham Lincoln, American Literature, and the Affirmation of Union" (1955), a Harvard Honors essay.

2. See Arthur Bestor, "The American Civil War as a Constitutional Crisis," in Lawrence M. Friedman and Harry N. Scheiber, *American Law and the Constitutional Order* (Cambridge: Harvard University Press, 1978), p. 234:

> But the abstractness of Constitutional issues has nothing to do, one way or the other, with the role they may happen to play at a moment of crisis. Thanks to the structure of the American Constitutional system itself, the abstruse issue of slavery in the territories was required to carry the burden of well-nigh all the emotional drives, well-nigh all the political and economic tensions, and well-nigh all the moral perplexities that resulted from the existence in the United States of an archaic system of labor and an intolerable policy of racial subjection.

3. The analysis of Lincoln's meanings that follows is not psychological in method. I have, however, greatly benefited from the findings of Dwight G. Anderson, *Abraham Lincoln, The Quest for Immortality* (New York: Alfred A. Knopf, 1982); also, George B. Forgie, *Patricide in the*

House Divided (New York: W. W. Norton, 1979), and Charles B. Strozier, *Lincoln's Quest for Union* (New York: Basic Books, 1982).

4. The destruction by the Revolution of the older "prestige order," based on inherited class or status, was accompanied by the development of an "indigenous class structure . . . based upon property." See Jackson Turner Main, *The Social Structure of Revolutionary America* (Princeton: Princeton University Press, 1965), pp. 282, 283. The loss of feudal status-criteria, and the loss also of the model of the hypostatic union (the union of persons in the Trinity), were correlative shocks contributing to the crisis. Emerson and Whitman attempted to recuperate the former development by reconstructing on a secular basis the empowerments lost as a consequence of the latter.

5. See John T. Irwin, "Self-Evidence and Self-Reference: Nietzsche and Tragedy, Whitman and Opera" in *New Literary History* 9, no. 1 (autumn 1979): 177–92. I fully agree with his notion of the "endlessly oscillating grounding" of self and text in Whitman, but not with his assimilation of Whitman's song to Schopenhauer's music.

6. In a conversation with the Reverend J. P. Gulliver in 1860, Lincoln specified two biographical moments in which his style was formed. As a child, he says:

> I used to get irritated when anybody talked to me in a way I could not understand. I don't think I ever got angry at anything else in my life. I was not satisfied until I had repeated it over and over, until I had put it in language plain enough, as I thought, for any boy I knew to comprehend. This was a kind of passion with me. . . . I am never easy now, when I am handling a thought, till I have bounded it North, and bounded it South, and bounded it East, and bounded it West.

The other moment he describes as the discovery of a means to make *demonstration* result, as Webster's dictionary promised, in "certain Proof." He supplied the means by secluding himself in his father's house "till I could give any proposition in the six books of Euclid at sight." Gulliver's report was published in the *New York Independent*, 1 September 1864, rpt. in James Mellon, *The Face of Lincoln* (New York: Viking Press, 1979). Lincoln's source for the "house divided" image as a logical contradiction is Tom Paine's *Common Sense*, 1:8 of *The Complete Writings*, ed. Philip Foner (New York: Citadel Press, 1945).

7. The centrality in Lincoln's mind, and the minds of his audiences, of the hermeneutic proposition—"the intention of the law-giver is the law"—is attested by its place in "The First Inaugural," Roy P. Basler et al., *The Collected Works of Abraham Lincoln* (New Brunswick, N.J.: Rutgers University Press, 1954), 4:263; hereafter cited as Basler.

Much of the Lincoln-Douglas debates, and other central arguments of Lincoln, notably "The Cooper Institute Address," are efforts to infer from indirect indications the intentions of the fathers who become archetypes of the hidden meaning-intending will of the singular person. Lincoln's God is also such a person. Divergence of interpretive inference is one of the obstacles to unanimity that, as I shall suggest, Whitman undertakes to abolish: "Have you felt so proud to get at the meaning of poems?" "Song of Myself," 11.32, 33 in Sculley Bradley and Harold Blodget, *Walt Whitman: Leaves of Grass* (New York: W. W. Norton, 1973); hereafter cited as Bradley.

8. Marianne Moore's "Lincoln and the Art of the Word" in *A Marianne Moore Reader* (New York: Viking Press, 1965) characterizes him as a "Euclid of the heart." The standard essay on Lincoln as a writer is Roy P. Basler, "Lincoln's Development as a Writer" in *A Touchstone for Greatness* (Westport, Conn.: Greenwood Press, 1973). See also, Edmund Wilson, *Patriotic Gore* (New York: Oxford University Press, 1962), pp. 119ff.

9. Lincoln's identification of the deontological distinction between right and wrong with the rhetorical authority of "logic" can be seen in the following reply to Douglas at Alton (Basler 3:315): "He says he 'don't care whether it [slavery] is voted up or voted down' in the territories. . . . Any man can say that who does not see anything wrong with slavery, but no man can logically say he don't care whether a wrong is voted up or voted down. He may say he don't care whether an indifferent thing is voted up or down, but he must logically have a choice between a right thing and a wrong thing."

10. F. O Matthiessen, *From the Heart of Europe* (New York: Oxford University Press, 1948), p. 90.

11. For Whitman on abolition, see Whitman's essays in *The Brooklyn Daily Eagle in 1846 and 1847,* reprinted in Cleveland Rodgers and John Black, *The Gathering of Forces* (New York: G. P. Putnam's Sons, 1920), 1:179–238. Note also Whitman's essays in the same volume on union. Whitman and Lincoln held the same political views, except that Whitman's attitude toward government and political parties displayed his aversion to units of social organization other than the individual and the whole. For the development of the Transcendental writers of the period toward the acceptance of abolition, see Daniel Aaron, *The Underwritten War* (New York: Alfred A. Knopf, 1973).

12. Basler, 4:264.

13. "I therefore declare that, in view of the Constitution and the laws, the Union is unbroken; and, to the extent of my ability, I shall take care, as the Constitution itself expressly enjoins me, that the laws of the Union be faithfully executed in all the States" (Basler, 4:265).

14. Taney in Dred Scott makes plain the primary function of the

Constitution as a regulative document that creates by secular means rights-bearing human beings, according to the principle of difference: "The words 'people of the United States' and 'citizens' are synonomous terms, and mean the same thing. . . . It is true, every person, and every class of persons, who were at the time of the adoption of the Constitution unrecognized as citizens in the several States, became also citizens of this new political body; but none other; it was formed by them, and for them and their posterity, but for no one else." See Henry Steele Commager, *Documents of American History* (New York: Appleton-Century-Crofts, 1949), pp. 339–45.

15. This was a conscious and practical matter. E. Merton Coulter (*The Confederate States of America, 1861–1865* [Baton Rouge: Louisiana State University Press, 1950], p. 10) cites a Georgia editor (*Atlanta Southern Confederacy,* 25 October 1862) who says of slavery that it made "the poor man respectable." It gave the poor "an elevated position in society that they would not otherwise have." For the specific legal requirement of respect by slaves see the Code Noir of Louisiana, cited in John Codman Hurt, *The Law of Freedom and Bondage* (New York: Negro Universities Press, 1962), 2:157, 158. More generally, "Slavery was seen as a model of dependence and self-surrender. For Plato, Aristotle, and Augustine this meant that it was a necessary part of a world that required moral order and discipline; it was the base on which rested an intricate and hierarchical pattern of authority" (David Brion Davis, *The Problem of Slavery in Western Culture* [Ithaca: Cornell University Press, 1966], p. 90; hereafter cited as Davis).

16. Emory Holloway, *The Uncollected Poetry and Prose of Walt Whitman* (Garden City, N.Y.: Doubleday, Page and Co., 1921), 2:69; hereafter cited as Holloway. For the functional analogy between body/matter/slave, and soul/spirit/master, see Davis, p. 304.

17. Holloway, 2:65.

18. See "Fragment on Free Labor" (Basler 3:462), and "Address before the Wisconsin State Agricultural Society, Milwaukee, Wisconsin," 30 September 1859 (ibid., pp. 471ff.).

19. Edward Sapir, *Language: An Introduction to the Study of Speech* (New York: Harcourt Brace, 1949), p. 224; D. H. Lawrence, *Studies in Classical American Literature* (New York: Viking Press, 1964), p. 170. For Cesare Pavese, see Gay Wilson Allen, *The New Walt Whitman Handbook* (New York: New York University Press, 1975), p. 317.

20. In "Democratic Vistas" at p. 981, *Walt Whitman: Complete Poetry and Collected Prose* (New York: Library of America, 1982).

21. "The Eighteenth Presidency" in Clifton Joseph Furness, *Walt Whitman's Workshop* (Cambridge: Harvard University Press, 1928), p. 109.

22. Cf. 15.171 of "When Lilacs Last": "And I saw askant the armies." The "crossing" moment, as in "Calvary Crossing a Ford," or the crossing of bodies in #5 of "Song of Myself," signifies for Whitman immediacy of access, unqualified by space or time. So, also, in "Crossing Brooklyn Ferry": "I see you face to face."

23. Basler, 5:535.

24. Ibid., p. 537.

25. On honor and dishonor as a zero-sum transaction see the "Epilogue" to Gregory Nagy, *Comparative Studies in Greek and Indic Meter* (Cambridge: Harvard University Press, 1974), p. 261.

26. Bradley, p. 714, 11.123–24.

27. The expression is William James's. James's "radical empiricism" is fundamentally explanatory of Whitman's epistemology.

> To be radical, an empiricism must neither admit into its constructions any element that is not directly experienced, nor exclude from them any element that is not directly experienced. For such a philosophy, *the relations that connect experiences must themselves be experienced relations, and any kind of relation experienced must be accounted as "real" as anything else in the system. . . . Radical empiricism,* as I understand it, *does full justice to conjunctive relations,* without however treating them as rationalism always tends to treat them as being true in some supernal way, as if the unity of things and their variety belonged to different orders of truth and vitality altogether.

William James, *Essays in Radical Empiricism and a Pluralistic Universe* (New York: E. P. Dutton, 1971), pp. 25–26.

28. Whitman's equivocation of the difference of sign and signified, word and thing, body and soul, "I" and "you" expresses an intention to rid the conjunctive transactions (whether seeing, loving, speaking, or political bonding) of all representational mediations. This is the reason of his use of Lucretian optics (as in "Crossing Brooklyn Ferry"), his interest in phrenology, his dislike of political parties, poetic diction, mythology, and so on.

29. "Celebration" in Whitman (as in "I celebrate myself") invokes the meaning of pluralization that inheres in all cognates of Latin *celebrare*. Pluralization as a solution to the bad faith of speaking at all (where silence signifies fraternal union, and speech interrupts that union) is vividly expressed by George Fox in *A Battle door for Teachers and Professors to Learn Singular and Plural:* "All languages are to me no more than dust, who was before Languages were, and I am redeemed out of Languages into the power where all men shall agree." Cited by Richard Bauman and Joel Sherzer, *Explorations in the Ethnography of Speaking* (Cambridge: Cambridge University Press, 1974), p. 146.

30. Basler, 4:90.

31. Basler, 5:537.

32. My discussion of Whitman is intended to show that a serious political poetry (like a serious policy of any kind) is not merely an advocacy, but an addition to the given repertory of conjunctive relationships, such that "literary" judgment about the poetry's success or failure constitutes an assessment (or "problematic") of the coming-to-pass, as an actual state of affairs, of the life that is its "subject." In this sense, a poetic structure is a political policy. Whitman identified for modernism, and for our time as well as I believe, the heuristic primacy of the structural features of poetry.

Hart Crane and Poetry

A Consideration of Crane's Intense Poetics with
Reference to "The Return"

The Return

The sea raised up a campanile . . . The wind I heard
Of brine partaking, whirling spout in shower
Of column kiss—that breakers spouted, sheared
Back into bosom—me—her, into natal power.[1]

Hart Crane was a poet who lived in and through the logic of the poetic principle, wrote poems that told stories about the impossibility of its imperatives, and died the death that always beckons when the exchange of natural for symbolic life is understood as a destiny without alternative. For Crane the only access to the poetic principle he could in the end imagine is the one that cannot be survived—not a regulated lover's relationship but a life-extinguishing identification, the imposssible response to the impossible demand.

Crane killed himself in the year I was born. And in the sunny library where I read of Caedmon, I also, as it happened, read Crane. Caedmon's vocation was claimed, as we have seen, by the central institution of his social world, Hild's Christianity. Crane's vocation was never claimed and its productions never donated to an instituted public world that could have contributed, reciprocally, a transcendental ground to his work as maker—a Genesis other than his own origin in "natal power."

First appeared as "Hart Crane's Intense Poetics" in *English Literary History* 48, no. 4 (winter 1981): 841–79.

The bitter logic of the poetic principle became, then, the structure of the story that he told about himself *and which is also told about him.*

But Crane was not slain by his practice of poetry. He died because he was unwilling to fail, by which I mean unwilling to view his life as anything other than the impossible response to an impossible demand. But poems are intelligible because they mark the difference between the actuality of the poem and the bitter logic of its principle—because they fail of, are different from, their purposes. Poems, even Crane's, are *possible* constructions. Crane's one subject is the deep desire to free the poem and the life from demands inconsistent with their inevitable common destiny in the actual world, to distinguish both art and life from the relentless sacrificial logic of the principle of appearance. He was able to do so in the domain of art, for a time, because its nature is forgiving. "But the death he imagined is not the death he died." He found nothing in his life of that nature.

I have given some time, in the long schoolroom, to becoming clear about this matter. Hence the following argument.

I

Throughout the criticism of Hart Crane's poetry there runs, responsive to his own intensity, the sentiment of something very important and uncommon at issue. Winters, Tate, Blackmur among early critics, and more recently Joseph Riddell, Eric J. Sundquist, David Bleich, and John Irwin, the former in ethical and aesthetic terms, the latter in various analytic languages, describe relationships between the catastrophe of Hart Crane's life and the nature of his work, different, I think, in degree and perhaps also in kind from such relationships in other authors.[2] It is agreed, whatever else may be in question in the matter of Crane, that he was, undeniably, a poet of stature, and that the sources both of his unquestionable achievement and of his equally unquestionable aberration (whether the latter be considered as an imperfection of his work, or his stopping of that work in death) are inextricably bound up with the sources of his monumental authenticity as an artist. Crane was not merely a poet; he was a poet of unmistakable gifts who staked everything upon poetry, who had no other presence in the world, and whose art attests a perilous extremity of ambition unaccountable except on the hypothesis of a life at risk. Indeed, Crane's singularity and claim arise directly from the conjunction in him of unmistakable authenticity and equivocal success—as if there were discovered in his life a degree of proximity to the sources of art inconsistent with the life of art itself. In Crane we see, I think, not only a pathology working out its implications in the context of a gift (a case common enough) but also something of the boundaries of poetry as an instrument for effecting human purpose. In this essay I wish to consider whether the harrowing cooperation of the authentic powers that Hart Crane brought to his art with the enormous need that he addressed in it does not indicate (as Crane himself from time to time felt that it did) some boundary at once of poetry and human hope—whether, in short, what you cannot have or be, you also cannot in well-formed poems say.

The four-line poem called "The Return," which this essay takes as text, was in effect a final communication, a suicide note. On one of the four manuscript pages relating to "The Return" Hart Crane's mother, Grace Hart Crane, searching like so many others for the "cause" of her son's death, notes (the annotation, now erased, is still sufficiently legible) that she found a version of this poem in his suitcase—on top—and asks whether it bears any "significance to his death."[3] This poem, to which his mother appended her awesome question, gives in brief the full cycle of her son's myth and life, and, insofar as it functioned in the event as a message to his mother across the boundary of death and life, includes her in fact, as it included her in imagination, in the central action of his life. The mother's initials on the manuscript page acknowledge the receipt of the message, completing as a final transgression by mother and son of the boundaries of fiction and experience, the cycle of departure from and return to source that the poem takes as its mythic subject and the poet acted out in the manner of his death. As would be appropriate for a final communication, the poem contains Crane's metrical signature, the rhymed quatrain that he used not only as a constituent of many of his characteristic poems but particularly as a structure signifying closure.[4] Hence, "The Return"—as the signature set to the work—was correctly placed by the editors of the Liveright *Collected Poems* (Waldo Frank, Grace Hart Crane, and Sam Loveman) at the end.

According to John Unterecker "The Return" was probably begun in the same creative period during which *The Bridge* was in large part written, commencing on the Isle of Pines in October 1926.[5] If this were the case, it would belong among the poems Crane thought to group under the common title *The Hurricane,* including "O Carib Isle," "The Island Quarry," "The Royal Palm," "The Idiot," and "Eternity." (To these poems that he names should be added as part of the hurricane group "The Air Plant" and "The Hurricane.")[6] But "The Return," not in fact mentioned in the letters, also shares its language and myth with Crane's latest works, an elegiac condensation of the history of his agon.

At the end of the prose poem "Havana Rose" (1932), for example, Crane assigns to the mantic doctor (the biologist Zinnser) a sentence that articulates the imaginary history of which "The Return" is an epitome, and that also became the program of Crane's death poem, "The Broken Tower."

> And during the wait over dinner at La Diana the Doctor had said—who was American, also—"You cannot heed the negative— so might go on to undeserved doom . . . must therefore loose yourself within a pattern's mastery that you can conceive, that you can yield to—by which also you win and gain mastery and happiness which is your own from birth.[7]

The sense of this oracle is approximately the following: ending at the beginning in the inheritance of the birthright—the return to "natal power"—this journey (the archetype is the *nostos,* the "return"),[8] which begins with the imprudence of refusing irony ("You cannot heed the negative") and passes through the loosing (or losing) of the self in "pattern's mastery," resolves in the end into the implicitly vortical shape (determined by the simultaneity of progressive and regressive vectors) of the hurricane marriage of discourse with origins ("mastery and happiness"). This marriage of discourse as mastery with source as happiness (the "kiss" of "The Return") defines the scene of authenticity to which Crane's poetry invites the reader—a scene primal, awesome, and ruinous like that to which "the bird of loudest lay" invites in the sovereign instance of "intense poetics" in English, the pseudo-Shakespearean "Phoenix and Turtle."

I shall suggest in what follows that this marriage does indeed require a "pattern" for its sanctioning, a pattern that Crane never found because in a profound way he never sought it (though he thematized it as an act of deferral again and again) and to which the structures he does use are related as substitutes and postponements that keep open the space of hope by leaving undefined the region in which discourse is possible. Poetry as discourse was for Crane, as for us all, an instance (and therefore a principle and history) of persons in relationship. Obscurity of discourse in his poetry was for him a postponement and equivocation of the decision as to what relationships are permitted and therefore possible—an equivocation that we as readers reenact when we dwell in the bewilderment of his style, and that we erase (but do not resolve) when we compel a "meaning." This is one function of the rhetoric that I have called Crane's "intense poetics."

Modern poetry, as apart from Crane's "slain numbers" we understand it, exhibits the lesser authenticity and greater poetic success of a true experimental art, one that defines the singularity of its motive in terms of a determinate set of outcomes encoded as structure. As such it was devised to set at a distance what Yeats in *his* marriage poem called, with reference to the dead Lionel Johnson, "A measureless consummation that he dreamed." Crane's intense poetics (by contrast) was defiled, unsanctioned, having the novelty of wild exploit rather than invention or experimentation and, inevitably, the strange authority, as I shall show at some length, of the imaginary themes of art rather than its actual imaginative forms. My concern, in brief, is to emphasize the nonexperimental (and antimodernist) characteristics of Crane's enterprise, to suggest that in the absence of the invention of new structures Crane's poetry tends to hallucinate or thematize structures (building, bridge, tower) and to develop a rhetoric of condensation, his well-known iconic "obscurity." In effect, Crane takes authenticity not as a sanction but as a subject, evolving a "difficult poetry" (a poetry without an intratextural interpreter, which therefore postpones meaning) of which the mode is the Longinian high or grand style, a style with inherent affinities to an earliness that preempts growth and leaves only metamorphosis as a strategy for change. This style, as I shall show, is the manner of utterance not of the imaginative singer of our poetry but of the imaginary subject (not of "Wordsworth" but of the solitary reaper, not of "Keats" but of the nightingale) and as such is inherently "obscure," obscure in a sense that can be stated. Finally, I wish to deal with Crane's central motive, the intense hierogamic kiss of absolute acknowledgment and the sense of immense comedic hopefulness he brought to poetry as both an inference from the nature of his art and as a discovery of its boundaries.

II

It is no longer in any way remarkable to suggest that, considered in the context of the poetic practice of his contemporary modernism, Hart Crane was not an experimental poet. At about the time of Crane's birth Yeats, to take the salient case, decisively redefined the idealist poetic enterprise that he had brought to high finish (but not to completion) in *The Wind among the Reeds* (1899), and in so doing passed judgment on the poetic task that Crane was compelled to labor at in the next generation. Yeats's ironic distancing (as in "Adam's Curse" [1901]) of his own death-bound early ambition (not now the *impossible* task, but only that task "most difficult" among the class of tasks *not impossible*) made Yeats as a poetic speaker the audience and interpreter, in effect, of his own early motive, and announced that ironization of questing that Eliot identified for his generation in the allusive poetics of "The Love Song of J. Alfred Prufrock" as the mark of high-modern structural innovation in poetry. The voices at risk internal to Eliot's *The Waste Land* could no more have spoken the poem that quotes them than could Joyce's Stephen have written *The Portrait of the Artist as a Young Man*. Crane, by contrast, spoke from the point of view not of the Daedalian survivor but of the Icarian overreacher, spoke not as the survivor in retrospect but as the mariner in course of the unsurvivable voyage. Yeats feared ("To the Rose upon the Rood of Time") that he would come to speak a "tongue men do not know," and so he changed the rules of the game; Crane really spoke that obscure tongue, refusing to change the rules. To have done so would have meant for Crane betrayal (modernism was in moral terms the treasonous friendship of which he obsessively complained) of the task set him by his great passion for consummatory validation, the obligation entailed by the great hope that brought him to poetry. Whether or not Crane's enterprise constituted a misreading of the medium that he practiced, whether what he wanted was within the gift of the art, is, as I have already suggested, one of the issues that the career of Hart Crane brings to mind.

Modernist experimentalism was precipitated by the discovery that certain central promises of poetry (as well as of the other arts) were impossible of attainment, shadowed by that "abridgement of hope" to which Paul Fussell has drawn attention.[9] If poetry were to go on it must change toward the ironic thematization of central aspects of its traditional function as a reconciling, honor-conferring, and perpetualizing medium. Crane, who sometimes mimicked or repeated but only very selectively participated in the high-modern innovation, refused to change the rules of the game as given (the "pattern's mastery") because he viewed those rules as the implicit fulfillment, the pre-text as it were, of the success he had not ceased to expect ("mastery and happiness which is your own from birth"). As a consequence we find him *pressed against* the logic of grammar (his well-known "logic of metaphor" is still the metaphorization of metaphor as logic), and against the resistant abstract "cable strands" of metricality that sustained the iconic and internally centered structures he imagined as responding to the purposes in view of which poetry justified the labor of its making. The result was that he achieved an agonistic discovery of the boundaries of the traditional art he practiced, rather than any redefinition of the structures of that art such as implied, in the case of Eliot or Williams or Stevens, a new avenue of practice. Crane's achieved work, his success, is an intense version of what he found; and his singular rhetoric is constituted by the compelled strategies of that intensity, the consequence of his unwillingness to relinquish what in his reading of the role and means of the poet he felt to be poetry's promises. No other poet, to my knowledge, tried with such relentless integrity to get so much out of the poetic means at hand as did Crane; and that is, as I see it, the beginning of an understanding of his claim on our attention.

III

The poems of Crane most marked by his characteristic manner belong to that rough class of poems called "difficult" to which also belong such diverse cases as "The Phoenix and Turtle," Blake's "The Mental Traveller," certain of Yeats's early poems, Roethke's "Lost Son," and some of the poems (to take a recent instance) of John Ashbery. "Difficult poems" are poems that lack an intratextual interpreter. As a class of limiting cases, they call attention to the extent to which the poems of tradition are themselves "readings" and administrations of already vanished (or phenomenally impossible) states of affairs. Crane's disposition to construct difficult poems in this sense, poems that leave undefined the relationship of their authenticity to any finite consequence or meaning, thus keeping open and unconstrained the reach of their discourse (they might mean everything, import the accessibility, the permissibility, of all relationships, *validate* the truth of the boundlessness of desire), delegated to the reader the role of the exegetical participant. Hence the reading of Crane's poems, as difficult poems, situates the reader internal to the poem, and assigns him or her the task of completing rather than deriving significance. (Hence also the critical tendency to find Crane's poetry incomplete, or imperfectly articulated by its symbols.)[10] Crane himself attempted to compensate for this feature of his poetry by making interpretations of his own structures. When he wrote for Harriet Monroe the famous exegesis of his Melville poem, he was doing the business of the culture that his poem omitted, seeking to provide not so much an access to the poem as a means of escaping from it. By analogy with Eliot's practice in "Preludes" ("Every street *lamp* that I pass *beats* like a fatalistic *drum*" [italics Crane's]), Crane implies that the "logic of metaphor" is provided by the inference of a middle term, the inference of a person in whom disparate terms of experience are integrated, a person whose ideal reconciling powers can exist *only* as an inference. This sensibility justified the logic of metaphor by disappearing, by vacating just that space in which as registration of personal presence (as lyric speaker in the traditional sense) the person as mind creates the interpretable world by accounting for the relationship of things in it. Crane's poems summon and await their reader much as the solitary reaper in Wordsworth awaits the exegetical deixis of the journeyer who says, "Behold her . . ."

Another consequence of Crane's practice of the "difficult" poem was his own production of "exegetical" poems (poems about other poets) as a countereffort to be the outside describer, the Daedalian survivor of enterprises like his own, or inversely as an effort to find his counterplayer and interpreter, the one who will be both inside and outside his own enterprise. *The Bridge* in its latter half—part IV (Whitman), VI (Dickinson), VII (Poe)—searches the tradition for an hermeneutic friend who might "close" the enterprise by stabilizing its meanings, but who must be a memorializer who can remember an event without betraying its authenticity. In the end, however, he finds even "Shakespeare" validated by indistinguishability from the hurricane authenticity of his subject, "pilot,—tempest, too!" In fact, Crane becomes in his poems about poets not an exegete or elegist (or like the modern Yeats a definer of possible life by contrast to impossible example, or like Keats on Lear a man interpreted by his master) but a transhistorical concelebrant at the same altar on which he himself experiences "transmemberment." Crane's poets are boundary demons like himself whose fidelity to authenticity (the "natal power" of "The Return") is measured by their unbornness, whose myths have no outside. When in his poems Crane does contemplate his own interpretation, he produces images of the textualization of the self as an agony of circumscription, or in his own word "conscription"—a mutilation, as we see in his terrifying uses of the word "engrave," or the word "counted."[11]

Crane's quasi sonnet, "To Emily Dickinson" (1927), closer in its language to Amy Lowell's sonnet on Keats than to the language of Dickinson herself, specifies Dickinson's subject as that "Eternity" which was in the hurricane poem so-called the name he gave to the white horse ("Like a vast phantom maned by all that memoried night / Of screaming rain—Eternity!") that stands forth epiphanically as the fact corresponding to the song of the "sweet, dead Silencer." Silence and whiteness (the white-ness of Crane's masterpiece *White Buildings* whose "Legend" is "As silent as a mirror is believed / Realities plunge in silence by") are the specifying features, the paradoxically obliterative marks, of that state of affairs, the truth and the fact, which his "difficult" poems solicit as desire and postpone as text—the world unqualified by the treacheries of meaning. As I shall have occasion to suggest later in this essay, Crane's language and subjects are always (like Dickinson, as presented in the language of Lowell) out of place, defiled, because as discourse they have not yet undone the exile that separates them from source—"Unwhispering as a mirror / Is believed."

To Emily Dickinson

You who desired so much—in vain to ask—
Yet fed your hunger like an endless task,
Dared dignify the labor, bless the quest—
Achieved that stillness ultimately best,
Being, of all, least sought for: Emily, hear!
O sweet, dead Silencer, most suddenly clear
When signing that Eternity possessed
And plundered momently in every breast;

—Truly no flower yet withers in your hand,
The harvest you descried and understand
Needs more than wit to gather, love to bind,
Some reconcilement of remotest mind—

Leaves Ormus rubyless, and Ophir chill.
Else tears heap all within one clay-cold hill.

Crane's exegetical poems tend to be hagiographic in character—the lives of witnesses who, because their truth is be-yond interpretation ("more than wit to gather, love to bind"), die in an act that like the Crane poem validates the truth of vast inference ("reconcilement of remotest mind") and preempts the lesser reconciliations of interpretation. The poem as a sign and the poet elegized by the poem tend to be equally silent, equally Silencers. Yeats's hagiographic poems in the same period func-tion, as I have suggested, to delegate away from the text, from the actual poem, the agonistic predicament of the dead and silenced subject. This Crane does not do. Instead, he reports "to" his "Dickinson" his *rediscovery in her* of the terms of his own enterprise ("The harvest you descried and understand"). In Crane's intense-poetics discourse functions as a repetition or condensation—the scene itself once again of the event referred to—rather than in the ordinary sense a mimesis or fictional displacement (or delegation) of a state of affairs. Structure in poetry is in the ordinary case an interpretation of meaning, or a repetition of meaning in another code. The irrelevance in Crane of structure to meaning calls attention to the "difficulty" of his poems, their status as instances, rather than accounts, of unsurvivable exploits. As in "The Phoenix and Turtle": "Death is now the Phoenix' nest."

The heroism of Crane's "Dickinson" is his own, and consists in persistence, like his own, in the "endless task" of responding faithfully to *all* the implications of "hunger." This activity drains the world of its terms (as the death of Shakespeare's birds took Beauty and Truth out of phenomenal existence), leaving "Ormus rubyless, and Ophir chill." If it does not do so there is only vacancy—"Else tears heap all within one clay-cold hill"—the vacancy that finds sentiment without an object. If it does do so, the one word that has vortically taken in all other words as the condition of its nominalization, leaves behind silence and a trace—the "difficult poem," manifest only insofar as it fails of perfect accord with its imaginary subject. Hence, Crane's poetic hagiography is a continuation rather than, as in Yeats's case or in Robinson's or Auden's, an interruption and ironization of the elegists intentions. "Eternity" is the moment of language's "clarity"—a clarity different from discursive intelligibility—obtained by the singer as "Silencer" whose life is the trace of an action, or a word, become true at the point of disappearance in death. All Crane's hero-poets—Dickinson, Melville, Poe, Shakespeare—repeat his posture as an agonist at the boundaries of possibility ("junctions elegiac") struggling with a medium (language and its artistic forms) that decays at the point of fulfillment of its promises, decays into the authority of its own signified—"O sweet, dead Silencer, most suddenly clear." Like the whiteness of the "white buildings"[12] the silence so often evoked in Crane is the inferential plenitude toward which his actual poems are the pre-texts, and in view of which his refusal of significant form is a postponement. In difficult poems there is, as I have indicated, no intratextual interpreter, and in Crane this absence opens a space in which the poem is not yet present and will never be.

IV

Crane's relationship to the forms he used was entirely ambivalent. On the one hand they were the necessary mechanisms of presence, and on the other deforming "gates of life." Like the terrifying (black and swollen) portals of emergence in his elegiac autobiographies,[13] poetic structures gave access to reality, and also withheld it; and the same was true for the poetic languages of tradition that he could not reinvent and could not do without. Crane precipitated upon basically nineteenth-century forms and diction-systems (not fundamentally different from those of Keats, Patmore, and Swinburne) a passion for consummation that crowded the small and unforgiving space of appearance (the term, the trope, the line, the stanza) with his verbal bricolage, the broken pieces of the vast gestures and uncompromising sentiments he would not give up and could not make fit whole in the secular window of his means. This crowding of the frame came to constitute a trope peculiar to himself—not the modernist "ambiguity," which hierarchizes, or ironically totalizes a plurality of meanings—but a singularly naive rhetoric of shadowed wholeness (the impossible simultaneity of all the implications of desire) that struggles merely to include all meanings in the one space of appearance. In short, Crane's structures do not, except in trivial cases, take the shape of his subject because there is no metrical order of desire in all its outcomes; and yet there is no shape of presence except the metrical frame, and its syntagmatic correlative the grammatical sentence.

Crane's crowding of the frame produces his characteristic intense version of traditional usage, a rhetoric of *condensation* that manifests itself both on the vertical axis of figuration or substitution (a matter that he was at pains to justify in his explanatory essays) and also in the horizontal axis of narrative (contiguity). As rhetoric, the intense poetics of condensation has the effect of precipitating "difficulty" by eliding the person who perceives (one remembers Crane's remarks to Harriet Monroe about "The dice of drowned men's bones": "These being the bones of dead men who never completed their voyage, it seems legitimate to refer to them as the only surviving evidence of certain messages undelivered, mute evidence of certain things, experiences that the dead mariners might have had to deliver"); as narrative, the poetics of condensation elides the human world by collapsing consequence into source, consummating the dominance of authenticity over structure. The true person of inference is the proportionless whole broken by the finite scalar frame of appearance of which metrical structure is the sign ("the broken world," "broken eyes," "Dawn's broken arch," "broken intervals"). The point of the manifestation of the person marks the moment of the preemption of consummation, hence (as I have said) the idealization of silence and whiteness as the ultimate refusal to appear, as the escape from all speech and the turning away of all light. In the moment of its release the eye is led, not along the wavering path of sentiment (the right side of the mountain in "The Island Quarry") but straight into the stone, putting an end to the monumental craving.

Crane's preferred type of fundamental narrative (of which *The Bridge* and "The Island Quarry" are as much instances as "The Return") is the *nostos,* the tracing of "the visionary company of love" back to the primal scene or source condition where it is an unbroken unity—"Back into bosom—me—her, into natal power." The effect of the rhetoric of condensation is to assign more and more of the content of desire to fewer and fewer terms, until all that truly is is finally condensed upon a single word. This is the rhetorical architectonic of Crane's vortex or spout. As there is finally only one word (as will be seen in the reading of "The Return" at the end of this essay), so there is also only one moment—the present. Crane's modernist contemporaries such as Yeats and Eliot tended to use the word *modern* in an ironic sense (the common usage until Whitman) as a term specifying the emptiness of *this* moment in history. Consistent with Crane's deironization of terms, the modern as present time has for him apocalyptic fullness. It is the moment of sudden actualization, perfect in proportion as it is like the inferential, totalizing, imaginary single word: nothing and all.

The scenario of "The Return" is restated (once again in terminal position) in the last sentence of the concluding paragraph of "General Aims and Theories":

> New conditions of life germinate new forms of spiritual articulation. And while I feel that my work includes a more consistent extension of traditional literary elements than many contemporary poets are capable of appraising, I realize that I am utilizing the gifts of the past as instruments principally; and that the voice of the present, if it is to be known, must be caught at the risk of speaking in idioms and circumlocutions sometimes shocking to the scholar and historians of logic. Language has built towers and bridges, but itself is inevitably as fluid as always.

Crane's shock to logic (its scholars and *historians*) is the situation of discourse at the point of the extinguishing of continuity in timeless presentness, where event is not recapitulated diachronically but becomes as language what language is in itself, "inevitably as fluid as always." Language as "natal power" receives back the towers and bridges of language as mediation (scholars' language and historians' language) in a consummation that is the intersection of sign and signified—the end of the quest at the moment of beginning. This poetics, which treats language in terms of its absolute freedom to be all things, in terms of the oceanic implication of its fluidity in which lies *per impossibile* the synchronicity of all its meanings, becomes associated in Crane's mind with the "present" and the "new."

Crane means by "the present" the place of the liberation of the will, technology being one of the symbols of that liberation, conferring speed that rivals time and the capacity to execute the wishes of dream; Crane means by "new" the competence ("This competence" as in "The Wine Menagerie") to journey across the particular space, fundamental to all issues about space in Crane (and Whitman) that separates persons, as "other" minds, one from the other.[14] Indeed, Crane situates in the present the consummatory energies that Yeats came to situate in the past. And Crane's technologizations of the past ("utilizing the gifts of the past as instruments principally") aligns the powers of the past with the will in the present, abolishing the historicity of tradition, but also condensing upon the present all the daimonic intensities of authentic earliness. For Crane, past and present, one mind and the other, meet not in myth but in fact. *New* as a cultural term carries from the time of the Gospels implications of subjectivity, the covenant reestablished within. In Crane's usage it implies ("New thresholds, new anatomies!") the transgression of the rule of subjectivity, which is of course the immiscibility of minds; as also in Crane's usage technology implies, not the triumph of structure, but its dissolution. In Crane's intense poetics the world has no outside, and language is seen (for example in "Voyages II") as from the inside, in its energies and earliness that have, like the inside of the body, no social form.

It was, of course, the high-modern habit to incorporate the past as an ironic measurement of an historically irreversible decline. Ambivalently conceived, the past was for Yeats ghosts on the wind, hostile to life, and also necessary to life. In the same way that Crane's imaginary poetics constructed states of reference identical to the reality he sought (short-circuiting the constraining social logic of mediation), so also in the name of the poetics of the "new" he undertook to write *as* his predecessor, ignoring the equally constraining and prudential history of styles, as if he had no body and no unexchangeable place in time. Crane's pentameter verse, for example, has in this sense a character precisely contradictory to the blank verse that opens the second part of *The Waste Land*. Eliot's poetry is devised as a system that measures its distance, as an ironic matrix of systems, from all other systems while at the same time bringing them antiphrastically to mind. Crane's by contrast functions to abolish the historicity of models, accomplishing his purposes and values, as he remarks in "General Aims and Theories," "as well . . . with the vocabulary and blank verse of the Elizabethans as with the calligraphic tricks and slang used so brilliantly at times by an impressionist like Cummings." The nature of Crane's stylistic anachronism can be seen by noting its similarity to the speeches of Melville's Ahab and Starbuck as lineated by Matthiessen in *The American Renaissance*. Of these speeches Matthiessen says:

> The danger of such unconsciously compelled verse is always evident. As it wavers and breaks down again into ejaculatory prose,

it seems never to have belonged to the speaker, to have been at best a ventriloquist's trick.[15]

But it is precisely the posture of speaking from the impossible point of view of the irrecoverably early and therefore imaginary past that constitutes for Crane the defiance of irony and distance upon which he founds his truth. Ahab was doomed to the vortex that swallowed up the Pequod. Crane interpreted and transvalued that vortex as "the vortex of our grave," the eye of perfected response.[16]

In "General Aims and Theories" (once again) Crane notes: "I have been called an 'absolutist' in poetry." He contrasts the sense in which he accepts this description with his understanding and repudiation of "impressionism." The impressionist, he says, "is really not interested in the *causes* (metaphysical) of his materials, their emotional derivations or their utmost spiritual consequences. A kind of retinal registration is enough." This distinction accords with Crane's practice. Crane is a poet of metaphysical cause, emotional derivation, and "utmost spiritual consequences" in the sense that his poetry abolishes mediation and absolutizes relationships. In the language of "The Return" the thematization of that abolishment is the hierophantic hurricane "kiss" that has no social or, in any ordinary sense, perceptual correlative. Crane's kiss of total response ("Kisses are,— / The only worth all granting"). is a social term that has no social meaning, as his poems segregate the language of social transaction (he is after all from first to last a love poet) into a strange region of elite discourse, the "absolute" region not of retrospect or anticipation but exploit. In this region he does indeed reach a boundary of discourse, an absolute that has no "poetic precedent," a "capture" (not a registration) of presence. Crane's "So I found 'Helen' sitting in a street car" (Apollonius of Tyana's displacement of Helen of Troy) constructs the impossibility of meeting Helen, or anybody else, by investing the present with the past in such a way that the subject matter of the poem is not the juncture between two terms but the impossible multiplied presence of both terms simultaneously.[17] As soon as the present—the space of meaning—becomes thus actualized, it becomes phenomenologically remote. Crane invests the present not with the intelligibility, but with the unreachability, of the past, and the past with the urgency of the present, thus burdening his hope (the enrichment of present time) with the unobtainability of memory and the unexchangeability of particular experience. Crane's logic of metaphor, just because it bypasses the social logics of inference that repeat prudentially the logic of history and language, destroys the very space of presentness and appearance that it is devised to obtain. By collapsing origin and consequence (between which all historical and psychological life is situated, and perhaps all poetic life as well) Crane founded his poetic enterprise on an (imaginary) mode of discourse prior to the structures of discourse as mediation ("Language has built towers and bridges, but itself is inevitably as fluid as always").

Connate with this intention is Crane's deironized use of the past (his instrumentalization of the history of styles, his treatment of the history of styles as an array of undisqualified possibilities). This is the poetics not of an imaginative state of affairs on which actual states of affairs can be modeled, but of an imaginary state of affairs that is normally in the history of poetry (and very distinctly in the modern period) seen from a measured distance. But Crane always treated his poetic models in a sense, in Matthiessen's term, ventriloquistically. His poetry is "literary" in a way that Eliot's, for example, is not. He was the captive, the "sexton slave," of the historicity of his models (whether modern, Victorian, or Elizabethan). Hence his models, of structure and style, were bitter friends indeed, an enemy element, at the most intimate point of self-presence. Insofar as they became his, he had destroyed their proprium. Insofar as he became theirs, his identity was in question. His search for nurturance in primordial lineage encountered, in the result, only more colonists and claimants, so that his poems present us with a speaker without a voice, ambivalent toward the terms of presence, the structures of his art.[18]

V

It has not been sufficiently realized that Crane is not a mystic but a realist for whom the fact of structure (metrical and grammatical), as the condition of presence, stands as the unalterable fact of "the world." Mystic language in Crane serves in place of the language of desire severely conceived, for which there are no other terms than "mystic" in the dialects of poetry. Crane's major poems put poetry in question, insofar as they are experiments that seek to discover whether there is anything a man can say (whether there is any poem) consistent with unconceded human hope. This is the cultural question that lies inside the intensity of Crane's poetics; and it is this issue that is at stake when we decide whether there is, or is not, a good poem by Crane among those (such as "For the Marriage of Faustus and Helen," or "Voyages," or "The Broken Tower") that are marked by the "absolute," the unrelinquishing intensities of his concern.

Precisely because Crane devised, in the modernist sense of the word, no "new" structures (nothing like Yeats's segmented integrations in "Among School Children," or Eliot's matrices of spatialized time as in *The Waste Land,* or Williams's metrically open line-frames as in "On the Road to the Contagious Hospital"), Crane tended in his poetry to hallucinate mechanisms, and structures, to repeat the problem of form as image as a way of searching for, voyaging toward, trying, and postponing a structural means of access to the space he sought, where all the powers and justly desired outcomes of sentiment would be simultaneously at home. These "Orphic machines"—the bridge, the tower, the airplane, the carillon, the hurdy-gurdy, the phonograph, the camera—function like poetic forms in that they produce experience and are burdened and deformed by desire. They are images of mind, and like mind (as other mind) portend knowledge:

> I saw the frontiers gleaming of his mind;
> or are there frontiers—running sand sometimes
> running sands—somewhere—sands running . . .
> Or they may start some white machine that sings.
> Then you may laugh and dance the axletree—
> steel—silver—kick the traces—and know—

"The white machine that sings" is one of Crane's many imaginal experiments toward a structure that can mediate source (like the severed head of Orpheus). In the above passage, that structure (or mechanism) is indistinguishable from other mind itself, both the goal of the quest for love and its means—conceived as the frontier of subjectivity, "new" because transgressed.

Traditional poetry (the poetry of insight rather than intensity) views inactual ideal states from the point of view of the achieved structures of the actual text that constitute, insofar as they are successful, stable mediations, interpretable interpretations, and therefore concessions to possibility. Crane by contrast wrote in the impossible ethos or intense position of the inactual ideal state (at the "frontier" of mind considered as borderless) and, inversely, *thematized* possible structures. Hence, the inevitability of the central and equivocal poem, *The Bridge*—a speculation based on Roebling's Victorian system, toward the possibility of "the curveship" (privilege and solving shape) that does mediate relationship absolutely. But technology for Crane (he is particularly concerned with the then new technologies of flight and electronic communication) became a parody and promise of transgressive psychological enablement, as did, in the bad end of his life, sexuality, drink, and poetry. Technology substituted for the novelty (the "new" state of relationship) that poetic structure could not finally concede him, and constituted experiment beyond the prudence of art. In a like manner, Crane attempted to construct ("hallucinate" would again be the appropriate term) genealogies, also myths or machines of access to origins correlative to the other high-modern administrations of history and archetype toward the provision of the sufficient terms of lyric presence. But for Crane these genealogies were always colored by consciousness, not of their nurturant fictionality as in Yeats, nor of their confident historicity as in Eliot or Pound (Crane's quotations were pressed out to the epigraphic margin), but of their impossibility. Crane, seeking identity rather than reference, ventriloquism rather than quotation or indirect discourse, registered in the many postures of extreme mutilation his poetry contains ("Blamed, bleeding hands") the real differences between wishing and having. It is not merely the case of the "Lie to us,—dance us back the tribal morn!" of "The Dance"—the anxious realism of "Lie" being the trace of an intratextual consciousness of the artistic equivocality of that poem, which has been so often noticed—but also of the admired early poem in the "wavering" line of "tears and sleep," "My Grandmother's Love Letters," where the effort is to assess the possibility of rescuing the present by voyaging to the source of the melting text of love.

My Grandmother's Love Letters

There are no stars to-night
But those of memory.
Yet how much room for memory there is
In the loose girdle of soft rain.

There is even room enough
For the letters of my mother's mother,
Elizabeth,
That have been pressed so long
Into a corner of the roof
That they are brown and soft,
And liable to melt as snow.

Over the greatness of such space
Steps must be gentle.
It is all hung by an invisible white hair.
It trembles as birch limbs webbing the air.

And I ask myself:

"Are your fingers long enough to play
Old keys that are but echoes:
Is the silence strong enough
To carry back the music to its source
And back to you again
As though to her?"

Yet I would lead my grandmother by the hand.
Through much of what she would not understand;
And so I stumble. And the rain continues on the roof
With such a sound of gently pitying laughter.

Like "The Return" this poem is a dream of rescue. For Crane rescue is the goal of the labor of the poem, paradoxical heroism of the doomed mariner. The almost unbearable condition of presence to the world, which the actual poems of Crane repeat as "difficulty," is the state of affairs from which he undertakes to save himself and his undistinguishable counterplayer ("me—her"). The effort to "keep" what in the intense poetics of lettered consciousness has been "pressed so long"—the effort to work out in poems the conditions of rescue from the murderous poetics of presence to the world—raises questions about the adequacy of all mechanisms of access to that source prior to art from which the "love letters" come. The rescue—from art, not to it—involves reference to a condition prior to the exile in language, prior to the mother (for poetry in Crane is not the conscious self-confirming and liberating father tongue, but the incestuously unconscious and implicating mother tongue). It is to that "natal power"—the power of the "mother's mother"—that this poem undertakes to reach, the "orphic machine" being the phantasmal instrument ("Old keys that are but echoes") that requires a strength from silence (the whiteness of speech, its truth and its transcendence) that proves unobtainable. This doomed orphic journey of rescue (Elizabeth is, of course, the mother of John, whose severed head, like Orpheus's, is found toward the end of "The Wine Menagerie") is enabled by a rare moment of spatial openness ("the world dimensional"), a moment of personal subjectivity that implies a confidence about identity that is the furthest reach of Crane's imagination. It emerges again only in Crane's death poem, "The Broken Tower," as "The commodious, tall decorum of that sky." Crane is the native of condensed, borderless, nonspatial, imaginary states of affairs, for whom the task of imagination is to produce the conditions of ordinary life—the labor of the hindered realist. The presence not of the mother but of the mother's mother awakens the sentiment of possible life and confident self-identification.

"My Grandmother's Love Letters" is a private elegy in the style of Patmore, Arnold, and Henley. But unlike the nineteenth-century author for whom the wavering right-hand margin implies the absence of theological assurance of transcendental reference, Crane expresses by the same metrical feature momentary release from an overwhelming objective prohibition ("stars").[19] Arnold's "folds of a bright girdle furled" becomes the "loose girdle of soft rain" (not yet the "screaming rain" of "Eternity"); and in the presence of a person (as in "Praise for an Urn") Crane's speaker becomes a person, in uncondensed dimensional space, whose body is the condition of the obtaining of his truth. But in this poem we also see the primordial discovery for Crane that the dimensional and undeformed body cannot execute the task of rescue, and therefore the reconstruction of the inevitability of a condensed poetics in which the hand is deformed, becomes "long"—not the instrument of the contingent and exilic "hand in hand" of the real fallen world of "wandering steps and slow" but of the impossible Edenic fusion of absolute relationship, of speed. Only in the absence of the stars can Crane be a self, and only in the absence of the self can he be a poet.

The deformation of the hand is required to obtain access to source, and Orpheus-like to carry power of rescue back into the world of consequence ("And back to you again / As though to her," where "her" is not now the grandmother but the mother). The effort at love through music exceeds the deformations possible to the hand; and the rescue of the grandmother is subsumed by the irony. Hereafter, the gentle poetics of irony, the region where there is room enough for an intratextual interpreter ("And I ask myself"), is replaced by the hurricane poetics of condensation that overburdens all structures and especially the structure of the most inevitable of Orphic machines, the natural body. In "My Grandmother's Love Letters," "Praise for an Urn," and "Chaplinesque," human space ("lucid space," as in "Praise for an Urn") appears and disappears. The sphinx of intense poetics takes up its stations on the threshold, and the prayer to the sphinx as muse is for access to feeling:

> (Let sphinxes from the ripe
> Borage of death have cleared my tongue
> Once and again; vermin and rod
> No longer bind. Some sentient cloud
> Of tears flocks through the tendoned loam:
> Betrayed stones slowly speak.)[20]

Crane's most "difficult" poems are, as I have pointed out, often preempted autobiographies ("Legend," "The Repose of Rivers," "Passage" are examples). In "Passage," in particular the argument with the laurel ends at the breaking of personal memory at the point of literate record. "What fountains did I hear? what icy speeches? / Memory, committed to the page, had broke." The enormous task of absolute relationship (the rescue of the personal world from mediation) brought Crane to poetry; but, under the burden of that task, poetry destroyed such access to sentiment and personal growth as would have promised a gratifying life in the world. As utterance obliterated by its style, Crane's poetry stands as a repetition of a countenance erased by its art of presence. The fate of the "hand" in Crane summarizes the outcome of the search for access to the world of persons, for the hand is the instrument of the secular bond and also the allegorical sign of the body as inscriber.[21] The question in "My Grandmother's Love Letters" addressed to the self ("Are your fingers long enough to play / Old keys that are but echoes . . . ?") contains inside it the issue as to whether there is any way of saying as an undeformed natural speaker what Crane's motive to art demands. As the response of a realist to an impossible demand Crane's poetic phenomenology of hands—"troubled hands," "reliquary hands," "snowy hands," "lover's hands"—confesses the incommensurability with human form of his labor at human validation.

In Crane, the story about structure—bridge, tower, tree, hand—follows as image rather than precedes as available creative knowledge the moment of the poem's construction. His thematized structures are less the outcome than the unfinished business of his invention. Poetic structure, whether the phantom modernism of *The Bridge* or the nineteenth-century French formality of "The Broken Tower," was unaccommodated to his meaning because no structure, the function of which is to bear meaning into the world of appearance, is free from the finitizations that are the sufficient condition of appearing at all. Like the hand and bridge and tower, language itself, under the weight of his concern, was deformed and became another hallucinated system wrenched from recognition (and therefore deprived of its power to confer recognition) by the poetics of intensity.

"Language has built towers and bridges, but itself is inevitably as fluid as always." The whole cycle of Crane's myth is the story about the dissolution of forms. The fundamental form of which all the other modes of structure are versions—erected, deformed, and finally dissolved—is language as the vehicle of acknowledgment.

> The sea raised up a campanile . . . The wind I heard
> Of brine partaking, whirling spout in shower
> Of column kiss—that breakers spouted, sheared
> Back into bosom—me—her, into natal power.

These lines are a "fragment" only because fragments are all that can appear; but they are also a "whole" poem in that they record their own disappearance antiphrastically. In "The Return" we find Crane's story about language and desire ("mastery and happiness," "towers and bridges") disentangling itself from exile, and resolved into the fundamental genealogy, the "natal power" that in any determinate manifestation it can only imply. As we have said, Crane's account of desire is "mystic" merely because it is extreme; and his account of structure and above all of language as a finite system under stress is realistic, referenced toward the question of possibility by its display of undisguised deformity. At the end of "My Grandmother's Love Letters" the speaker, in the ambiance now of the mockery of the rain, leads his grandmother "Through much of what she would not understand." The sense of mockery and unintelligibility responds to the terms of a solution to the problem of the source of love incompatible with the human use to which that solution is to be put. The consciousness of a hope inconsistent with any outcome of desire invades even Crane's most lucid poem of sentiment. Under the burden of hope the structure of relationship itself dissolves. What is the nature of that hope?

Unlike the cultural vortices of the Eliot/Pound/Lewis axis, Crane's "whirling spout" represented the all-consuming experience of acknowledgment that seemed to him the one proper subject of poetry and the sustaining condition of life. His dream of rescue was a story about the restoration of relationship between persons. He had no other subject. The resort to poetry for the execution of this subject was an inference from the fact that poetry is founded on, and justified by, solutions to the questions of persons in relationship (across the distance of otherness to one another, and across the distance of death). Whatever the accident of biography that pitched Crane toward the poetic art, he addressed poetry in terms of the great imaginary promises to which the tradition of the imagination points: honor and immortality.[22] His originality consisted in supposing that the promises of poetry and its actual life in the world could be indistinguishable.

For Crane acknowledgment was a crisis, both of mind and of representation, in which existence was altogether at risk. This crisis presented itself whenever Crane encountered the paradoxicality of the unqualified relationship he desired—a relationship that draws into itself, vortically, the totality of experience, admitting no secondary subject, no space of digression, no otherness. The high-modern poetry of Crane's contemporaries aspired to a putative universality of reference ("Let us go then, you and I," "Something there is that doesn't love a wall"). Crane's poetry aspired to a totality of existence ("And yet this great wink of eternity . . ."). In this inherently obscure (because inward-referenced) vortex all relationships are condensed into one relationship, all words into one word, all moments into one moment. This single "flower" is not merely an occasion of experience but the occasion that replaces all other occasions of experience, and in view of which all other relationships are judged. This vortical relationship has the name of all other relationships, as in Yeats the vortex or gyre is the shape preliminary to the subsumption of all shapes. In the vortex exile ends. And, in the sense in which it is not survived, so ends also the inherent paradoxicality of story. The vortex has no outside, as in "The Return" there is no station of the speaker except the creative source itself in which the "me" and the "her" are one in the perfected acknowledgment of copresence at origin. As Crane's hope is an inference from the promises of poetry (honor and immortality), so the image of his hope is an inference from the mechanisms of lyric individuation that requires a recapitulation of the self from the point of view of origin. In this sense the seriousness of the lyric person (Crane's intensity) is always incestuous, and therefore, like Crane's style, touched with abhorrence and disfigurement, portending an autonomy that is not "elite" (as Crane's poetry is sometimes called) but inimical to civility in the largest possible sense. The rescue contemplated, however, is not incest but the nurturing of the "me" and the "her" at a common bosom, the "natal power" of both.

As an allegory of discourse the vortex has no interpreter; it is the most difficult of all poems. The "whirling spout" or tower-column (like the bridge and indeed all Crane's thematized structures, white machines) is the momentary suspension of language in the human world before its descent (return) into the fundamental fluidity ("fluid as always") that is language's estate when it is, as it were, for itself. From this we understand the *nature* of a language (I shall deal with its tradition in the next section of this essay) iconic of source, inherently obscure—such as Yeats points to but does not enact as exploit in the famous interrogation, "How can we know the dancer from the dance?" "Consummation" is an alien subject in English, as the anomaly of "The Phoenix and Turtle" reminds us. The intense poetics of consummation as Crane practiced them are correspondingly alien and uncommon, defining the boundaries of poetry as a means for modeling or anticipating experience. Insofar as poetic structure, and the decorum of speech, are the form and principle of the entrance into appearance of the poetic subject matter, Crane's motive has, in proportion as it is perfected, no intelligible saying or human sentence. The motive of authenticity (as Yeats learned and Eliot preached) is not a poetic motive at all.

Crane's poetry, then, is an exposition of the fate of structures—the body of man, man's language, man in language (the poet), and the things of man's making—when brought into service of the unconceded comedy of human enhancement ("Let us unbind our throats of fear and pity") of which the central act is fundamental acknowledgment—the "kiss."

VI

The style of Crane's poetic enterprise is the "high" style, or more precisely (as I shall explain) the *imaginary style,* of which Crane's anachronistic high styles are modal signs. Beyond any embodiment in actual poems the motive of poetry is, in the tradition, a constant allusion. On this allusion or idealization Crane (by an inversion) has attempted to model the fact of his text. Both Winters, early on, and, more recently, Joseph Riddel remark that what Emerson proposed the poet should do Crane really does. The matter can, I think, be stated more generally. The nature and function of "poetry" (as eternal, divine, regenerative, honoring, etc.) are generalized in poetry's apologies, not from the fact of any text in history, but from the imaginary, inactual, or true poem that the actual poem carries inside it and alludes to ("Let there be . . ."; "Sing, goddess . . ."; "Behold her . . .") as, for example, the song of a solitary reaper is carried inside Wordsworth's actual poem, "The Solitary Reaper." Wordsworth's actual poem, to pursue the example, is infected as a pseudoballad by the oral nature of the imaginary and true ballad inside it, but is itself precisely the finite, intelligible, ironized shadow of the infinite, unintelligible ("Can no one tell me that she sings?") substance of which, as the real poem that comes to hand, it is also the trace of access.

Crane's practice reverses the relationship between the actual and the virtual or imaginary poem in the tradition. In effect, he puts poetry in question by making a severe moral interpretation (a liberal interpretation) of its promises. *He attempts to identify the actual poem with the nature of the imaginary or virtual poem, and to array the former (the actual poem) with the latter's putative features, so that the poem he writes has the nature of the poem (the siren song, or the voice of the nightingale) to which the poet of tradition, and particularly the Romantic tradition, alludes.* The lyric speaker in the poem of tradition is the intratextual interpreter of the virtual poem, who both recalls it and postpones it as a state of affairs (as in Dryden's "Alexander's Feast" or Yeats's "After Long Silence": "That we descant and yet again descant / Upon the supreme theme of Art and Song"). Crane's version as "difficult poem" of the virtual song—the supreme theme—in which (by the inversion) the natural speaker is only an allusion has therefore no intratextual interpreter. In the tradition, it is not a model of possible states of affairs but rather the apocalyptic moment of the "untuning of the sky." Taken as a model of a possible state of affairs, the virtual poem is, in a sense, a hurricane.

The state of affairs in literature that finds an actual work that has inside it an inactual utterance of another sort is a perennial trope of poetic structure. Novels as fictional *books* tend to have real libraries inside them, whereas poems as fictional *speaking* tend to have inside them the source of utterance or speaking itself, whether as lady or bird or god, wind or tower. Poetry, therefore, tends to be closer to the natural, or (as Adrienne Rich has remarked) the psychological unconscious, than fiction; and the imaginary poem is the voice of the authenticity of language rather than its reference, the signless or silent voice of the thing signified. In poetic practice, the closer the actual poem comes to the virtual poem, the "higher" the style. The virtual poem is the trace of "natal power," and the high style is inevitably involved with earliness. Genesis and the Homeric exploits of Poseidon are juxtaposed in Longinus as instances of the grand or sublime in literature.[23] Crane's Columbus, like Freneau's (and like Melville's Ahab), is a high-style speaker because his transaction is with earliness and founding. The Bible (especially the Gospels) is the archetypal work of one kind that gives an account of works of another kind, the work of God. The voice of Wordsworth's "leech-gatherer" (the account of which is modeled on the biblical accounts of the voice of God—the sound of many waters) resonates as the high style ("lofty utterance"), but when taken inward becomes "like a stream / Scarce heard; nor word from word could I divide." This untranslatable voice of Wordsworth's daimon is the central "obscure" language of our civilization. It is primordial (Whitman's "hum of the valved voice" is another example) and prior to exile; it is weighted with what Owen Barfield calls "archaism" and manifests the iconic obscurity of existence prior to its meanings. In it time and space do not exist, and its name, if it has one, is unity.[24] In this authenticity Crane robed his discourse, making his styles repeat the implications of the imaginary poem that constructs only its own source.

The high style was, of course, the enemy gesture for the central poets of modernism. Yeats survived it as an early self, Pound shattered it as structure and reconstituted it as myth, Stevens mocked it as "magnificent measure." Crane's speaker does not survive his early self, is himself shattered, and makes the playing of "Old keys that are but echoes" the activity effective for redemption. But it all hangs by a thread. The sound of mocking laughter is everywhere in Crane and turned against the speaker, not delegated away. The imaginary enterprise, dragged into the real world under the auspices of intense poetics, is absurd, hypertrophic, a solecism. The high style, as the sign in the modern world of the virtual poem, is by its nature out of place; and, like the divinity that attends it, out of place it is also defiling. The reader who functions in Crane's intense poetics as the survivor self, and who must complete the dyadic trope of enclosure (providing the real discourse in which the imaginary can have manifest existence) is repelled or embarrassed because he is called upon, not to interpret the difficult poem, but to finish it. This act of supplementation is the correlative for reading of the specific difference that difficulty makes in the poem. Stylistic solecism (language out of place) is the literary equivalent of defilement (the ritual consequence of the transgression of boundaries), as philosophical idealism is its conceptual equivalent.[25] Crane's style requires of his uneasy readers tolerance of proximity to undefended authenticity, and the ability to endure the absurdity of imaginary states of language without ironizing them by a meaning or dismissing them by a judgment. What the imaginary style invites is acknowledgment of the man in the defilement of his authenticity, most authoritative in effect when his "failure" is greatest.

A principal event of Crane's later creative period was the hurricane on the Isle of Pines in 1926. That hurricane (with which, as we have noted, "The Return" is associated) had the character of a transgression of the boundary between experience and art because Crane felt himself to have, by his birth as it were, a Longinian disposition toward "hurricane poetics."

> I write damned little because I am interested in recording certain sensations, very rigidly chosen, with an eye for what according to my taste and sum of prejudices seems suitable to—or intense enough—for verse. . . . One should be somewhat satisfied if one's work comes to approximate a true record of such moments of "illumination" as are occasionally possible. A sharpening of reality accessible to the poet, to no such degree possible through other mediums.

A little earlier on in the same brilliant, but also truculently self-justificatory letter, he remarks in response apparently to an accusation by Winters of philosophical (and moral) opportunism:

> You seem to think that experience is some commodity—that can be sought! One can respond only to certain circumstances; just what the barriers are, and where the boundaries cross can never be completely known. . . . I can't help it if you think me aimless and irresponsible. But try and see if you get such logical answers always from Nature as you seem to think you will! My "alert blindness" was a stupid ambiguity to use in any definition—but it

seems to me you go in for just about as much "blind alertness" with some of your expectations.

If you knew how little of a metaphysician I am in the scholastic sense of the term. . . . It's all an accident so far as my style goes. It happens that the first poem I ever wrote was too dense to be understood, and I now find I can trust most critics to tell me that all my subsequent efforts have been equally futile.[26]

Crane's conception of poetry, by contrast to prose, as singularly adapted to the registration of "intense" sensations, and his disposition, an "accident" that befell him at the very beginning of his experience of composition, toward a style "too dense to be understood" are (as we can now see) vitally related. Obviously, the disruptive boundary between "intense" experience and ordinary experience defines for Crane (as for Longinus) not only the difference between poetry and prose, but also the difference between his own kind of poetry and other kinds. The segregation to poetry of ideal or philosophical subjects and to prose the account of social fact was a late-nineteenth-century decision reflected, for example, in the work of Crane's autodidact predecessor Stephen Crane, and in the work of the Symbolist contemporaries of the young Yeats. It persists in contradiction to the modernist program in the popular conception of poetry to this day. Crane's antimodernist difference consisted in the employment of the high subject to put the adequacy of poetic structures in question on the ground of their own promises. The "heroic pathos" (Riddel's phrase) of Crane's poetry results from the sense conveyed of an enterprise conducted (and not randomly) beyond the limits of its possible outcomes, with that tolerance of flaws that Longinus predicted for the artist of sublime occasions whose motives "often go beyond the boundaries by which we are circumscribed."

As Crane notes, his preference for intense subjects began with the beginning of his poetic career (note, for example the two quatrains called "The Hive" [1917]). It persisted down to the palinodial death-poem, in signature quatrains, of 1932, "The Broken Tower." Our elegiac four lines, "The Return," is an exposition—"suddenly clear"—of that preference for intensity, the return (not versing, but re-versing) of structure into authenticity. In this context, we have observed the relationship between Crane's "difficulty" and the imaginary or virtual poem of tradition, and between the imaginary poem and the high style. The anachronism (disjunctive earliness) of the high style ("Infinite consanguinity it bears") implies the urgent relevance of the question of origins to every moment of consciousness, making the work of bornness and validation the unfinished and preemptive business of mind both in love and art. Crane's subject was the establishment not of culture, but of existence itself, the Reconstruction of the primal scene with the intention of undoing the dismemberment of birth by the "transmemberment" of song that traces "the visionary company of love" back to the hurricane kiss of beginning (which might be any moment of experience)—and then to begin again. There will be a "new threshold" (a new birth) and a "new anatomy" (a new body). The only moment "intense enough—for verse" is the moment simultaneously of destruction and creation that requires a "new" language, not the cultural instauration of Pound's pseudoapocalyptic "Make it new," but the respeaking of the traditional imaginary language of creation, poetry prior to its poem, mind prior to the difference of other minds. There can be no other meaningful occasion of verse. Eliot's speaker is posthumous of civilization; Crane's is prior to the measured consanguinities of civilization. Crane's poetic procedure is not the ironization of styles, but a dismantling of styles, the decreative analysis and exhaustion of poetic means through the overburdening of fundamental concern. The hierogamic kiss of primary acknowledgment discountenances all states of language except the "natal power" of the mother tongue beyond imagining.

The high style is intrinsically early because it is referenced back toward the earliest instance of the art (the epics of origin and foundation, such as Virgil's, with which Crane compares *The Bridge*), and toward the point of the emergence of discourse from mystery (the oracle and sacerdotal riddle—"Remember, Falcon-Ace, / Thou hast there in thy wrist a Sanskrit charge / To conjugate infinity's dim marge— / Anew"). The high style is always also the limit of a prohibition, being not merely discourse that is by implication totalistic and at the incestuous boundary of origin (the bottom of the sea), but being of course also by its nature a repetition of the already accomplished, the prior poetic act that Crane did not ironize by quotation. Crane's identic repetition of styles, like his figural compressions and his synesthesias, reexpresses preemption of difference, of development, his intransigent refusal to be born in *this* form. The primal scene in Crane—"white, pervasive Paradigm"—has no structure. Therefore, structure was for him an alien element, keeping him *in representation* but always *outside* his motive. In *The Waste Land* Eliot developed a structure in which nothing can be out of place. In Crane's anachronistic and dysfunctional rhetorical pastiches ("prayer of pariah and the lover's cry") nothing can be in place, for nothing that is still in discourse can be at home. From this situation (a mind without a realm) he was required to make thematic a principle of representation (abstract, metadiscursive) in which the anxiety of energies out of their proper place might be held or covenanted absolutely; but it is primordial, a word not yet constrained by reference. Crane was a poet of first creation, continually soliciting origin, the highest style of all.

> The imaged Word, it is, that holds
> Hushed willows anchored in its glow.
> It is the unbetrayable reply
> Whose accent no farewell can know.

When Crane speaks of the "accident as far as my style goes," he is talking about a psychological formation (whatever its biographical basis) that compelled him to put culture in question more severely than it was put in question by his contemporary moderns. What was at issue for Crane, as I have said, was personal existence itself. "The Return" was the history and principle of his world.

VII

The Return

> The sea raised up a campanile . . . The wind I heard
> Of brine partaking, whirling spout in shower
> Of column kiss—that breakers spouted, sheared
> Back into bosom—me—her, into natal power.

Interpretation of Crane's poems tends to specify the terms that are constituent of his world by procedures more internal to the linguistic facts of his text, and at the same time more abstract, than is the case with less "difficult" poetry. This occurs, as we now see, for several reasons: first, because the reader is presented not with the traditional finite and internally interpreted structure that bounds and mediates an infinite allusion (language in its liquidity); but with, in effect, an infinite structure (unbounded, liquid) in which finite structures, like the campanile, rise, are burdened, and fall. The reader must supplement the poem, endure its undefended and illogical energies, rather than "gather its sense." The reader is ambiguously internal to the poem, a part of its project. Secondly, the surface of the poem is designed to exhaust the finite procedures that the reader brings to it. All poetry is in some sense uninterpretable; but the "difficult" poem is *situated* on the virtual uninterpretability of the poetic text, the "infinite consanguinity" of its elements. In a context signifying states prior to difference that functions by a rhetoric that elides the separated individuality, the making of difference (which cannot be avoided) will have no end. The sense of Crane's text (the response it anticipates) must lie in the acknowledgment of its authenticity. Such a response will be mediated by a theory of its "difficulty" that does not erase or neutralize the complexity and peril of the terms of presence at the extremity of demand. Crane anticipates not a meaning but an answer, a candid glance, a kiss.

"The Return" is a message from death, uttered like many of Emily Dickinson's poems from the imaginary station ("death"), with the authority of authenticity itself—"natal power." The past tense in which it is cast negotiates a difference, therefore, not merely temporal. As a poem in the imaginary mode, "The Return" is an exposition (in the condensed rhetoric of intense poetics) of the *nostos* morpheme /re/, which has inside it the rescue of the world as the story of the success of desire ("kiss"). The condensation of more and more meaning upon less and less language (the "crowding of the frame"), until all is found in nothing or silence, is arrested in Crane's most characteristic practice at the level of the morpheme, the almost atomic trace of the imaginary (or divine) "unfractioned idiom." The morpheme (in this case /re/) stands as an instance of the one word of which all other words are images, the Word within the word, or "imagined Word." The assonance of all words with this word is not a question of sound alone, but of sound making sense (the remotest "reconcilement" will be of mind); and there is by implication no end to the reduction. "Criticism" cannot complete the analysis, because the reductions criticism can make are mere signs of the nonfinite reduction of all to one that is the "meaning," thematized in the poem by an action ("Back into bosom— me—her, into natal power"), that ends in an elision of process ("..."). Inside the /re/ is the "me" that becomes inverted (inversion or reversal is for Crane the process of decreation, the vortical rotation) in the "heard," as "brine" and "partake" are in "shower," and as "breakers" is in "sheared." And, finally, as "me" is in "her," and both in "power."[27] At the oceanic bottom of the rhetoric of condensation the morphemic element manifests, as I have suggested, the "infinite consanguinity" (Ezekial's sound of many waters, Wordsworth's "stream / scarce heard; nor word from word could I divide") that is momentarily betrayed ("plundered momently") by the fact of mortal language (the actual poem) and recovered in the elision of the "return," the ambivalent rescue of silence that takes the actual poem inside it.

In Crane, mind takes world inside it, and gives back a transient image ("a moment on the wind") in which the mind is in the world as a campanile, an Orphic machine, the fragile disappearing differences of the speaking person. The "campanile" is a structure and a word out of place, raised up and then canceled, made futureless. The hurricane wind (a parody, as R. W. B. Lewis notes, of the Romantic "corresponding breeze") enters as the assault of eternity (passionate hope) on the structures that manifest it and that, as in "The Broken Tower," it will overburden and break. The "I," as the tower that will be broken, is introduced postpositive to (inside) the winds. The hierogamic sacrament of "brine" as salt wine of the sea ("partaking" as participation and dismemberment) is heard (overheard as the primal scene is overheard) under the eternal auspices of the "ing" participle, which introduces chiastically the atemporal presentness of the grammatically multistable "kiss" (a grammatologically emphatic form of the existence copulative "is"—also noun as verb in present tense, verb as static arrest of noun). This participatory sacrament becomes the marriage deep in the language as it now unfolds—the /her/ of "herd" ("I heard") passing through the /she heard/ of "sheared" into "me—her," while "partaking" passes by way of "shower" and "breakers" back into "natal power" ("natal" being iconic of decreative reversal, /na/ becoming /al/).

Chiastic doubling, as in the second line of "The Return" ("Of brine partaking, whirling spout in shower"), constructs a disjunctive figure in terms of the "ing" suffix so that "partaking" as present-making participle is bound back toward "wind," but "whirling" has its principal grammatical bond prospective toward "spout," creating an empty space in which the consummatory kiss transpires ambiguously inside and outside of grammatical time. This kiss is the boundary of discourse; and here ensue the "breakers," the sense of shore as limit and therefore breaking, from which the "me" and "her" are swept ("sheared," implying "she heard," as at the beginning of the first line "I heard") into the rescue of "natal power." The "kiss" is the point of obscurity (the primal scene that is both overheard, as Mill says poetry must be, and transgressively participated in by the speaker), where the inside and outside of discourse are confused, and definition equivocated. This kiss, the moment in which the speaker is begotten and consummated, projects the relationship between the "difficult" poem and the reader in trouble with respect to "interpretation" because he is situated both within and without the text. The analysis of Crane's language of desire as it imitates and, at the same time, approaches and thematizes the oceanic nature of its reference situates the reader, as I have said, internal to his text. Its rhetorical formality manifests boundlessness, and its structures are at once intrinsic to its meanings and utterly (philosophically) alien to them. They are the structure of what has no structure, no "earthly shore."

Hence, Crane did not experiment with "open form" in any significant poem. The meter of "The Return" (the four-line stanza of Rimbaud's "Le Bateau ivre," Tate's "The Mediterranean," and Masefield's "The River"—the first and fourth line being the French Alexandrine and the second and third English pentameter) is an instance of his "hand," his desituate formality.

He refused to devise a structure that dissimulated the resistance of reality to desire. This sense of form is expressed by Valéry in terms appropriate to Crane:

> As for the arbitrary nature of these rules it is in itself no greater than that of the rules of language, vocabulary, of syntax. . . . The exigencies of a strict prosody are the artifices which confer upon the natural language the properties of resistance, of matter that is alien to our spirit and, as it were, deaf to our desire.[28]

Crane's insistence on the historicity of syntax, forms, and styles (which produces that sense of grammatical coherence and referential obscurity that Winters noted early on) is the measure of what I have called his "realism," an inability to concede any aspect of desire ("happiness") or of the facts that are deaf to our desires ("pattern's mastery"). The homelessness of the whole spirit in the "broken world" of art thus produced (in the absence of modernist concession to the weak mystification of open-form speculation toward merely secular infinities, or the greater "treachery" of the modernist ironization of hope) makes of Crane a passionate ghost, a "returner," a revenant. "Cathay" is the empty space of the dwellinglessness of a mind that finds no rest in any structure faithfully conceived, of the poet who is not *in* his poems as Hopkins is, or Lawrence or Thomas. Crane's unsatisfied spirit is still abroad ("LOST AT SEA") because never at home in the texts that manifested it. This uncanniness of Crane, the sentiment to which the equivocation of boundaries gives rise, is found in Keats's revenant fragment, his return of the hand:

> This living hand, now warm and capable
> Of earnest grasping, would, if it were cold
> And in the icy silence of the tomb,
> So haunt thy days and chill thy dreaming nights
> That thou wouldst wish thine own heart dry of blood
> So in my veins red life might stream again,
> And thou be conscience-calm'd—see here it is—
> I hold it towards you.

Critics of Crane have been disposed, as I said at the beginning, to assume relationships of cause and effect between his philosophic and (I would add) stylistic decisions, and his suicide. Blackmur put it this way:

> Crane had, in short, the wrong masters for his chosen fulfillment, or he used some of the right masters in the wrong way: leeching upon them, as a poet must, but taking the wrong nourishment, taking from them not what was hardest and most substantial—what made them great poets—but taking rather what was easiest, taking what was peculiar and idiosyncratic. That is what kills so many of Crane's poems, what must have made them impervious, once they were discharged, even to himself. It is perhaps, too, what killed Crane the man—because in a profound sense, to those who use it, poetry is the only means of putting a tolerable order upon the emotions. Crane's predicament—that his means defeated his ends—was not unusual, but his case was extreme.[29]

This is incorrect. Crane's means that were defeated by his ends were poetry's means, and the ends were poetry's ends, the "hardest and most substantial." Riddel is closer when he observes:

> For his own part, Emerson wrote poems which almost literally were dedicated to defining what this poet must *be*, not to rendering what this poet does *see*. They are essentially verse essays in poetics, poems which explore the role of the poet but never dare to assume that role.[30]

Crane did assume that role. He devised the forbidden language not of the familiar metapoetic imagination, but of the virtual poem in its difficulty and strangeness. Blackmur's remarks, and the tendency of Riddel's otherwise acute analysis of Crane's "poetics of failure," assume either (Blackmur's case) that the poet must constrain desire to the criteria of civility ("a tolerable order"), whatever the truth may be of the demand of sentiment, or (Riddel's case) that the involvement of the poet as speaker and as the subject of his own elegy (the song of himself) in the problematics of presence is gratuitously (or pathologically) destructive to the man in history. But the psychological causes of Crane's suicide could not have been determined by, or healed, in the context of his art. Crane did not misinterpret the nature of poetry or misunderstand its means. He put them to the test in the form in which he found them on the basis of a demand neither gratuitous nor ill, as the expectation of loving acknowl-edgment and the correlative certitude of self-presence is an expectation neither gratuitous nor ill.

What is at stake in Crane, as my comments are intended to suggest, is the Columbus discovery of a limit of discourse that is also a limit of experience—a discovery only possible if, like Columbus, the voyager supposes there is really something there (a passage through, *per impossible*) where the culture assumes just the end of the world. This discovery can only be made if the goal of poetry, as Crane profoundly demonstrated, is not the "poem" but an investigation (not finally a text but an exploit) of the relationship between the means of presence, of which poetry as it comes to pass is a case, and the high hypothesis of human hope that the poem keeps in mind and of which the pathology that put Crane's life at risk made him aware. What Crane discov-ered is that presence is not its own accomplishment, and that the imaginative culture that keeps alive inside it the seed of its imaginary motive and validity was not, in the world (family and nation) in which he lived, whole. This discovery could only have been made by a radical fidelity to poetry's ends and a relentless disposition to postpone versions of its means, the ironic struc-tures of well-made and decorous poems, which would have con-ceded those ends. The political and ethical systems in the poetry of Pound, Eliot, Yeats, and Frost are not on the whole admira-ble. Crane by contrast did not accept premature hierarchiza-tions or relinquishments in order to sustain the structure and protect the "intelligibility" of his art.

The great *nostos* archetype ("return" as rescue through rees-tablishment of fundamental relationship) of which Crane's *The Bridge*, his "Voyages," and his "The Return" are displacements takes, in the history of literature, two forms: one is the return to the remembered place (like Odysseus's return to Ithaka); the other is the return to the unremembered place of origins (like Socrates' return to the Idea, or Shelley's "Die, / If thou wouldst be with that which thou dost seek!" or the Columbus landfall of *The Bridge*). The return to the remembered place through the good use of time leads to an enhancement of the mortal self, involving an internalization by the voyager of his own past and then its revalidation in the external world (recovery of Ithaka and remarriage with Penelope). The return to the unremembered place is by contrast sacrificial, requiring and justifying the destruction of time and the self at home in time. Both are comedic systems, but the latter is accompanied as in Crane's versions by an inability to delegate away from the self (whether to the god as in the Mass, or to the dead her-friend as in the elegy) the immense losses attendant on a self-realization so absolute, a growth so vast. The return to the unremembered place is the archetype of Dante's *Paradiso*. The "shower," penultimate in our "The Return," but which concludes Crane's death poem "The Broken Tower" ("The commodious, tall decorum of that sky / Unseals her earth, and lifts love in its shower"), repeats the image at *Paradiso XIV,* where the consolation of the resurrection of the body is argued:

> Qual si lamenta perchè qui si moia,
> per viver colassù, non vide quive
> lo refrigerio dell' eterna ploia.

> Whoso lamenteth that we here must die to live
> up yonder seeth not here the refreshment of
> the eternal shower.[31]

The eternal showers ("eterna ploia") restore the body whole. In Crane, however, symbolic restitution does not compensate mortal loss, and his poetry everywhere remembers the dismemberment inherent in transformation. Crane has no language, as the mere poet he was, to effect the purposes of self-validation in this high sense, and he had no permission to relinquish the enterprise. Yeats and Eliot dealt with this predicament in culturally atavistic ways, through affiliation with the vanishing institutions of Church, aristocracy, national (and other) mysticisms. Crane's "failure" is evidence of his fidelity to the secular means at hand.

Throughout Crane's poetry there is an effort to imagine time, to devise return from the unremembered to the remembered place—to make the imagination work in terms of the structure of possibility given:

> Bind us in time, O Seasons clear, and awe.
> O minstrel galleons of Carib fire.

> Bequeath us to no earthly shore until
> Is answered in the vortex of our grave
> The seal's wide spindrift gaze toward Paradise.

Crane's palinodial effort, to return from the imaginary authenticity that was his station, and, as a use of the power with which that authenticity invested him, to make of inevitable death ("our grave") a morally adequate response to paradisal expectation, is the final indication of his cherishing of the real secular state of affairs. The scene of answering (the glance, the adequate return, of which the linguistically embedded sign was the decreative rhetoric of reversal, as in the skewed sequence of the last two lines of "Voyages II" cited above) was obsessive in Crane and defining of him. The bridge was the answerer as hurricane windflower ("O Answerer of all, —Anemone"). By contrast to the scene of answering in the tradition, however, in which the God seeks answer of man's harmonies, Crane spoke on behalf of the central authenticity of his humanity as the "divine" child in search of a mortal response—a structure—that would render intelligible his "melodious noise," unseal his earth. We see his enterprise as in the reversal of a mirror in Milton's "At a Solemn Music":

> That we on Earth with undiscording voice
> May rightly answer that melodious noise;
> As once we did, till disproportion'd sin
> Jarr'd against nature's chime, and with harsh din
> Broke the fair music that all creatures made
> To their great Lord, whose love their motion sway'd
> In perfect Diapason.

"Diapason" comes down to Crane ("Take this sea, whose diapason knells / On scrolls of silver snowy sentences" ["Voyages II"]) from Milton through Dryden's "Alexander's Feast" as the full sound of reality in accord with desire, the "new" creation. This sound was for him (as for Milton) a music, a high style of speaking, man's reconciliation with source of the other person by whom we are made human. In the vital palinode or retraction of his death poem ("The Broken Tower") Crane redefines his notion of a mortal structure capable of reciprocating his hope. The Babel-tower of the primal scene that "Broke the fair music"

("The steep encroachments of my blood left me / No answer")
itself breaks down and there arises ("lift" is Crane's term for the
return of things to their proper place) a new space described in
the classical Augustan language of scalar reconciliation ("com-
modious," "decorum"). The terms of this unsealing contain the
terms of "The Return" and go beyond them to the representa-
tion of a personhood, commensurate with Crane's sentiment of
human destiny, capable of making answer to death in a smile, a
kiss, or a music—capable of reading the difficult poems of im-
penitent seriousness. At the end of his last poem the genesis
event occurs and the hurricane abates, becoming the nurturant
rain that brings up ("lifts") the green world:

> The commodious, tall decorum of that sky
> Unseals her earth, and lifts love in its shower.

The death Crane imagined was not the death he died.

NOTES

1. The text of "The Return" is drawn from *The Collective Poems of
Hart Crane,* edited with an introduction by Waldo Frank (New York:
Liveright Publishing Company, 1946), p. 159. Other texts of Crane's
poems are from *The Complete Poems and Selected Letters and Prose of Hart
Crane,* edited with an introduction and notes by Brom Weber (Garden
City, N.Y.: Anchor Books, 1966). "The Return" was excluded from the
latter on the grounds that it was a fragment. Hereafter cited as *Complete
Poems.*

2. This essay is in accord with the analyses of the four younger
critics named, but differs (I think) in its interpretation: David Bleich,
"Symbolmaking and Suicide," *University of Hartford Studies in Literature*
10, 70–102; John T. Irwin, "Naming Names: Hart Crane's 'Logic of
Metaphor,' " *Southern Review* 11, 284–99; Eric Sundquist, "Bringing
Home the Word: Magic, Lies, and Silence in Hart Crane," *ELH* 44, 376–
99; Joseph Riddel, "Hart Crane's Poetics of Failure" in *Modern American
Poetry: Essays in Criticism* (New York: David McKay Co., 1970), pp. 272–
301. Bleich has established the right psychological etiology for Crane,
in the region of differentiation failure. Irwin has provided an analysis of
Crane's verbal behavior on the basis of his motive to renominalization. I
have benefited from Sundquist's introduction of Heideggerian terms.
Riddel's analysis seems to me the most comprehensive, especially in the

matter of the implications of a life lived close to the problematic of representation.

3. The manuscripts of "The Return" are recorded as D75, D76, D77, D78 in Kenneth A. Lohf, *The Literary Manuscripts of Hart Crane* (Columbus: Ohio State University Press, 1967). The page in question is D76.

4. For a discussion of the quatrain in Crane, see Herbert A. Leibowitz, *Hart Crane: An Introduction to the Poetry* (New York: Columbia University Press, 1968), chap. 9. A short list of poems from Crane's mature work of which the quatrain is closural includes "Legend," "My Grandmother's Love Letters," "Recitative," "For the Marriage of Faustus and Helen" I and III, "At Melville's Tomb," "Voyages VI," "To Brooklyn Bridge," "The River," "O Carib Isle," "The Broken Tower." This list is merely by way of example. The stanza is either constituent or closural of many of Crane's poems from the earliest period. It was also the stanza he tended to see in other writers. (Cf. "From Haunts of Proserpine, *Complete Poems*, pp. 264–66.) The stanza was effective for Crane because the four vertical lines provided the least sufficient number of units that could manifest the chiastic reversal that was for him the decreative conclusion of the poetic enterprise, the return.

5. John Unterecker, *Voyager: A Life of Hart Crane* (New York: Farrar, Straus and Giroux), p. 464. Hereafter cited as Unterecker.

6. See Crane's letter to Winters (July 18, 1927) in *The Letters of Hart Crane, 1916–1932,* ed. Brom Weber (Berkeley and Los Angeles: University of California Press, 1965), pp. 298–302. Hereafter cited as *Letters.*

7. *Complete Poems,* p. 188.

8. The best guide to the study of this great trope of narrative is Douglas Frame, *The Myth of Return in Early Greek Epic* (New Haven: Yale University Press, 1978).

9. Paul Fussell, *The Great War and Modern Memory* (New York: Oxford University Press, 1975), chap. 1 and passim.

10. Questions of the value and meaning of Crane's poems arise (as will be discussed at some length below) for reasons different from the reasons that raise such questions in the case of other "moderns." In the case of the other moderns such questions tend to disappear in time. In Crane's case they are inextricable from his presence in the culture. Insofar as Crane's poems do not anticipate "completion" in terms of the structures in which they are framed, insofar as they are devised to postpone semantic closure, or situate the reader internal rather than external to their own constructive processes, they are both unforgettable (like an obligation that cannot be extinguished) and forever "unacceptable" by mind. It is not merely a question, as in some sense it is in the case of Eliot or Pound, of in time seeing the structure. It is a matter

of enduring the uncanny liminality of the presence Crane's poems negotiate. Hence, the inappositeness in Crane's case of exegetical normalizations, or judicial dismissals. Crane's poems, as will be pointed out, present us with another sense of the word *new*.

11. Crane's incorporation of metadiscursive languages into his poetic idiolect is another strategy toward the establishment of an intratextual audience of his exploit. But meaning in Crane is thematized rather than embodied as structure in his poems, and as theme always finds meaning hostile (like structure) to hope ("I could not pick the arrows from my side"). See in this connection his use of such words as "spell," "scribble," "number," "conjugate," "groove," "idiom," "recite," "Stitch," "scan," etc. Note also Crane's use of terms for textual classification as titles. Such are "Legend," "Recitative," "Paraphrase," "Postscript," "Interludium," "Passage," "Pastorale."

12. The title *White Buildings* arises, as has been noted by David Bleich, in "Recitative," Crane's poem about the relationship of writers and readers. *White* for Crane ("And gradually white buildings answer day") describes the world as whole because prior to meaning, reflective of all light, and therefore simultaneously the world on which all can meet and "the world that comes to each of us alone." The "difficult" poem is "white," the world that "answers" (see part VI of this essay).

13. This major class of poems in Crane includes "Legend," "Passage," "Repose of Rivers," "Voyages III," "National Winter Garden" (where the infant is aborted), and, of course, "The Broken Tower." In Marvell's phrase, these are the poems of the "iron gates of life." In them the crowding of the frame, metrical and grammatical (the gates of life), the conflict between the motive to manifestation and the means, is most severe. The impossibility of growth deflects Crane toward a recuperation of its conditions—toward a repetition of his genesis, got right because an act of his own will.

14. The passage is well-known:

> New thresholds, new anatomies! Wine talons
> Build freedom up about me and distill
> this competence—to travel in a tear
> Sparkling alone, within another's will.

15. F. O. Matthiessen, *American Renaissance: Art and Expression in the Age of Emerson and Whitman* (London: Oxford University Press, 1941), p. 426.

16. Crane is quite explicit about his intention to devise a "new *word,* never before spoken and impossible to actually enunciate" (*Complete Poems,* p. 221). What I am at pains to show is the relationship between this impossible station, and the traditional structures of poetry.

17. The high modernist "juncture without copula" functions only

in the absence, or Teiresian attenuation, of a lyric speaker. Crane's practice does not allow the "spatialization of form" but rather condenses vortically all terms upon a single occasion of speaking, a lyric exploit—a thing done only in the interstices of possibility.

18. Though it is beyond the scope of this essay, it is useful to note that this state of affairs is the residue of a colonial situation. Crane's search for a native genealogy becomes an incestuous return to "natal power" in the absence of a working national culture of poetic styles. Crane's sense of "sundered parentage" is a description both of an historical and a psychological state of affairs.

19. "Star" means for Crane the preemption of relationship as a result of the dominance of prior meaning, the tradition of the interpretability of experience. See, for example, "Cape Hatteras": "Stars scribble on our eyes the frosty sagas," "The stars have grooved our eyes with old persuasions," "Stars prick the eyes with sharp ammoniac proverbs."

20. This much-commented-upon passage of intense rhetoric means: Let (in the sense of new creation, the "Let there be. . . ." of Genesis) the sphinx as principle of "difficulty" be hindered ("let") so that speech, facilitative of sentiment, can do the business of relationship. It is another case of "travelling in a tear" within the will of the other.

21. The complexity of Crane's "hand" references orders itself along the conflictual bipolarity of hand as inscriber, and hand as instrument of direct sensuous relationship, in much the same manner as in Jonson's "Farewell, thou child of my right hand, and joy."

22. Honor is the acknowledgment term, and immortality is the continuity term. Even in the oldest versions, their conjunction is "impossible" in natural life. In the *Iliad,* another story about a young absolutist, you can have *kleos* as immortal image only at the cost of *nostos,* return to "natal power."

23. See chapter 9 in *Longinus: On the Sublime,* translated by T. S. Dorsch, in *Aristotle, Horace, Longinus: Classical Literary Criticism* (Penguin Classics). Subsequent citations of Longinus in this essay are also from Dorsch.

24. The best recent discussion of this tradition is in Margaret W. Fergusson, "Saint Augustine's Region of Unlikeness: The Crossing of Exile and Language," *Georgia Review* 29, no. 4, 842–65.

25. Three among many reasons words as such are out of their proper place in Crane are as follows: (1) morphemes in Crane's poems have more vital relationships, in many cases, to other instances of the same morphemes, than to the words in which they occur; (2) words themselves often have more vital affinities to other instances of the same words than to their grammatical contexts; (3) words are driven together in the condensed rhetoric that elides particles of relationship

in the interest of creating the inference of nontemporal states of affairs. In addition Crane's polymathic lingo is devised as the dialect of no community or class of persons. Among the boundaries Crane equivocates are the cultural taxonomies inherent in grammar, and in the natural decorum of language communities. For the anthropology of defilement as things out of place, see: Mary Douglas, *Purity and Danger* (New York: Praeger, 1966), chaps. 1 and 2.

26. *Letters,* p. 302. Quoted by permission of Brom Weber.

27. The working with /re/ is not local to "The Return." Study of "Voyages" I, II, and III yields a vast system of /re/ and /er/ reversals, as in "fragment"/"scattering," "trust"//"cordage," "cruel"/"eternity," "sceptered"/"terror," "prodigal"/"dark," concluding again upon "her." The system in these poems is summed in such words as "superscription," "reliquary," and "transmemberment." It is the morphemic system that determines the presence of these words in the poem.

28. Paul Valéry, "Fragment of a Preface for the *Adonis* of LaFontaine" (1920). See *Selected Writings of Paul Valéry* (New York: New Directions, 1964), pp. 139, 140.

29. R. P. Blackmur, *Form and Value in Modern Poetry* (Garden City, N.Y.: Doubleday, 1957), p. 275.

30. Riddel, p. 295.

31. This is the translation of the Temple Classics edition that Crane read in 1930 (Unterecker, pp. 625, 633, 634).

The Poetry of Robert Lowell

When Robert Lowell early in his life undertook to bestow himself in the name of poetry on Allen Tate, as Crane had twenty years before, Tate was said to have responded, in effect, that one such obligation in a life was enough. Lowell inherited, and consciously reenacted in his generation, that ambiguous victimage to a master discourse that Crane had seized upon, without permission, and made in his way magnificent. Crane killed himself, as I have noticed, in the year I was born.

Robert Lowell—monumentally gifted, privileged, and afflicted—performed the poet's vocation before my eyes when I was a college student. He enacted the spectacle of authenticity and, in the end, exercised great authority in the long schoolroom of poetic practice at the time I set to work. The character and validity of his judgments remain to be thought through.

Robert Traill Spence Lowell (1917–77) was the central poet of the first post-modernist period in Anglo-American poetry. His literary generation, born in the second decade of the century (including Randall Jarrell, John Berryman, Delmore Schwartz, Charles Olson, Robert Duncan, Elizabeth Bishop, Dylan Thomas), took in hand the question of the continuity of the culture after the Second World War, as Eliot and Pound had taken in hand the continuity of culture after the First World War. Lowell was a great worker at his art and, after 1946, a famous man in American letters. But, like the rest of his generation, he left a less determinate answer to the questions that poetry addresses than did his high-modernist predecessors.

From *American Writing Today*, edited by Richard Kostelanetz (Troy, N.Y.: Whitson Publishers, 1991).

The literary masters whom Lowell encountered on the American ground, and whom he acknowledged, formed a heterogeneous group of stylistically singular and, on the whole, ideologically nativist practitioners, among whom were Allen Tate (b. 1899), Hart Crane (b. 1899), William Carlos Williams (b. 1883), Theodore Roethke (b. 1907), Robert Frost (b. 1874), and, by an accident, Ford Madox Ford in Ford's later years. From these men and others Lowell took his meticulous, severe, and arduous sense of the poet's work. He did not, however, take from them a sense of the poet's role that, as in Yeats or Stevens, supplanted the social identity of the writer. For Lowell a particularly complex and marked social identity was always the primary allegory of his meanings.

Born into an insecure collateral branch of a family unmistakably identified with the political and social domination of American Protestantism and with the moral ambiguities of American industrialism, Robert Lowell struggled not with any insufficiency of identities but with their multiplicity and stigmatizing unexchangeability, their bewildering superfluity, their demonic constraints—the gifts of the God, Jehovah, that could not be put off. Assigned a name borne at once by an American city, a president of Harvard, and two earlier American poets, Lowell identified his personal nature with history at a catastrophic moment in history—as the inheritor, neither of power nor knowledge, but of a will imprisoned among external and ungovernable energies. His last and most ambitious poem, the song of his self, is called with bland but relentless appropriateness just *History*. Robert Lowell's poetic commission was, from the beginning, of a satiric and prophetic character, a national judgment and at the same time a personal rectification of genealogies, modeled not on the high-modernist examples, but on nativist and formalist impulses that flowed, on the one hand, from Tate and Crane and, on the other, from the New Critical phase of American post-modernism promulgated by John Crowe Ransom.

Thus, Lowell, as poet and as disempowered inheritor, set out to reconstruct by poetic means a self whose purview was nothing less than the whole human world—public, inescapable, identified, insane, certainly not the fertile cultural "ruins" of Eliot, but by contrast a brilliant American rubble of dead fact.

Robert Lowell's first book, published at Cummington, Massachusetts, in 1944, was called *The Land of Unlikeness*. The title is an Augustinian phrase supported by an epigraph from Saint Bernard *(Inde anima dissimilis deo / inde dissimilis est et sibi)*. It is borrowed from (or repeated in) a chorus at the end of Auden's Christmas oratorio, "For the Time Being" (published in the same year):

> He is the Way.
> Follow Him through the Land of Unlikeness;
> You will see rare beasts, and have unique adventures.
>
> He is the Truth.
> Seek Him in the Kingdom of Anxiety;
> You will come to a great city that has expected your return for
>   years.

The Land of Unlikeness contains twenty poems, beginning with "The Park Street Cemetery" ("The graveyard's face is painted with facts") and ending with "Leviathan," in which the Protestant capitalist culture, indistinguishable from the culture of war, is identified with the lineage of Cain. Lowell took more than half of the poems in *The Land of Unlikeness* into *Lord Weary's Castle* (1946), the book that established his reputation. Although the poems in question were strenuously revised for the later volume, the basic analysis of history remains unchanged.

Such innocence as history can manifest is subverted (literally, the Boston subway does run under the graves of the Old Granary burial ground) by the Protestant individualist and materialist innovation that founded and now rules America. Such are "The Children of Light" who "wrung their bread from stocks and stones / And fenced their gardens with the Redman's bones." This paternity is in itself unredeemable, or redeemable only by the reference outside of history to the transcendental Mother, Mary, who will restore the genealogy disrupted by paternal violence. *The Land of Unlikeness* announces all the features of Lowell's later style.

Redemption (not "meaning," but a nurturant and tranquil relationship between mother and a son, a right ordering of the energies of love and trust) can only come from outside the present and the at hand. Accordingly, the formal *order* of Lowell's poetic language comes theatrically from outside of the natural language in the form of measured traditional structures, premodern, archaic, in effect miraculous. In an introduction to *The Land of Unlikeness* Allen Tate speaks of Lowell's style as "bold and powerful . . . the symbolic language often has the effect of being *willed;* for it is an intellectual style compounded of brilliant puns and shifts of tone; and the willed effect is strengthened by formal stanzas, to which the language is forced to conform." This is correct. The "unlikeness" of the world to its right form is repeated in the *alienness of structure to experience,* leading to a style of violent imposition, the counterviolence of the will of the son directed against the paternal violence of fact and the presented civilization.

The figure of "unlikeness" in Lowell's *The Land of Unlikeness* announced his central trope: the specular meeting of the self as history, in the present, with its own irrecoverable prior authenticity, the past, the ancestors—as in a mirror that gives back, not an image of the actual person, but an impossible paradigm, an encounter without recognition—the face of the speaker as child seen reflected in the glass of the portrait of a numinous ancestor. The result is sealed in the exclamation of "the Fat Man in the Mirror": "O it is not I." In Yeats, history can reverse itself. But in Lowell, inescapable encounter with the past cannot become recognition in the present by any process inherent in the self. Because there is no possibility of new knowledge, tragedy eludes Lowell. Like the satirist in general, Lowell is a comic writer, anticipating only apocalypse (at first), and then ironic endurance. Nonetheless, it is the curing of the genealogy, the restoration as innocence of the energies of the past, and the sanctioning of love through the reconstitution of the family that Lowell pursues, first by sacred and then by secular means, through three marriages and a score of volumes. In the end, however, he refused to regard poetry as healing—a just reading of the meaning of his own practice. In the book published in the year of his death, thirty-three years after *The Land of Unlikeness,* Lowell records—still in theological terms—his judgment as to the best one can do:

> Is the one unpardonable sin
> our fear of not being wanted?

For this, will mother go on cleaning house
for eternity, and making it unlivable?
Is getting well ever an art,
or art a way to get well?

Lord Weary's Castle (1946) and the book that followed it, *The Mills of the Kavanaughs* (1951), describe, first, a conversion, the recapitulation and universalization of the discoveries of *The Land of Unlikeness,* and then repudiation of that conversion, a contraversion, the abandonment of both an institution and a style. *The Mills of the Kavanaughs* ends with a poem the title of which announces where he has got, and where there is to get: "Thanksgiving's Over." The poem, one of Lowell's very strong works, concludes upon a question and an answer: "Miserere? [pity?] Not a sound."

The self-characterization of the high-modern poet was in general atavistic (Yeats, the Druid master; Eliot, the Anglican postulant; Pound, the reactionary Populist; Stevens, the Republican). Lowell literalized this formula. A radical satirist in a Protestant world, itself founded on dissent, Lowell represented himself as an émigré from the archaic interior of American cultural space. He emerged in the forties in the only disguise possible to the rebel against a liberal dispensation: the archaic intruder. Gothic, aristocratic, anachronistic, Catholic, the epigone as scapegoat, he undertook by sacrificial self-transformation to recover the innocence of the world. The epigraph (in Latin) that precedes *Lord Weary's Castle* is a prayer for restoration of holy sanity: "Accept, Lord, gifts in remembrance of your saints: so that, as their passion made them glorious, our devotion may restore our innocence." Here, indeed, the *willed* nature of Lowell's style, joined with the Christian idea of the cosmic efficacy of the choices of the person, produces a speaker central to the well-being of the race—an Agamemnon, Prometheus, or Hamlet, on whose right relationship to the gods depends the fertility of the field, the health of the kingdom.

The primary sentiment in Lowell's world is fear, its color his pervasive yellow. In the form of evangelical and redemptive anxiety in *Lord Weary,* that fear has meaning. And the obsessive deliberateness of his style has appropriateness in his early work, as it does not in his later, as the gesture of a mind responding to sacramental obligations. *Lord Weary's Castle* begins ("The Exile's Return") with the homecoming of the prophetic wanderer to postwar Belgium, a world of disrupted lineage ("Ancestral house / Where the dynamited walnut tree / Shadows a squat, old, wind-torn gate")—a world therefore of unredeemed fact. This is a world, like the *Inferno (Voi ch'entrate)*, but where (unlike the *Inferno*) redemption is still a power of the will. *Lord Weary's Castle* ends ("Where the Rainbow Ends") with the announcement of the sacrament of the Eucharist as a promise of peace: "What can the dove of Jesus give / You now but wisdom, exile? Stand and live, / The dove has brought an olive branch to eat." As we have observed, the sense of cosmic centrality that sacramental privilege gives Lowell as a poetic speaker justifies the immense scope of *Lord Weary's Castle*. The moral implications of right choice in a Christian universe makes sense of Lowell's stylistic insistence, his obsessive enactment of choice as technique.

Lord Weary's Castle begins in 1945, announcing the postwar and postmodern world with the same monumental deliberation with which Eliot announced the modern world (also postwar) in *The Waste Land*. Lowell's method is however not the "mythic method" of Eliot and Yeats (which implies after all, a fittedness of past and present, an effective continuity of lineage); but neither is it in any new way immanentist or strictly secular. The past as "history" that speaks through and agonizes Lowell's personae amounts to a sort of poetic demonism that does not succeed either in revising modernist poetic impersonalism or in continuing and developing it in significant ways. The agonistic courage of Lowell's procedure results from the laborious and painfully unmistakable persistence of his poetic speaking *in the absence of a formal idea intrinsic to his subject.* ("History" for Lowell in itself has no form.) Intensity of style and monumentality of project (the centralization of an historical self without its mythic amplification or cognitive illumination) produces as subject a victimization of the self precisely at the point at which the self becomes visible, becomes the subject of his art.

Hence, all spaces in Lowell's poetic world, like all occasions of his speaking, are the same insofar as they are enabled by the one crisis that speaks for him—the moment of terror when the two images, the self and its ancestor, the present and the past, confront one another. This is the moment of "madness" and of art. There is no private space in Lowell, hence in a strict sense no "confession," no recuperation, and no absolution. The self is identical with history, and history both remembers and is incapable of using its own powers and images. "The Lord survives the rainbow of his will."

Published in 1951, *The Mills of the Kavanaughs* is the most experimental of Lowell's books. It consists of seven poems (apparently his whole output since *Lord Weary's Castle*), all of them dramatic narratives in which the world becomes manifest through the narrow aperture of an extremely specific station of consciousness. The title poem, for example, is preceded by a note that reads in part: "An afternoon in fall of 1943; a village north of Bath, Maine. Anne Kavanaugh is sitting in her garden playing solitaire. She pretends that the Bible she has placed in the chair opposite is her opponent."

Lowell is not an obscure writer, because he is not in the philosophical sense profound. Rather he is *difficult*, and that difficulty arises from and repeats the paralyzing specificity with which he experiences the world. *Identity is the cage in which his persons are displayed, and that captivity which keeps them in representation keeps them from joy.* This is the bitter logic that is Lowell's principle subject. "Life's a cell," as the girl screams in "Thanksgiving's Over." The only possible principle of organization in Lowell's world is the person. The person, however, always a captive in consciousness, is (once again) like an inhabitant of Dante's *Inferno*, both inextinguishable and overwhelmed by the alien facts of which consciousness consists in an unredeemed world. Only violence can make the connection. Like the electric chair of "West Street and Lepke" in *Life Studies*, the poem becomes an "oasis" in the "air" of lost connections.

In *Lord Weary* Catholicism provides a supplement to the inadequate mediations of mere conscious life. In *The Mills of the Kavanaughs* Lowell undertakes to become human by a construction of "real presence" less dependent on institutional authorization than the Eucharist, namely dramatization. The female soul that is the principal speaker of that book endures, in several forms, bereavement of the empowering grammar of male relationship that contributes genealogical intelligibility. The obsessive tightening of the form, the notable and extreme archaizing of discourse in *The Mills of the Kavanaughs* fails to compensate the bridegroom's violent betrayal of hope. Lowell's poetic dramatizations lack the freedom of the difference between actor and role. *They have no true alterity, as his early Eucharistic imagination had no true sacredness.* At the end of the different but related transformative efforts of *Lord Weary* and *The Mills,* Lowell abandons strict metricality together with the adoration of the Virgin. The self overwhelmed from without in his first three books becomes the self-describing soul in *Life Studies.* Lowell at this crucial moment ceases to construct the poem as a supplement to experience. He now undertakes to gain access to experience through its repetition.

In the literary community of the 1950s Lowell seemed the only poetic writer capable of meaningful self-revision. *Life Studies* (1958) offers a new style for a new reality, the new reality announced in the refusals and impossibilities of *The Mills of the Kavanaughs,* but left there unperformed. "Much against my will / I left the city of God where it belongs." In the opening poem of *Life Studies,* Lowell's speaker announces the "bodily assumption of the Virgin Mary." The impersonality and transcendental experiments of Lowell's earlier poems had left undecided the question whether there was to be found in the scope of his genius any alternative to poetic modernism. *Life Studies* was Lowell's effort to settle the issue by producing in effect a truly secular art such as modernism could only, as it were, imagine.

Life Studies itself consists of four parts, of which the second is a prose memoir. The first part addresses the implications of the corporealization of the object of love, the "bodily assumption of the Virgin." Lowell's development as a whole consists of a life-long struggle to assimilate the implication of that secularization, and *History* in the end becomes merely the late stage of a vital process first stated in *Life Studies* and never concluded. Lowell's conception of this process can be seen in another poem early in *Life Studies* called "The Banker's Daughter." In this poem Lowell's speaker is identified with the sexual woman, a mother out of shape ("such a virtuous ton / of woman only women thought her one"), out of shape and engulfing—the self-generating female soul of Lowell's open-form poetry—who drives out the king (Henri IV). The banishing of the same king, the good soldier, and his supplanting by the promises and powers of the woman, the desire for form, and the exploitation of its terrible elusiveness—these themes of the opening of *Life Studies* come to a climax in a poem called "A Mad Negro Soldier Confined in Munich": "I had her six times in the English garden / Oh mama, mama, like a trolley-pole / sparking at contact, her electric shock— / the power-house!"

Part 2 of *Life Studies* is a strong autobiographical prose piece that accounts in a clear narrative style for the anxiety of a mind seeking its relationship to its own style and the imaginative wealth of its world in the absence of a central principle of order that, if it existed, could make that mind and wealth accessible by giving it a determinate structure. "91 Revere Street" is the story of Lowell's failed warrior father ("the Commander") who has to go to school to learn to cut meat. Correlatively "91 Revere Street" is the account of a mother in search of a style of self-presentation in the world the father has left disordered, the female soul once again doing the whole work of civilization. In this family the child is indeed an intruder who seeks mastery by the arraying of archaic resources, by an alliance, as it were, with the dead for the purpose of rescuing the intelligibility of the living.

It should not therefore be surprising that part 3 of *Life Studies* consists of a set of poems that effect the substitution of a literary genealogy for a natural one—George Santayana, Delmore Schwartz, Hart Crane, Ford Madox Ford. Ford Madox Ford is the true warrior, author of *The Good Soldier* ("Was it war, the sport of kings, that your *Good Soldier,* / the best French novel in the language, taught / those Georgian Whig magnificos at Oxford, / at Oxford decimated on the Somme?"), whose mortal pathos embodies the ambiguities of the prose model that Lowell has accepted. Throughout Lowell's life his politics, insofar as politics enters his poetry, consists of the search for the *real* Commander, as absurdly in "For Eugene McCarthy": "I love you so . . . Gone?"

The fourth part of *Life Studies* bears out the title of the book and identifies Lowell's meaning, the drawing from the naked life, the body. Of these poems two are most distinguished, "West Street and Lepke" and "Skunk Hour." In the former we see a poem constructed from the zero point of coincidence between the language of the ordinary life of the world and the language of poetry. The poem begins in the leisure of casual repose and mounts toward that oasis of significance where meanings arise, that violent threshold where experience yields its meanings, in this case the electric chair. The indistinguishability in Lowell of representation and overwhelming sensation here marks the strange failure of this masterful poet to give an account of the reconciled state that should be the fruit of his new stylistic discovery. In the same way, "Skunk Hour" records the failure of the older strategies of order, and finds the moment of self-discovery in the parodic ancestral mirror of the animal eye, as before in earlier poems a similar confrontation without recognition was registered in the mirror glass of the human portrait.

For the Union Dead (1962) and *Near the Ocean* (1967) are paired works marking the end and outcome of Lowell's stylistic experimentation. Thereafter poetic structures function in Lowell as neutralized principles of the mere endless speaking of a world whose only conceivable forms are either smaller or larger than the scope of the lyric poem and by implication of the individual self. *For the Union Dead* enacts the project of *Life Studies*, as *Life Studies* puts in place the project rendered inevitable by *The Mills of the Kavanaughs.* Now the fallen world in which discourse and experience approach one another is imperiled by the experimental indistinguishability of those two great principles. It is for this reason that *For the Union Dead* contains many of Lowell's most difficult poems, poems of hallucinated lostness of the cognitively empty space between meaning and experience. This is a realm of "suffering without purgation." As in "Eye and Tooth," the field of perception becomes itself a space of suffering. The endings of the poems of this period manifest a world that cannot be shut out and cannot be made sense of—a world that has no closure except the exhaustion of the mind that experiences it.

> Nothing! No oil
> for the eye, nothing to pour
> on those waters or flames.
> I am tired. Everyone's tired of my turmoil.

The most progressive discovery in this book is the consciousness of the desirability of sentiment even in the face of overwhelming threat ("Fall 1961"):

A father's no shield
for his child.
We are like a lot of wild
spiders crying together,
but without tears.

In the title poem of the book, "For the Union Dead," the absence of formality leads to a sense of inversion, the reversal of inside and outside, a drowned and subverted world—precisely that deluge against which the formal will in *Lord Weary's Castle* asserted precarious dominance. The hero's "angry, wrenlike vigilance," "his lovely, / peculiar power to choose life and die" is now lost in the no-difference of a world where outside and inside, up and down, are indiscriminable. This is captivity.

The title poem of *Near the Ocean*, returning to formality, is a dream of escape. The book divides in half, the first six poems being original in the ordinary sense of the word, and the last six being translations (Lowell's term is "imitations") of Horace, Juvenal, Dante, Quevedo, and Góngora. The poems in this volume of greatest interest are the first two parts of the title poem and "The Vanity of Human Wishes," a version of Juvenal's Tenth Satire (a poem to which Samuel Johnson's imitation gave large standing in English letters).

The first section of "Near the Ocean" is called "Waking Early Sunday Morning" and is a parody of Wallace Stevens's monument of early modern secular confidence, "Sunday Morning" (1915). It begins:

O to break loose, like the chinook
salmon jumping and falling back,
nosing up to the impossible
stone and bone-crushing waterfall—
raw-jawed, weak-fleshed there, stopped by ten
steps of the roaring ladder, and then
to clear the top on the last try,
alive enough to spawn and die.

These octosyllables cast the mind of Lowell's reader back to one of his earliest poems, appearing both in the *Land of Unlikeness* and *Lord Weary's Castle*, called "The Drunken Fisherman." In that poem Christ was the "rainbow" trout hunted by the mortal heart betrayed by history. In "Near the Ocean" the apocalyptic fish is more remote, being a secular metaphor neither as accessible as the Eucharist nor as truly a part of nature. The sense of history motivating the old desire to "break loose" is laid out at the beginning of Lowell's imitation of Juvenal later in the volume:

> In every land as far as man can go,
> from Spain to the aurora or the poles,
> few know, and even fewer choose what's true.
> What do we fear with reason, or desire?
> Is a step made without regret?

The singularity of "Waking Early Sunday Morning" is its fidelity to and captivity in the hyperbolic impressionism that marked his early dramatic monologues and is now made to serve the desolate skepticism of a lyric speaker:

> I watch a glass of water set
> with a fine fuzz of icy sweat,
> silvery colors touched with sky,
> serene in their neutrality—
> yet if I shift, or change my mood,
> I see some object made of wood,
> background behind it of brown grain,
> to darken it, but not to stain.

The desire for escape (from the skull, the lyric "cell," the "world") still throws the speaker back upon the transcendental model ("When will we see Him face to face?"), and the meter of the poem mirrors the hymn structures ("stiff quatrains shovelled out four-square") that at least "gave darkness some control."

The structure of the poem is itself a retrospect upon unworkable solutions. It is the countertruth to the windowless simultaneity of life and art in "For the Union Dead," but it is inefficacious in the face of the world of fact:

> No weekends for the gods now. Wars
> flicker, earth licks its open sores,
> fresh breakage, fresh promotions, chance
> assassinations, no advance.
> Only man thinning out his kind
> sounds through the Sabbath noon, the blind

> swipe of the pruner and his knife
> busy about the tree of life.

As always Lowell's speaker is interrupted by history in his reflective self-discovery. The speaking is pitched forward by the speaker's unwillingness to penetrate either history or the self. Lowell has no psychology, as he has no politics, only the truth-bearing sentiment of fear in the presence of forces inside and outside the self, forces that are out of human scale and beyond "control." The archaic intruder is not at home, having been incarnated against his nature, and like the old model of his God dying in the Incarnation, in the prison of the skull, the private Golgotha, the Golgotha of privacy.

The second section of the title poem of *Near the Ocean* is a parody of Yeats's "Prayer for My Daughter" called "Fourth of July in Maine." It is dedicated to an aged "cousin" Harriet Winslow (the mother's family name) after whom Lowell named his daughter. About this figure as about the daughter there hangs an air of exemption from the terror. *In the figure of Harriet is wrapped up all Lowell's competent imagination of ease and satisfaction in the world.* The two Harriets clearly know in their several ways both sentiment and its place in the world. They stand as delegates toward a future in which Lowell cannot find himself and for which he has a voice scarcely used. In the effective genealogy of those women whose names are inside one another lies obscured a future for poetry that Lowell has bequeathed unexplored to his successors—the space that he has left unentered, to which his voice scarcely reached, as by contrast all the spaces that he did fill with his voice can only be entered in imitation of him, in service of his desolating mastery.

After *Near the Ocean* the work of Lowell shatters into five hundred or so satiric epigrams in sonnetlike form, the fragments of a broken mirror all of which reflect only the one face. These compose all the works of the 1970s, except the last *(Day by Day)*. They constitute *Notebook, For Lizzie and Harriet, The Dolphin,* and *History.* Lowell has now come to *assert the unexchangeability of immanent fact for any meaning.* He has identified the structure of representation with the real. His large late work is therefore a parody of epic, for the premise of epic is the *inherent* structure of the whole human world. What is true now for Lowell is only the voice. Lowell had chosen poetry, as I think, for its atavistic promise of authenticity—a genealogy outside of history, a lineage that included the Holy Spirit—by which to repair the guiltiness and disability of the life he remembered. In the end the passion for genealogy and authenticity remains, but the expectation of its actualization as transcendental order has been lost. *Only the self that speaks is real; and the self that speaks, speaks only of the bitter truth of representation.* Lowell experienced his honesty like a disease, and his disease as a form of honesty. His integrity consisted in lifelong endurance of an externally enforced collision between the irreducible "unlikeness" he perceived (the unlikeness constituted as the logic of the poetic principle) and his monumental desire for a world in which to be at home. His late and endless sequences of short sonnets—assertions of the momentary relationship of things actualized in the picture of a person, or the disparate elements of experience bound together, if at all, by the insufficient knowledgeless fact of "the same voice"— enact the treadmill of a powerful will without an intelligible truth. He cannot stop, stay married, affirm anything except himself. Seldom in the history of representation has so powerful a voice found in the end so little to say. There is both magnificence and waste in the spectacle.

Notebook, first published in 1967 and revised in 1970, contains in its revised form 309 of Lowell's sonnetlike poems. It announces the most marked discontinuity in the sequence of works Lowell so deliberately laid upon the line of his life. In Lowell, as we have seen, mind and the world are never "fitted" to one another, as they become, for example, in Lowell's younger contemporary A. R. Ammons. Though Lowell was as acute an observer of nature's regime as ever wrote English poetry, natural process for him lies only in the perceptual field as a failed allegory for the processes of personal acknowledgment, love, and fame. The difference between minds (the sentiment of love's imperfection and also of its natural triumph) in Lowell is madness—the madness of the mind disempowered by its great models in love, mother and father, and at the same time driven by an energy that, because it contemplates no good outcome in the social world, seems bound in guilty fidelity to an "unlike" personhood not in human scale. The scale of this energy in Lowell is potentially sublime. *Notebook* (and its shaped sequel *History*) is, as I have indicated, an epic project in the scale of a great motive, actualized from the shattered perceptual outlook of the natural man not exempt from the body of flesh and reason that the true sublime, as Kant reminds us, interrupts. Lowell's man cannot, as Yeats hoped, embody truth. It would destroy his body. Nor can he exempt himself, as Stevens proposed, by an art that makes a difference from life, that relieves the "pressure of reality." Art is bound to life and therefore baffled by the representational system that is correctly named experience.

Though Lowell from first to last is a poet the substance of whose art is the person, he cannot engage persons or make sense of relationship as a form of knowledge. He either identifies with persons (his pseudodramatic inhabitation of the lives of the great) or combats them by insisting on their unreachable otherness. (The poem wholly in quotation marks seems his characteristic invention.) In 1973 he split the *Notebook* into three parts. *For Lizzie and Harriet* contains the poetry memorializing the former beloved, as it were the natural person past and future (Elizabeth Hardwick and their daughter Harriet); *The Dolphin* (mostly new poems) records the unstable and largely allegorized new marriage, another version of the symbolic bride. What remains, his story, becomes *History*. In this manner he separates the beloved from his central poem and finds *within* the beloved a dichotomy that portends, if life permitted it, an endless fragmentation.

The split between the mortal and the immortal beloved, *Lizzie and Harriet*, on the one hand, and *The Dolphin*, on the other, is a traditional procedure in modernism. The development, in Yeats for example, is from the allegorized woman to the immanent body of the world. Lowell's singularity is the severity with which both are judged as incompletely realized, incompletely taken into life. The scene of *For Lizzie and Harriet* is "the mind which is also flesh." The restlessness of Lowell's speaker with the mortal marriage, the "Dear Sorrow," seems accounted for by the implicit severity of her criticism of the gothic hyperbole by which he exchanges life for style even at the moments of greatest intimacy. Here in the clarity of her challenge to acknowledgment, his style evacuates its qualities:

> Lizzie, I wake to the hollow of loneliness,
> I would cry out *Love, Love,* if I had the words:

> *we are all here for such a short time,*
> *We might as well be good to one another.*

Lowell has no style of repose, no way to live both as a poetic speaker and as a reconciled, morally acknowledged, and conceded social and sexual person. "Man," he says in his second of his "Dear Sorrow" sequences, "cannot be saved outside the role of God." And in the fourth:

> Do I romanticize if I think that I
> can be as selfish a father as Karl Marx,
> Milton, Dickens, Trotsky, Freud, James Mill,
> or George II, a bad son and worse father—
> the great lions needed a free cage to roar in.

If it is part of Lowell's heroism and accomplishment to press art hard against the life lived, then it must be concluded that he does not obtain a credible account of life under the pressure of the motive to art. He remains the gothic intruder whose life is hallucinated by "the role of God." *For Lizzie and Harriet* begins with the birth of Harriet, the daughter, in "Summer" and ends just beyond "Late Summer" with an "Obit" for the marriage from which the child came. This child is the future beyond Lowell's ability to experience a future consistent with his motive to art, not a possible occasion of art for him but perhaps the best inference his art awakens.

The counterwork of 1973 (as I have indicated) to *For Lizzie and Harriet* is *The Dolphin*. Its subject is not the mortal love and genealogy, the immanent destiny, the birth of the daughter, but a return to the dynastic conception, a resymbolization of an earlier state of the Lowell self—not, in other words, the birth of another, the daughter, but of the self-mirroring son. The Lizzie of the countervolume speaks in *The Dolphin* wholly in quotation marks. Her utterance is separated and distinguished by the terms of its remote mediation: "Records," "Communication," "Voices," "In the Mail," "On the End of the Phone." It is the voice not his own that loves him. By contrast, the lyric voice in *The Dolphin* is vagrant, searching for its lost authority. The singular apparition of Racine in *The Dolphin*'s last and best poem mocks the interminable patrol:

> Racing, the man of craft,
> drawn through his maze of iron composition
> by the incomparable wandering voice of Phedre.

In his early writings Lowell's demon was his madness. It is now his sanity. Always a demonized writer, the compelled activity of self-record is now seen as a betrayal of life rather than an instrument of its redemption. "Everything's real until it's published" is a characteristic sentiment of the poetry in *The Dolphin*. It declares the end of the confessional enterprise. Indeed, with the exception of some few vitally symbolized stanzas, the poetry of *The Dolphin* is inept and casual, compromised by the posture of a man who does not speak the truth to either lady— "the hangman's-knot of sinking lines." The sense is of scribal automatism, a keeping on with writing that is a postponement of the truth. *The dead end of the confessional mode is the identification of art with consciousness, and the disabling of consciousness by identification with art.* The empty endlessness of self-awareness without recognition becomes what Lowell in his culminating work calls *History*.

Lowell began as the poet of New England, not in the way of Frost the genius loci but in the manner of the Jeremiad preacher, the disturbed conscience of the place. At the end of his career the genealogy of the catastrophe he saw around him had become coterminous with the totality of history, and at the same time somehow specified within the implications of the names and persons of history rather than its processes. *History*, his major work—his story, a satiric dismemberment of epic—is accordingly a mere sequence of reperceptions (more than 360) of the same moment of aberration, viewing through the same window of personal obliquity not a calculus of forces articulated in ideologies (e.g., the Protestantism and Catholicism of *Lord Weary*) but the endlessly repeated deformation of personal energies, the energies of individuals all of whom are, in the captivity of his unmistakable voice, himself. If there is a point of intersection between lyric structure (the account of a self by a self) and the structure of *History*, it lies in an implication similar to that of Nietzsche when he said: "At bottom, I am all the names in history." For example:

Caligula 2

My namesake, Little Boots, Caligula,
tell me why I got your name at school—
Item: your body hairy, badly made,
head hairless, smoother than your marble head;
Item: eyes hollow, hollow temples, red
cheeks roughed with blood, legs spindly, hands that leave
a clammy snail's trail on your scarlet sleeve,
your hand no hand could hold . . . bald head, thin
    neck—
you wished the Romans had a single neck.
That was no artist's sadism. Animals
ripened for your arenas suffered less
than you when slaughtered—yours the lawlessness
of something simple that has lost its law,
my namesake, not the last Caligula.

The Lowell who speaks in *History* constructs (confesses) a story beginning in the primordial pre-texts of the culture ("Man and Woman," "Bird?" "Dawn," "In Genesis," "Our Fathers"), and rotating at its center on the discovery of the moral uselessness of a past in which he is himself always present, and always the same. The central poem of the vast sequence is "Mother and Father 1": "I hit my father." The structural device that characterizes this sequence—a device touching the syntagmatic relationship of elements rather than the prosody of representation—is what Lowell called "Surrealism," which is to say the juxtaposition of the contents of consciousness (and therefore experience) without securing the meaning of their relationship—once again a strategy of confrontation without recognition:

Mother and Father 2

This glorious oversleeping half though Sunday,
the sickroom's crimeless mortuary calm,
reprieved from leafing through the Sunday papers,
my need as a reader to think celebrities
are made for suffering, and suffer well. . . .
I remember flunking all courses but Roman history—
a kind of color-blindness made the world gray,

though a third of the globe was painted red for
   Britain. . . .
I think of the ill I do and will;
love hits like the *infantile* of pre-Salk days.
I always went too far—few children can love,
or even bear their bearers, the never forgotten
my father, *my* mother . . . these names, this function, given
by them once, given existence now by me.

The gathered events of memory are displayed without assessment of their interrelation, hence without the entailment of tragic conclusiveness. Such a habit of consciousness sustains the ongoing of representation in the mode of comic or satiric registration rather than the shaped riskiness of judgment. The self-absolving tone of Lowell at this point serves only its own prolonged presence in the world, rather than the penetration of cause by art on behalf of life. Lowell's skepticism, at bottom the decision by which he is characterized by his own hand, seems a willful postponement of majority. In this sense, the "realism" of Lowell's *History* is inferior to the imagination of Yeats's *A Vision* (another sorting of a world of names), or to the extravagant and costly overdetermination of Crane's *The Bridge*. In the motiveless inclusiveness of Lowell's disobligated structure (his sequences of rhetorically colored sonnets) the terrors that arise seem arbitrary, as they are found to be uncaused.

The difference between *Notebook* and *History* (aside from the strenuous revision of many of the stanzas) is the chronologizing of the elements. Lowell's last book, as it turned out, was called *Day by Day* (1977). At the beginning of this book the myth of Odysseus's return articulates the sentiment of "coming home," and also of a life posthumous of emergence, a life capable of the conciliation of past and present because it is no longer obligated to act. There is here a marked seriousness about the thinking through of experience and a greater intelligence about structure than in the other works since 1967—less mere representational opportunism and more struggle with the resistance of the world to meaning. *Day by Day* is at once elegiac and clear sighted, a profounder secularization of the motifs of mother and son—son and the loves that the mother has permanently shattered into multiplicity. In *Day by Day* Lowell gives an account of his latest style as if it were felt by him to be an instrument no longer responsive to his purpose and not yet replaced by a more powerful means. As in "Shifting Colors":

> But nature is sundrunk with sex—
> how could a man fail to notice, man
> the one pornographer among the animals?
> I seek leave unimpassioned by my body,
> I am too weak to strain to remember, or give
> recollection the eye of a microscope. I see
> horse and meadow, duck, and pond,
> universal consolatory
> description without significance,
> transcribed verbatim by my eye.
>
> There is not the directness that catches
> everything on the run and then expires—
> I would write only in response to the gods,
> like Mallarmé who had the good fortune
> to find a style that made writing impossible.

This nostalgia at the end for a style that resists discourse, for a structure that opposes rather than conspires with experience, *for an effective intention,* declares the exhaustion of a motive that began in *Lord Weary's Castle,* and before in *The Land of Unlikeness,* to see the world transformed, made innocent, aggregated in a Holy Family through which as a just inheritance the good promise of life could flow.

Lowell's last poems are the end of a transit of styles that began with *Life Studies* as a disencumbering of mediations, an empowering of the self toward the object of desire. What he learned (though the inference he draws from what he learned is not clear) is that experience represented at the point of coincidence between world and mind really has no meaning and no end; it confers no consolation—yields no story but the account of its own production as story. And that is not a story adequate to human hope. For Lowell, I think, the great moderns—Yeats and Eliot—had exhausted the implications of transcendental fidelity without healing the pain of life he felt so keenly—a pain that now awaits a new poetic insight, the possibility of which he kept alive by the patience of his labor at utterance but the truth of which he left to be found again by another.

The Jew as an American Poet
The Instance of Ginsberg

The argument of this sequence of arguments turns here, at the point of the earliest text (1962) in this book. The writing of it followed close upon the sunlit library moment with which we began. The question put to the poet and therefore the poet's question was why are things as they are and not another way. The answer? Because of the ubiquity of the poetic principle and the continually reconstructed logic of representation that constitutes the structure of the poetic principle. Thus the poet's question becomes: Is there another logic consistent with the poetic principle, or only this one?

Let us say that in every generation there are two classes of poets: first, the "strong" poets who search the resources of the art, its logic *as given,* in the interest of an outcome responsive to the impossible obligation to *sing something* framed always in the "strong" formulation of that obligation: "Sing something *other.*" Such poets produce to the world, as if for the first time, the implication of the poetic principle, and seem to exhaust the possibility of world-realization by poetic means within the métier thus constituted—as if without alternative. Dickinson and Baudelaire were such poets, as well as Tennyson, Yeats, Lowell, and I think Plath, who was born in my own year—and also Celan. Such poets enact captivity to the logic of which I speak. They bequeath, each of them, an inimitable example. They seem, however, to bring the art they practice to an end. Above all, they realize (as did all the grand "high moderns") that the price of new knowledge by poetic means is the overcoming of

From *Judaism,* 1962.

art itself. They are the better poets *because they can be judged.* Because there is a poetry of the kind they intend.

For there has never yet been a poetry of another kind. Why? If the truth of the world is always other than it has been thought, then truth's poetry must be other than has been thought. But there is no such poetry, or it is *inactual.* Hence the terror of the demand, "Sing me something," now discloses its reasons. Something—"a song"—always by implication "a new song"—is demanded (on pain of death)—which has never existed in the world.

And let us say there are also poets who undertake to do just that—to sing *a new song such as never has existed in the world.* They enter into the space of origination (as Whitman did, but not Dickinson; as Stein may have done, but not Stevens) and undertake to change the codes. Insofar as such poets succeed, they are poets indeed but less poets than the others, hard or impossible to judge as poets because there are no exemplars or artisanal paradigms—or the paradigms deform the instances.

The great artifact that Western civilization found (or begot, not certainly "made") is the Jewish God who always demands "Sing me something," but never demanded a poem. The distinguishing predicate of this god is sanctity.

The sacred classifies both the God and the poet. (We say "Holy is the Lord of Hosts"; and we also say "divinus poeta.") "Sanctity," itself unrepresentable, specifies precisely difference itself and is the beginning and the end of representation. Perhaps the study of sanctity is the beginning of an understanding of the other (inactual) poetics that does not repeat the logic of representation. The beginning of that study can be glimpsed in "Holiness" (chap. 9).

Historically, the question of another poetic can be put in the form: "Why is there no Jewish poetry?" (see chap. 7). In my time in America, the answer to the question begins with the instance of Allen Ginsberg.

The Jew, like the Irishman, presents himself as a type of the sufferer in history. At a mysterious moment near the end of the nineteenth century the Irish produced a literature of international importance, without having previously contributed a single significant poem in English. The Jewish poet in America today [1962] resembles the Irishman in England during the 1890s. From a literary point of view, he is emerging from parochialism into the mainstream of writing in English, and he is bringing with him a cultural mystery arising out of his centrality in history as a sufferer, and also out of his relation to a vast body of literature in another language. The Irish at the end of the nineteenth century discovered rather suddenly that their political experience had a symbolic relation to modern history as a whole, and that their ancient literature provided an inexhaustible resource of mythology by which to interpret that history. The Jewish poet in America at this time is engaged in the attempt to express the meaning of his own historical centrality, and he too possesses a vast body of literature in another language—the *Zohar*, for example—which constitutes a symbolic resource as yet unvisited in English literature.

None of the Anglo-Irish poets of the Celtic Renaissance began as celebrants of the Irish subject matter, or practitioners of a style that might be called peculiarly Irish. They, all of them, "went Irish" when it became professionally useful for them to do so. Similarly, there is a tendency at the present for Jewish poets, whose work appears at first under culturally neutral auspices, to present their work again (Karl Shapiro is the most obvious example) as *Poems of a Jew*. In the case of Allen Ginsberg, the development is quite clear. His earliest poems (reprinted as *The Empty Mirror*, Totem Press, 1961) are culturally anonymous. His first published volume of poems (*Howl*, the Pocket Poets Series, 1955) draws its title from Blake, and presents itself as part of a completely formed artificial subculture called "Beat" that takes the place of the lost real ethnic and political subcultures that in the past succored and gave identity to the outcast by forming a community of outcasts. Ginsberg's most recent volume, *Kaddish*, is presented under an aggressively Jewish title despite the fact that it is in no simple sense a Jewish book.

The Beat movement, which is now more or less done with, is antinomian and predominantly mystic in substance, and Ginsberg, though still from a position within the movement, is quite clearly invoking the Jewish cultural mystery as a new ground for poetic identity beyond the disintegrating coterie that first gave him notoriety and a language.

Ginsberg's poetry belongs to that strange and almost posthumous poetic literature that began to be produced in America after the Second World War, and in which the greatest figure is the spoiled Calvinist (Catholic), Robert Lowell. The characteristic literary posture of the postwar poet in America is that of the survivor—a man who is not quite certain that he is not in fact dead. It is here that the Jew as a symbolic figure takes on his true centrality. The position can be stated hypothetically from the point of view of a European survivor who has made the Stygian crossing to America: "Since so many like me died, and since my survival is an unaccountable accident, how can I be certain that I did not myself die and that America is not in fact Hell, as indeed all of the social critics say it is?" Ginsberg's poetry is the poetry of *a terminal cultural situation*. It is a Jewish poetry because the Jew is a symbolic representative of man overthrown by history.

It must be remembered that the image of the Jew in America as it underlies the poetry of Ginsberg is not in any sense the same as the image of the Jew in Europe, such as we find, for example, in the poetry of Eliot. Eliot's Jew is a familiar figure resembling Shylock and the Ugly American. Eliot's Jew is the phantom of a dead cultural situation. Ginsberg's Jewish protagonist is the apotheosis of the young radical Jewish intellectual, born out of his time and place, possessing now neither social nor political status. Having exhausted all the stratagems of personal identity, sexual and ethnic, he is nonetheless determined to celebrate his state of being and his moment in history.

From a general point of view, what Ginsberg says in *Kaddish* is that there is no longer any wisdom in experience. In a conversation not long ago with another poet of the "Beat scene," I was astonished to learn that Ginsberg is regarded as a "Dionysian" writer. One must hope that the Dionysian man has more joy in his ecstacy. *Howl*, Ginsberg's only major poem [then and now], is a lament for the passing of experience as a resource for wisdom. In Ginsberg and the Beat writers generally the word *wisdom* is an important technical term. If there are two traditions of wisdom education, the first proposing that the greatest wisdom arises from the most intense transaction with experience, as exemplified, for instance, in the story of Oedipus; and the second, that wisdom arises from the least transaction with experience, Socrates and Jesus being examples—then Ginsberg represents a culture that has exhausted the first of these resources and that has turned, with hardly more certitude than the mere assertion, to the second. Ginsberg represents himself as the last wise child in a secular culture, whose missions it is to reconstitute the relation of the world and its soul.

The symbol of the ultimate transaction with experience for Ginsberg, as for Sophocles, is possession of the mother. Nothing, needless to say, could be more predictable from the point of view of the popular sociology of the Jewish family. But what represents Ginsberg's point of view as entirely desolating is that he documents the death of the mother, and therefore of the ground of experience itself, as a source of value. At the end of the great sentence that constitutes the first 150 lines of *Howl*, the speaker has reproduced the crime of Oedipus, and found guilt without transformation. The New York of Ginsberg is a kind of Thebes through which the poet wanders like a king become prophet by some terrible and inappropriate transformation: but beyond this Thebes there is no Colonus where the prophet becomes a king once again outside of life. In *Kaddish* Ginsberg laments the death of the mother herself, the ground of all being both physical and ethnic. In *Kaddish* the archetypal female is a mutilated and paranoid old woman ("scars of operations, pancreas, belly wounds, abortions, appendix, stitching of incisions pulling down in the fat like hideous thick zippers"), an old woman, haunted by the image of Hitler—and dying, obscene and abandoned, in a sanatorium.

This is Ginsberg's version of the Jewish mother and, simultaneously, of the Shechinah, the wandering soul of Israel herself. Ginsberg is the last dutiful son of Israel reciting Kaddish at the grave of his mother and of the symbolic image of his people. The mysticism of Ginsberg is peculiarly Jewish in the same sense that the *Zohar* is Jewish. As Gershom Scholem has recently shown, the origins of Zoharistic mysticism lie deeply embedded in Christian gnosticism. For Ginsberg, as for the Jewish mystic in general, the gnostic attitude represents the attempt of the Jewish mind to reconstitute itself outside of history. The Jewish mother in *Kaddish* fantasizes herself hunted by friend and enemy alike, by her own mother, by her husband, by Roosevelt, Hitler, by Doctor Isaac, by history itself. She possesses an insane idealism of which her son is heir, and in the end she dies in a fashion so ignominious as to be pornographic. Ginsberg erects on her grave an image that is no longer ethnic and that therefore is no longer obsessed by the mystery of the Jewish people in history. To Naomi dead he cries out:

> O glorious muse that bore me from the womb, gave suck first mystic life & taught me talk and music, from whose pained heat I first took Vision—
>
> Tortured and beaten in the skull—What mad hallucinations of the damned that drive me out of my own skull to seek Eternity till I find Peace for Thee, O Poetry—and for all humankind call on the Origin.
>
> Death which is the mother of the universe!—Now wear your nakedness forever, white flowers in your hair, your marriage sealed behind the sky—no revolution might destroy that maidenhood—
>
> O beautiful Garbo of my Karma—

In his poetry Ginsberg attempts simultaneously to document the death of history itself, of which the Jewish people personified by Naomi is the symbol, and to erect a new ground of being beyond history, of which his own poetry is the type and of which the symbol is the mother, or Israel, transformed as (gentile) muse.

Curiously enough, Ginsberg finds a tradition for his peculiar form of Jewish gnosticism in the history of American stylistics. Ginsberg, and to some extent the Beat movement in general, regards himself as the heir of the American transcendentalist rhetoric. He himself refers to his style as "Hebraic-Melvillian." The transcendentalism of Emerson, founded as it is on the *Metaphysics* of Leibniz rather than on the *Ethics* of Spinoza, provides a national strain upon which Ginsberg, who is at once casual and profoundly serious about his references to history, attempts to graft his "Angelical Ravings." This mixture of nationalism and ethnicism represents the peculiar position of the American Jewish poet who regards himself as simultaneously native and, in the special sense that always pertains to the Jew, alien.

Significantly, Ginsberg's attempt to trace his particular form of transcendental ambition to Whitman is, in all but the grossest sense, absurd. The Whitmanian style is founded upon the celebration of the secular world as an inexhaustible resource of sensation and identity. The world of Ginsberg, on the other hand, is the world of the ruined mind presiding over the death of its physical being and attempting to refound itself in a new reality. The culture of Ginsberg's poems, despite his attempt to naturalize it, is fundamentally an international or extranational specter. *Kaddish* opens with a Neoplatonic reference to Shelley's *Adonais,* a prophetic memory of the Hebrew anthem, and echoes of Christian apocalypse. Ginsberg's style recalls successively Yeats, Hart Crane, William Blake, the Jacobean prose of the Authorized Version, the ecstatic prose of *Moby Dick,* and translations from the thirties of the Chinese wisdom literature. Whereas the national image in Whitman is a stable symbol of an ideal form of the self, Ginsberg's reference to America is an effort to naturalize a fundamentally alien and precariously grounded consciousness. For Ginsberg the poetic identity must supersede the ethnic identity if the poet is to survive.

Ginsberg's poetry, insofar as it is American poetry, represents an attempt to refound moral culture from a point of view outside any given tradition. *The form of his poetry—that of the enormous unifying syntax of the single sentence—is proposed as a model or archetype of some new language of personal being.* Like the Jewish Kabbalist, Ginsberg regards his words and indeed the letters of which they are composed as living things that in their form represent the recreation of "the syntax and measure of poor human prose." The ideal of unity in the self, which is intended to effect a legitimization of both the body and the soul in terms of one another, finds its source in the English poetic tradition in William Blake. Blake himself drew on Swedenborg, Law's translations of Böhme, Milton, and other sources many of which are themselves identical with the culture out of which Jewish mysticism arises. Ginsberg gathers together in his peculiar way all these ancient cries of ecstatic being, and lays them down on the page as a kind of epitome of failed hopefulness.

The enemy in Ginsberg is Moloch, who is quite simply the image of the objective world of which the economic culture of America is the demiurgic creator. Moloch, or Capitalism, destroys the soul and drives the "angel" to a frenzied search for new worlds. Similarly, in the Jewish mystical tradition, the neophyte attempts to uncreate himself and to return back along the developmental continuum to the womb and primal substance in which he had his origin. Curiously, the symbols that Ginsberg employs to identify the moral enemy are in part the symbols by which the Jewish role in culture is traditionally defined. Throughout Ginsberg's writing there is an ambivalence toward Jewishness that should be recognized, as it seems to be an emphatic part of his public statement.

The death of the Jewish mother in Ginsberg's *Kaddish,* and the succession of cultural generations implied in the burden of identity laid by the mother on the son, is unquestionably the most momentous record in English of the problem of the passing of the older sociology and meaning of the Jewish family-centered culture in America. But the mysticism with which Ginsberg faces the problem of the death of Israel is, perhaps, less momentous than the poetry that he makes the vehicle of that problem. There is, as I stated at the outset, no major tradition of Jewish poetry in America, as there was before Robert Lowell no major tradition of Catholic poetry, or as there was before Yeats no major tradition of Irish poetry in England.

On the one hand Ginsberg uses his Jewishness as a way of representing the general condition of the culture of value in America. On the other hand, he represents himself as the only surviving son of a Jewish universe that died with the death of his mother. We may note that the Jewish symbology becomes available in American poetry just at the point at which the Jewish poet finds it necessary to document the death of the Jewish cultural fact.

The earlier poetry of Ginsberg, that represented primarily by the volume entitled *Howl,* is a great deal more buoyant than the poetry that we are here considering. Between *Howl* and *Kaddish* Ginsberg has lost his humor and gained a kind of horror that even he cannot accommodate to the necessary reticence of the poetic mode. Ginsberg's chief artistic contribution in *Kaddish* is a virtually psychotic candor that affects the mind less like poetry than like some real experience that is so terrible that it cannot be understood. In America, which did not experience the Second World War on its own soil, the Jew may indeed be the proper interpreter of horror.

Allen Ginsberg himself was too young to experience the Second World War either as a soldier or civilian. For him, as for other American poets in this decade, the extreme situation, the American analogy of the bombed city and the concentration camp, is mental illness and the horrors of private life. In this sense the Jewish family, as Ginsberg represents it, becomes the type of the private suffering of the American soul. The tendency of recent American poetry to represent the terrors of history in terms of purely mental agony is almost universal. This is the subject of Snodgrass's *Heart's Needle*, Sexton's *To Bedlam*, and, most recently, Dugan's *Poems*. Ginsberg's image, however, is more extreme than any of these, and I am inclined to think that it is the Jewish theologic mystery that makes that stern agony inevitable.

Now I should like to return to the general problem of Jewish poetry in America with which I began. It is clear that Ginsberg uses Jewishness as a way out of the cultural cul-de-sac of the Beat style, and as a way into the soul of the American intellectual. It is clear also that Ginsberg can entertain the Jewish subject matter only as it is in the process of being transformed into something else. Quite possibly the documentation of the death of Judaism is, and will always be, the characteristic Jewish subject. However that may be, Ginsberg has had the sense to perceive that the only significant Jewish poetry will also be a significant American poetry. The fact that Ginsberg seems to be a Jewish poet less by design than by the habitual candor of his nature is the sanction for such Jewish meaning as truly exists in his verse. What is happening in Ginsberg is that a sense of the disintegration of past cultural identities has led to a return to even more ancient symbols of moral being, the matrix of medieval Jewish mysticism. The death of the mother in *Kaddish* represents the death of parochial culture, and the poem emerges at the point when it is necessary to lament that loss and to refound identity. Ginsberg represents a brilliant though uncertain invasion of the American literary community by the Jewish sensibility in the process of transcending parochial definitions. It is an irony, though not necessarily an unproductive one, that the poem of the Kaddish should be recited for the death of the archetypal Jewish mother, articulated for that purpose in the language of Yeats and Whitman.

Jewish Poetry Considered as a Theophoric Project

I do not, in fact, wish to ask or answer the question, "What is Jewish poetry?" The poetry of a nation or a world is whatever comes to pass in its domain in the name of poetry, and can neither succeed nor fail. But let us suppose for a moment instead—as a "mind experiment"—that there never has been any Jewish poetry. In the same way, one might suppose (and in my view should) that there never has been any poetry at all—of any kind.

Then—in the quiet that ensues—let us ask (remembering that for this moment it is a Jewish poet who is asking, searching his nature), "What should Jewish poetry be?" After all, "Every tribe has its music." And poetry (the music of the tribe) appears as a vocation, a calling from the "above" and the "outside" to a singular destiny in language. Consider, then, that the Jews are a God-bearing (a theophoric) people. Surely their God is the one great, inalienable, and determining collective construction that they have contributed to the history of civilization and maintained. What, then, is the God-bearing, the theophoric poetry, that is the destiny of the Jews? What is its nature, and what is the *prospective* importance of such a poetry to the world?—Even if there is not such a poetry, the *idea* of such a poetry (which we can perhaps reach to, however inactual it may be) pertains profoundly to its nature.

Please understand that it is in no sense my intention to divert admiration and love from the "Jewish poetry" of the past or of

Reprinted from TIKKUN MAGAZINE, A BI-MONTHLY JEWISH CRITIQUE OF POLITICS, CULTURE, AND SOCIETY, 251 West 100th Street, 5th floor, New York, NY 10025.

the present. Rather, it is my intention to say that in the nuclear age all poetry must change its characteristics (in this sense there is good reason to suppose, for a moment, that there has never yet been *any* poetry) and that the Jewish world-construction—specifically, the Jew's knowledge of the Jew's God and His culture of sanctity—possesses a regulative power, in proportion to His radical abstraction and priority, not inscribed elsewhere in the world's inventories of cultural terms. I intend to say that, insofar as the Jew has kept the Torah, the Jew has kept it also for this.

I shall begin, therefore, by indicating something about the relationship of two categories of our discourse, the *fictive* (to which poetry as representation belongs) and the *sacred,* all that is indicated in Hebrew by forms of the root KDS (the subject of chapter 9, below).

Everyone remembers how at the beginning of the Greek (and therefore the Western) *literary* system Hesiod—a shepherd on Mt. Helicon—met the poetic voice. It appeared like a gang of girls descending toward him as he climbed up from the hard place—Ascra—where he was born. All cultural systems begin with a first calling from above, and the Hesiodic instance is the originary scene of gentile poetry, inscribed by and inscribing the first named poet of the West. The calling by the Muses produces in the man, Hesiod, a singer who restates the structure of power in the human world by *re-producing* things as they are in a form of words, and by marking that reproduction (or representation) with the signature and authority of Mnemosyne, mother of the Muses. Things and persons so reproduced become part of cultural memory. They die as things and persons and are reborn as signs. We also remember (we are reminded by Torah at Genesis 12) that Abraham too was called and that the calling of Abraham was the inaugural moment of the biblical narrative. The calling of Abraham was the beginning not of the fictive but of the sacred system of texts constituting the culture of holiness (reiterated and sealed at Genesis 22, the Akedah) in which things die to be reborn, as members of that class of facts of which God is also a member.

The calling of Abraham by the divinity of the Old Testament who is *not memory but Presence* (such is the originary moment of the Western *theological* system) restates the structure of the world by reversing the processes of reproduction (in the narrative, often, literally usurping them), taking back the children. Thereby, the sacred narrative intends to withdraw the world into its source in Divinity—that is, not into appearance, of which the representational correlative is the Gentile fictive or mimetic or imaginative or poetic, the bitter logic with which this book is concerned, but into the sacred that has no representational correlative and no existence but Presence, its own term and explanation. In *fiction*—the production of the "subject" called by the Muses as is the poet Hesiod—the reference of words is problematized, raised up but only halfway up, making room for a plurality of texts, demanding the speculative difference of poetry and also philosophy. In *holiness*—in the domain of sanctity—all reference is rotated and abolished (the disappearance, as we shall see, of Isaac) so that the holy thing becomes a member of that class of things of which (as I have said) divinity in itself is a member. As it is written, "Holy is the Lord of Hosts."

Poetry in the usage of Western language may sometimes be called "divine" or sacred; but for the Jew *there is always a sense* (a profound understanding beneath all other understandings) *that the category of the sacred and the category of the poetic repel one another*—because the poetic defers the sacred, which is, nonetheless, the destination of all things. It is this *sense*—the use of it, its prospective civilizational productivity—that I wish very briefly to indicate. My remarks are *speculative* in that I assume a constrained, a rationally obligatory, relationship between the *theological* understanding of the world that the Jewish people keep (the keeping of which founds their existence as a people) and their *cultural* practice. And speculative, also, in that I wish to project a commission for Jewish poetry of a kind that may never yet have existed.

A recurrent name in the Bible, and tradition, for the locus of history (more precisely, the locus or site of *opposition* to history in the place of its occurrence) is Moriah—where Moses encountered the burning bush, where the Temple was built and destroyed, where (typologically) transpired the agon of Adam and Christ, history's threshing floor bought by David from Arauna, the Jebusite, as an altar for sacrifice—which became our contested Jerusalem. The rabbis unpacked its name (Moriah) variously—as "the teaching place," "the place of fear," "the place of Myrrh," "the place where God sees." It is also (of course) the place whither God commanded Abraham to go (the second calling of Abraham, exegetical of the first) in order to sacrifice his son. I will recur to the meaning of Moriah as the place of the Akedah, the schoolroom of history, and the sign of the culture of holiness that it has been the singular commission of the Jews to keep.

But first I wish to say that to the question, "Why a *Jewish* poem?" the Jew must reply, "Because the Jewish people, like all other peoples, requires *a place to be* (a teaching place, a place of Myrrh, a place where God sees), and the Jew's place is the word." But the Jew's word (as I wish you for a moment to consider it) is hard, not like the split word of the gentile nations who know the little word of the muse (the word half-raised up, divided—signifier and signified), or (again) who know the little word of the muse (as fiction), *and* the big word of the god or God. The Jew's word, strictly speaking, is One (holy, sacred, *Kadosh*), and is unlike all other words in that it does not signify by difference but rather serves the Master who is difference— which is to say, existence itself.

Hence, the Jew's one word (the Jew's poem of which I write) does not "create," for that would be redundant, but repeats the one word that is. In the (biblical) culture according to which the father of "all who handle the harp and organ" is in the genealogy of Cain (Gen. 4:21), the universe—by reason of its existence—can have only one monologic rationality. For example, the *midrashim* (as collected by Louis Ginzberg) that refer to the destruction of the temple in 586 attest that *Adonai designed* the intention of Nebachadnezzar to destroy what Solomon built; and even the letters of the alphabet (capable of an infinity of alternative combinations) when summoned to testify to the reason of that event are mute. History repeats a single figure, first inscribed in the Creation itself (the first devastation) and thereafter in successive expulsions, forcible removals, ravagings. Thus, Jewish poetry *cannot* be autochthonous. The project of "Jewish poetry" repels the founding of its discourse—its place for the people—in the incommutable earth of the national language. For "the earth is the Lord's." The Jew's word is the name of the nation; but the nation is not, as among the gentiles who speak of "American poetry," or "Greek poetry," the name of the word. Thus, neither the term *Jewish poetry* nor the practice of whatever the term indicates can be symmetrical with the poetries (imaginative and local) of the "nations."

The gentile poet is called by language in all the openness—the ontological problematicity, as it is—of language's relation to the world. The Jewish poet (the Jew's *great* poet whom I wish speculatively to summon to mind) is called monologically by Presence itself. The correlative but severely contrastive figure in traditional Jewish narrative to the gentile muse (daughter of Memory) is the Shechinah, whose name means *dwelling*—the dwelling of the name in the world: the Jew's place to be.

In 1950 Schlomo Spiegel (professor of medieval literature at the Jewish Theological Seminary) published a twelfth-century Hebrew poem, a *piyyut* (liturgical poem) by R. Ephraim of Bonn on the slaughter of Isaac and his "resurrection"—that is, on the text of Genesis 22, the Akedah or "binding of Isaac" at Moriah. The poem contains twenty-eight quatrains, the fourth line of each of which is a quotation from the Bible. I will quote five stanzas in Judah Goldin's translation:

> Then did the father and the son embrace.
> Mercy and truth met and kissed one another.
> O my father, fill your mouth with praise
> For He doth bless the sacrifice.

> I long to open my mouth to recite the grace
> Forever blessed be the Lord Amen.
> Gather my ashes, bring them to the city
> Unto the tent, to Sarah.

> He made haste, he pinned him down with his knees.
> He made his two arms strong.
> With steady hands he slaughtered him according to the rite.
> Full right was the slaughter.

> Down upon him fell the resurrecting dew, and he revived.
> The father seized him to slaughter him once again.
> Scripture bear witness! Well grounded is the fact:
> And the Lord called to Abraham, even a second time from
>   heaven.

> The ministering angels cried out terrified.
> Even animal victims, were they ever slaughtered twice?
> Instantly they made their outcry heard on high.
> Lo, Ariels cried out above the earth.

Isaac has vanished from the altar on Moriah (in Bible no account is given of Isaac's descent [v. Gen. 22:19]), and Abraham is filled with fear that an imperfection of his own in the sacrificial procedure has marred his response to the commandment of God. But the ram is supplied, and the event thus described is recommended, by Ephraim of Bonn to his posterity with the prayer: "Recall to our credit the many Akedahs / The saints, men and women, slain for thy sake. / Remember the righteous martyrs of Judah / Those that were bound of Jacob." This latter expression ("bound of Jacob") is understood to refer to those slain "for the sanctification of the name" (the traditional language by which martyrdom is expressed in theological Judaism).

The *name* of God, in which the rationality of history resides, is represented by the Shechinah who summoned the Jews at the inaugural moment of the people, and who signifies and constitutes the culture of holiness that refers all events not to appearance (as in the case of the culture of poetry) but to being as Presence without qualification of differences (as, for example, between appearance and reality).

The historical *reference* of Rabbi Ephraim's poem is remote—the atrocities done to whole communities of Jews in Germany and France by the Crusaders during the eleventh and twelfth centuries. The historical *occasion* of Schlomo Spiegel's book was, of course, immediate—*ha shoah*, the "holocaust." In Rabbi Ephraim's poem (as in the "Books of Disasters" of the period, Spiegel informs us) the horror of the slaughter of the Jew is *for the Jew* (as his tormentors understood) neither the pain nor the loss of life, but precisely the defilement arising from ritually impure techniques of killing, intentionally practiced by the barbarous Christians. The priority of the duties of sanctity, among which is ritual purity, even (or especially) to life is the Jew's faithful response to the singularity of the Jew's word—the word that cannot be split and to which all things are referred as to their origin.

I want to say two kinds of things in context of R. Ephraim's poem and Schlomo Spiegel's commentary: first, with respect to the relationship of written paradigms (including Bible and poetry) to history; and second, with respect to the God-bearing culture of holiness that I am proposing as the scene of Jewish

mind—the mind, including poetic mind, that it makes a differ-
ence to call Jewish.

First: Rabbi Ephraim's Jew, in the monocausal (monological)
culture of Jews in the eleventh century, is responding to a *repre-
sentational crisis* defined by the fact that Abraham in the story did
not kill his child, while the people of the book were actually
suffering the slaughter of their children—indeed, felt obligated
to kill their children in order to avoid ritual impurity and to
secure the sanctification of the Name. In the sense that what is
authoritatively written (scripture *or* poem) has value because it
supplies the rationality of WHAT HAPPENS, the Bible, as the
narrative (pre-) text of R. Ephraim's poem, has been put in
question on its own ground—experience that by *putting the child
to death* precisely falsifies sacred story, the *ground* of history of
which God is the author. (We have seen the same state of disso-
nance in Shakespeare's account of the story about Philomela in
chapter 1, and Milton's "On the Late Massacre in Piemont,"
chapter 2 above.)

Second: R. Ephraim's poem *responds* to the representational
crisis precipitated by the inadequacy to history of the authorita-
tive narrative—biblical story as the paradigmatic, pretextual ra-
tionality of history—by resituating history in the domain of holi-
ness that is its home. Having acknowledged the innocence of his
child and received acknowledgment of his own innocence, Abra-
ham in the poem decrees that the place (Moriah) be called
Adonai-Yireh, "The Place where Light and Law are manifest. /
He swore to bless it as the temple site / For there the Lord
commanded the blessing."

The gentile poet is called *once,* by Mnemosyne (transpersonal
memory), mother of the Muses. The patriarch, Abraham, by con-
trast, is called *twice* (Genesis 22, following upon Genesis 12), the
first time, like the poet, to representation or story ("Get thee out
of thy country"). The second calling of Abraham, however,
("Take thou thy son . . .") is to the *culture of holiness,* the ground of
the Jew's meaning, the God-bearing or theophoric project that
the Akedah founds—a culture (perhaps, the only one in the
inventory of civilizations) capable of bringing to mind and there-
fore regulating a violence as great as the violence of the creation
itself, because it is capable of bringing to mind what the words

Bereshit barah adonai (in the beginning God created) can bring to mind—existence *and also nothing.* To this bringing to mind of existence itself, the inactual Jewish poet I have in mind is singularly called. It is her part or his part, the poet's part, in the theophoric—the God-bearing—project of the people.

The Jewish poet who invokes the Shechinah has an obligation to construct the place where "Light and Law are manifest," to which the nations may come because it is where they are. The obligation is the same as the obligation to the intelligibility of experience, the covenant. And the place of holiness is the ground—neither heaven nor earth—upon which the paradigms of experience (the adequacy of the constructive mind to history) can be restored, where loss is given back as meaning and where the People and the peoples are equally at home.

The poetics that constructs the poetry of which I speak founds itself in the (biblical) power of thought that *can* situate itself in *the punctual moment before* all beginnings ("Suppose for a moment there has never been *any* poetry at all")—the moment before the poetries of memory and the daughters of memory have "built for themselves solitudes." Let us call this order of discourse (this Jewish poetry considered as a theophoric project)—the logic of which is other than the representational logic of gentile poetry in the West (for example, the logic of representation narrated in the story about Orpheus or the story about Philomela)—by the name of Being (being in itself) whose presence is *dwelling.*

The word that indicates her—Shechinah—first became current, as I understand it, as the name of God in the Aramaic translations of Bible during the first and second Christian centuries as a displacement or translator's term. The dwelling or home her name indicates is precisely *the homelessness or placelessness of the word,* existence itself and only that. She mediates between the above and beneath by being exactly both—the Light and the Law—as she is presence itself as well as its sign. As such her nature is the contradiction of representation. Raised in the beginning from the text, she is seen everywhere in Jewish history, but most often in Jerusalem itself—Moriah. As existence itself and absolute presence (adorned with all its losses), she is the thing to be feared and, also, the ground of an obedience that frees from fear because it constructs (perpetually reconstructs) the person. As the indicator of the difference between nothing and something—memorial of the creation—her presence regulated an order of force unanticipated by the culture of representation—an order constituted only in the culture of holiness that inscribes the most abstract God.

It is she, Shechinah, who carried the Law to the people when Israel chose the Law, and it is for knowledge of her that the people should look to the Jewish poet and the Jewish poet to his or her own nature—as a creature of the *other* poetics that can be brought to mind *only if* (for a moment) we stop the poetries that have been, and begin again. For she is also the presence of Proverbs 9: The Wisdom who has "builded her house." She has hewn out her seven pillars. The construction thus indicated is the place of teaching where the adequacy of the paradigm is renewed in the culture of holiness: the Temple on Moriah built and destroyed, the body of Isaac sacrificed and restored.

Finally, in the speculative silence of these remarks, consider whether there cannot come to mind a poetry of (and in the place of) evil. Consider whether the theophoric, the God-bearing, poetry of the Jewish poet cannot by reason of its nature as God-bearing reach to the evil of history—because the God it bears is the place of that evil, and the structure entailed by the otherwise unstatable difference that is his nature states the magnitude of the violence which civilization must regulate.

Of this poetry I will say only the following: Whether the "poet" I struggle to bring to mind is a Jew or not a Jew makes no difference. Whether the poetry is mystical or nonmystical makes no difference. It is not an overcoming. But it is a beginning of the work toward which the Jew, if the Jew takes thought, is particularly called.

Nuclear Violence,
Institutions of Holiness,
and the Structures of Poetry

It looks as if before long we should have more places worth seeing here than in Europe—were it not for the fatal absence of history. But I recur to my axiom—that not only all society but most romance rests on the death of men—and where the most men have died there is the greatest interest.

Holmes to Laski, July 28, 1927

Then in turn answered him the courier Argeiphontes: "Aged sir, neither have the dogs eaten him, nor have the birds, but he lies yet beside the ship of Achilleus at the shelters, and as he was; now here in the twelfth dawn he has lain here nor does his flesh decay, nor do the worms feed on him, they who devour men who have fallen in battle. It is true, Achilleus drags him at random around his beloved companion's tomb, as dawn on dawn appears, yet he cannot mutilate him; you yourself can see when you go there how fresh with dew he lies, and the blood is all washed from him, nor is there any corruption, and all the wounds have been closed up where he was struck, since many drove the bronze in his body. So it is that the blessed immortals care for your son, though he is nothing but a dead man; because in their hearts they loved him.

Iliad, XXIV, 11. 410–23 (translated by Richmond Lattimore)

Nuclear science has conferred on the human community an unalienable capacity for precisely measureless violence—a capacity that will remain a virtual empowerment even if there are no actual nuclear devices on the face of the earth. Consequently, there is required *a culture of nuclearism* capable of pro-

---

From *AGNI* 29–30, (1990).

ducing the infinite deferment of that virtuality. The word "culture," as I here use it, is intended to specify the kind of collective artifact the human community has devised, in the interest of its continued life, to manage (or regulate) other empowerments that the alliances of mind with nature, divinity, and its own inhuman force have placed among the choices of the human will. Two such historical "cultures" that are functionally related are *first*, the institutions of "holiness," by which I mean the religious administration of creational violence. (Such violence in the Judeo-Christian cosmogony, because it is founded in the difference between nothing and something, is absolute in character.) And, *second*, the structures of poetry mediate between the validating forces that ground representation within and without the persons, and the regulative requirements of the (scalar) countenance of humanity. Divinity on the one hand and the constructive mind of man (including the kindred violence of science and art) on the other continually threaten to subsume in themselves the totality of the facts of reality, among which is the human world that in their interrelationship they found.

Both the institutions of holiness and the structures of art, insofar as they offer models of deferment of absolute empowerment, function by reason of the cybernetic (or regulative) operation of *a check—a limit to the practice of power that can be expressed as the imageability of the person.* In the Gospels, for example, the imageless omnipotence of God manifests itself in human scale as the person of Jesus, the "human form divine." Between the nonnarratable inconceivability of the absolutely powerful God and the life of the community, the holy person intervenes (the cybernetic mechanism is "covenant") with the effect, on the one hand, of deferring the bearing of divinity on humanity (i.e., the apocalyptic subsumption of the world in God), and on the other of producing the possibility of access by the covenanted community through the mind of the individual to the power of source. The rules of the construction of this regulative social form—this check—are the same as for the construction and maintenance of the human image. They constitute the culture of holiness.

The operation in a *poetic* context of the check of which I speak is exemplified in *Iliad* XXIV, where the gods establish a limit to the defacement of Hektor's body, not only against the dogs, the carrion birds, the deliquescence of the natural body, and the devouring worm, but above all against the barbarism of Achilleus, a daemon of human presence in whom the violence of the production of the honorable image threatens to overwhelm the conditions of its conservation. The passage in question (an epigraph of this paper) attests a miracle of narrative reflexivity that enacts the text's maintenance of its own existence as representation, as constitutive narrative, and at the same time thematizes the regulative function of the poem in history.—What, from the point of view of this argument, is the purpose of the *Iliad?* It is this: *the establishment of a limit to violence at the point of the defacement of the human image.* ("Yet he cannot mutilate him.") The specific occasion of this passage is the moment at which the ordered life of the universe is seen to depend upon protection, from obliterative rage, of the recognizability of the human form.

This limit of defacement I will call the *eidetic check,* invoking the Homeric word *eidos,* signifying the form or fashion of anything, its lovely, order-conferring, and ultimately world-maintaining countenance. It is what the heroes view with amazement when they see one another. The mechanism of the eidetic check is the fundamental moral formation, and the rules of its construction supersede and implicate all other ethical rules.

The absence of the eidetic check constitutes the historical singularity of nuclear barbarism (even by contrast to adjacent technologies of harm such as chemical, and notably biological warfare, which appears to generate its own restraint). The reconstruction of the eidetic check within the nuclear context would constitute, as I have indicated, the establishment of a nuclear culture. Poetic culture is a primary custodian of the human image, and is *structured like* other custodial formations, such as civil order (chap. 3) and the religious institution (institutions of holiness—especially chap. 9, below). The labor of establishing that image in its function as the limit of violence is deeply a part of what poets and critics intend.

What is discussed as "nuclear violence" is not this weapon or that but destruction under the sign of totality, inscribed where the regulative finitude of the human form was. In a sense, poetic structures and the institutions of holiness produce "history." But poetic structures and the institutions of holiness are also *subject* to history considered as the sum of the dynamic processes that generate, and alter across time, the relationships within the human community of forces and institutions (their kinds, empowerments, legitimacy, accessibility).

For the study of the disappearance or disablement of the eidetic check, the most important of these history-factored processes is secularization. By secularization I mean the delegitimization (and consequent disempowerment), in the high culture, of the institutions of holiness, and the resulting liberation of the autonomous human will from the regulative alienation of transcendental relationship. The religious principle of story functioned to produce the human world (that is to say, history) through maintenance of the difference by reference to which the human form was established, for example, the difference between God and his creatures. The loss of the difference between the holy and the profane (the God and the man) disables the principle of story itself—that mechanism of reflexivity whereby "history" negotiates its own maintenance through the thematization in story (as religion) of the cybernetic limitation of the human will. *Of the free or unregulated will there is no human form, and therefore no narrative.* From this point of view, the question of the existence of God and the question of the existence of man are the same question.

The correlative disruption in the sequence of *poetic* structures was the breaking of the millennial canon of the metrical line, with the attendant blurring of the lineaments of the countenance in modern poetry, and compensatory efforts to reconstruct surrogate "ceremonies of innocence": among them, Romantic and modernist ideologies of organicism, impersonalism, and openness, and the peculiarly American epistemologies of immediacy. This state of affairs was (of course) synchronous with the scientific integrations that conducted absolute violence from the regulative virtuality of apocalyptic dream to the actuality of atrocity—above all, the special theory of relativity (1905), which by equating matter and energy both expressed and enabled the elision of all appearance, that is to say, the "created" or human world, the skin and superficies which I love. Paradoxically (it is once again the bitter logic I speak of) the motive (the reason for doing it) is liberational: to desacralize nature and mind intends to admit the human will directly to its world.

Likewise, the motive of poetic openness intends to release experience from the alienating domination of abstract pattern.

The crisis of representation in the context of secularization—that is, the absence of the god who keeps the human image from the predation (the dogs and carrion birds) of the logic of image production—is expressed by Justice Holmes's axiom: "where most men have died, there is the most interest." At the moment of greatest interest (epic, the romance of conquest, or tragedy) death produces the image.

On this issue the obvious cases are also the most authoritative. For the kinship of poetry and violence is established at the beginning of the poetic record—as we observed in our discussion of the Greek founding stories of poetic production (chap. 1). That is to say, the poetic record at its beginning takes as its subject the processes of its own production, and also judges them. Homer's poem both feeds on the violence required to establish the person as representable (the culture of the warrior class) and compensates (as honor) the losses incurred.

The final thematic recovery is violence-driven memorability; and the beginning of the transaction of memory, thus constructed, with history, is of course the *Iliad* itself. Internal to the *Iliad* the losses entailed by the violence of image production are compensated by the legitimation of an economic exchange whereby the honor image—the *eidos*—replaces the actual human loss. That loss is *possible to be willed* because the exchange of death for highest value offers immortality (the endless continuation of the image) to which the person has otherwise no access. The refusal to will that loss—the other possible outcome of the awesome decision to fight or not to fight, the ethical moment of the epic and perhaps of poetry in general that weighs the symbolic benefit of the image against its organic cost—threatens the counterloss of the human form of the world. Thus, beneath the horror of the violence of poetic construction (e.g., Homeric warfare) there lies the greater horror of another obliterative violence that poetic violence defers.

Insofar as the imageability and commemorability of the person is accomplished by acts of violence (the characterizing civility of a warrior class, on which our Western language of value is founded), and insofar as the poetic medium is the mechanism of the transmission of the image, *poetic culture and the culture of war are one culture.* But so long as the exchange of the image for the organic life of the body is tolerated, the nature of immortality as image-bearing text functions as a limit to the violence of its production.

Internal to the story of the *Iliad* (and indeed any traditional poem adapted to serve the continuity of the community) there is a check to the scope of violence, upon which all the powers of the Homeric world, except Achilleus, concur. The defacement of the person of Hektor by Achilleus is the only act in the whole atrocious story that could subvert the reproduction of the image, the *eidos.* The sign of the intention of poetic story to regulate obliterating force is the refusal of the God to allow that act.

The interest of story ("where most men have died there is the greatest interest") must come to an end at the *moment before* the perfectly interesting moment of the death of all men. The moment before that moment is the moment of art, the triumph of *poetry as culture.* It is the moment of the poem as artifact—*the picture of the person,* the imperfect trace of the only thing with a right to perfection. Nuclearism, absolute violence, as it is warfare without regulation and therefore not warfare at all, actualizes the motive to presence without the constraints of representation. As such, it is the primordial enemy of that immortality the laws of which are the same as the rules of the construction of the human image. The rules of immortality define the sufficient condition for maintaining the value of the human image. They are the rules of patience, the willingness to dwell in likeness and therefore to defer forever the thing itself.

The regulative function of the processes of representation— the culture of poetry—was constructed in the *Iliad* as an inseparable part of history's great machine for the production of human interest, namely warfare. Encoded in the text of the poem from its beginning, therefore, is the actual regulative science our civilization has devised counter to the science of absolute violence. That counterscience is the courtesy with respect to materials that characterizes poetic practice. Courtesy is always one possible model of a historical *culture* of nuclearism.

But postnuclear poetic innovation (the heuristic of poetry after 1945) has been driven by the intention *to get violence also out of the process of representation.*

Characterized by "open," free or decentered, forms and by

the solicitation of the point of least difference between the natural and the artistic version of speech—the thing itself and *not the likeness*—postmodern poetic innovation has intended the abandonment of abstract patterns such as the metrical line—*as if the violence of the structure of the image were greater than the violence that opposes the image altogether.* If for the poet exchange of the absolute claim to actualization for its symbolic and regulative diminishment as representation is blocked, then the work of the poet and the critic must be (it is thought) toward the identification of a new structure of representation that can reconstitute the conserving decorum of warfare and poetry (the culture of structure) in the context of the dialectic of liberation. It is worthwhile lingering on the rationality of this problem.

Every poem of tradition (that is, every poem that serves to produce a future), every actual poem of the kind that comes to pass, *indicates* a virtual poem that the actual poem (the text at hand) postpones, as it were forever. In a familiar master work, (for example) Wordsworth's "Solitary Reaper," the represented speaker (who also represents and thus anticipates the reader)— the man who says, "Behold her, single in the field"—obtains the munificence of the unrepresentable girl's untranslatable song by the concession implied in the professed incapacity of his report (*his* song of another kind) to include the great song that "overflows the vale." The virtual poem, thus *indicated but not represented* ("Will no one tell me what she sings?"), imports a boundless version of human worth that the mechanism of representation defers, and thus recovers in human scale. But absolute human value (the unexhangeable worth of the person) may function as an absolute sanction incompatible with the postponements of representation—as pure science does, or as the whole body does, or pure sentiment, or fundamentalist religion. And it is the sanction of this higher value—the greater poem, the thing of greatest interest not to be deferred—that constitutes at the present time the rationality of the rebellion against the traditional institutions of poetic structure, the "measured consummation" of representation that intends *the unjust civility of human scale.*

Deep inside the acknowledgment of human limit (the eidetic check, the limit of defacement) that poetry by the rule of the countenance constrains is the same paradox of civility that policy confronts. The two terms of that paradox consist of, on the one hand, the postponement of limitless empowerment exacted by civility as courtesy that accommodates the limit placed on the individual in a social world; and, on the other, the boundless sanction that the intuition of absolute value (the ground of civility as right) casts over the person. In the name of that value, Achilleus in his rage against the slayer of his friend attempts to deface the body of Hektor, and thus attempts also to overthrow the culture both of warfare and representation on which the intelligibility of his world of persons is based. It is in the name of that value also that the open or free counterpoetics of immediate presence attempts to get violence (the warfare) out of representation.

It has been noted that nation-states by their nature stand in relationship to one another as anarchic equals, rather than as civil individuals subject to the hierarchies that pertain internal to any social order. Equalities are unstable, and perfect equality unimaginable, whether as a political state of affairs (where everyone is equal no one has rights), or as a state of affairs in art (where virtual and actual poem coincide, there is no representation). In the absence of strategies for the resolution of anarchic equality in some terms consistent with the conserving stability of civil hierarchy, conflict becomes absolute because it has no regulative principle—no poetics: it is a zero-sum game of total domination on the one hand, or obliteration on the other. At such moments, the *requirements* of image construction (entailing the unjust civil hierarchy) and the *purposes* of image construction (the conservation of the whole person whether considered as a nation or as an individual) are in conflict. At such moments, the bitter logic of the poetic principle becomes the central issue of civilization.

Such historical moments, when the institutions custodial of the human image fail to conserve that image, are *eidetic crises*—crises of constructive rationality precipitated by the successful production of an artifact (a revolution, a God, a weapon, a science) that costs nothing less than everything, in the sense that the new achievement *delegitimates* the constructive bases of the image of the person in the interest of which it was undertaken. Such are the generative moments of the great monuments—

including literary masterpieces. We can hear the cry responsive to such a failure of care by the poetic principle in Milton's "Where were ye nymphs when the remorseless deep / Closed o'er the head of thy loved Lycidas?" Nuclear empowerment presents an eidetic crisis, one in a succession of such crises, including the eighteenth-century social revolutions that produced the Napoleonic armies and romanticism, and the technological revolutions that gave us the warfare of the machine gun, the campaigns of Grant, the strategies of the Somme, and the art of modernism.

The present need to control force, to postpone the perfection of the world, inherits the great artifactual achievement underlying the revolution I have called secularization—and completes it. From *Lycidas* to *The Waste Land* the reconstructive strategy of the poetic response to eidetic crisis has been the reaffirmation of the transcendental ground of the person. The deepest moral intention of our present poetic civilization prohibits this, and thereby repeats rather than compensates the historical loss.

Just as the revolution that broke the canon of the poetic line intended to get the violence out of representation, so the revolution (the same secular impulse) that broke the religious institution (under the sanction of liberation) destroyed at the same time the structure of mediation (of delegation and alliance) by which the deepest human imagination of creation and destruction was made accessible in the scale of human life. In the Judeo-Christian tradition, the model of the recovery of human energy in human scale is the binding (or sacrifice) of Isaac (the Akedah, at Genesis 22). And the Akedah is repeated as the "Great Code" of Western art in the incarnation and crucifixion of Jesus. The *interrelation* of the mediational strategy of the poetic line (the deferment of perfection) and the mediational strategy of the institution of holiness (religious delegation, the giving back of human creative power—man's significant son—to the source of creative power in order to receive it again in human scale) is everywhere attested.

It is Zeus, in our Homeric example (again, our epigraph *Iliad* XXIV, 410–23), who commands the conservation of the body of Hektor against the violence of Achilleus. *Holiness* is a term (more precisely a determinator) importing the rotation of all reference toward source, as *poetry* is a term importing the subsumption of all reference within the transcendental measure and infinite postponements of art, the referential problematicity of representation. But just as warfare and representation ("where the most men have died there is the greatest interest") are kindred, so the archetype of obliterative warfare is religious warfare, the offering up of the other to the one holiness of the God—as in the biblical formula of deracinatory violence sanctioned (in Joshua and elsewhere) by the "holiness" term *cherem*. (The implication of this word is the subject of chapter 9, below.) The competition of immortalities, that is, religious communities, because it is driven by the obliterative logic of the absolute motive in all presence, is also the most accurate model of nuclear warfare.

Modernist poetics—Yeats, Eliot, Stevens—undertook to reconstruct holiness and metricality on particularist (Anglicanism) and surrogational grounds (Stevens's "abstraction"), and also modernism takes on as urgent concern approximate "ceremonies of innocence." Post-modern poetry—appalled after 1946 by the modernist complicity of poetic construction and violence— has fallen back on minor forms that equivocate the constructive process altogether, in the interest not of the regulative image but of the anarchic fact. We have disabled the *eidos,* the representation of the countenance, which alone may have the power to control the violence entailed by its own construction. Thus we have withdrawn from *the great business of poetry, which is to keep the story that we tell from being true.*

The sign of obliteration is very interesting. From the moment when Truman destroyed Hiroshima and Nagasaki to "send a signal" to the Russians after Potsdam, nuclearism has been inscribed as a sign, a determinator, that like holiness cancels, or changes the meaning of, all other signs and inscriptions, a sign that preempts all reference. In the policy of deterrence it is inscribed in the space of regulation where *the human image* was and must be. Nuclear violence is now an inalienable potentiality of the human will; we require, therefore, as I have said, a culture of nuclearism—a strategy of infinite deferral. The culture of nuclearism will be the same as a poetic culture in the nuclear age. For the sign of obliteration is the same as the sign of immortality—the sign of poetry. Both are versions of the human countenance, the first in its anarchic historicity and the second in its poetic form. As a state merely of history, nuclear violence produces the rational paralysis of an insoluble problem. Considered as the work of poetry, it engages the only profound engine of collective humanity, the creativity that finds the human image: As, at the end of Dante's *Divine Comedy,* the problem of knowing the human meaning of the primal light is considered, first, as insoluble when understood as the rational impossibility of constructing the area of a circle from its radius—but then seen as solved by finding it painted with our likeness, *nostra effige.*

Holiness

Holiness, in Hebrew *kodesh,* indicates the highest value, or—more precisely—what can be said by men (or angels) when God comes immediately to mind, as in Isaiah 6:3: "Holy, holy, holy is the Lord of hosts." Holiness is the word by which men describe God and therefore the ultimate doxological predicate, because it is the word by which God describes himself. "You shall be holy, for I, the Lord your God am holy" (Lev. 19:2). Hence, *holiness* is the abstract term taught man by God to mark God's difference and the nature of everything that comes to be included (obedient to the absolute imperative implicit in the idea of "highest value") within his difference.

The vital life of holiness in the human world is primarily *transactive.* The root of the word *holiness (k-d-sh)* occurs most often in the Bible as an adjective, the result of an ascription (for example, "holy ground," "holy nation," "holy name," "holy spirit," "holy mountain," "the Holy One of Israel"), or as a verb that commands or accomplishes the inclusion of something within the category of holiness (as in the sanctification of the Sabbath, or of Aaron and his sons, or of anything consecrated to the Lord, such as a beast or a house or a field). In this latter sense, words formed from the root of *holiness* are related in function to words meaning to *sacrifice,* and especially to the root *ḥerem,* which is found in relation both to cult and also to God-commanded warfare, as in Leviticus 27, 28-A. "Every proscribed thing is consecrated to the Lord" [kol herem kedosh kedoshim] and Joshua 6:16–17: "For the Lord has given you the city. The city and everything in it are to be proscribed *[ḥerem]* for the Lord." The transactions of holiness, by which anything is included in its category of which God is a member, may be violent in proportion as the difference between God and his world as established in the creation is severe. The pacification of the transactions of holiness depends on the right use of freedom.

More generally, the supreme human work (man's service and creativity) is the voluntary performance of the transactions of holiness, which reciprocate and complete God's creation of the world by restoring it day by day, fact by scattered fact, to his nature. The specification of such work, as in the 613 *mizvot,* or commandments, defines *a culture of holiness,* a system of transactions by which through the mediation of holiness man and God come to be included within the precinct of the same term. The Jew affirms this each time he recites the blessing that accompanies the performance of a commandment: "Blessed are you, O Lord our God . . . who has sanctified us by your commandments." As Philo remarked: "That which is blessed and that which is holy are closely connected to one another."[1] Holiness therefore specifies the coincidence of the wills of man and God and defines the freedom of both. That freedom expresses itself as the voluntary, continuous, cooperative maintenance of the world—sanctification, Kedusha.

The "highest value," which holiness indicates and which the transactions of holiness produce, is not in its fundamental nature ethical value, because the actions of holiness are performed in the relationship of man and God and not in the relationship of man and man, which is the plane where ethical meanings occur. Indeed, inclusion in the category of holiness erases the intrinsic nature of a thing and returns it, as in the restoration of the literal meaning of a text from the alien intentionality of interpretation, to the source of all being, where it has in itself (intrinsically) no nature at all except its freedom. From the standpoint of human experience, therefore (the point of view of language), *holy* is not in the ordinary sense a predicate, a word that asserts something about a term, but the sign of the withdrawal of all reference into its source, a determinator of the radical disablement of metaphor and the absolute preemption of the truth of discourse at the supremely privileged moment of reference to reality. Hence, when the Lord is in his holy temple *(be-heikhal kadsho),* all earth must be silent (Hab. 2:20), because the order of sacred structure has superseded all other order; the meaning of all terms has been preempted by the Holy One—nothing has a name of its own to say.

As in the sacrifice of the productions of earth in cult, the production of the *holy* effects a rotation of the significance of words toward the origin of significance in God, who is outside of experience and therefore outside language. As he is aniconic—without image because perfectly free—so also he is antimetaphoric—a "man of war" who defeats comparison. "Who is like you, majestic in holiness?" (Ex. 15:11). That which enters the class of things of which he is a member ("holiness") loses its provenance in nature and history at the moment it is restored to the precinct of divinity. Hence, the rationality of martyrdom in Judaism is expressed as "the sanctification of the Name" *(Kiddush ha-Shem).* This is the case because martyrdom, as the willed assimilation or sacrifice of the person to the category of the holy, repeats in a radical form the structure of all acts performed in response to the divine commandment to sanctify the world and therefore the self, even the keeping of the Sabbath. And, indeed, all such acts have in the course of history become the occasion of martyrdom. "Why art thou brought out to be killed?" "Because I have performed the rite of circumcision upon my son." "Why art thou to be stoned to death?" "Because I have observed the Sabbath." "Why art thou led out to die by fire?" "Because I have studied the Law."[2] As God is the immaterial source of material life and the nonnarratable source of narrative, so also is he the nonethical source of the ethical. Hence Maimonides, in *The Guide of the Perplexed,* is free to explain the human utility of the *mizvot* only after first demonstrating that no term that can be predicated of anything else can be predicated of God—that is to say, after having first ensured that the meaning of the *mizvot* as transactions of holiness cannot lie in human use.

The most common name for God in rabbinic usage (derived, it would seem, from Second Isaiah and Jeremiah) is the Holy One of Israel *(yhvh kedosh yisrael).* The Holy One, who, as we have seen, repels all metaphoric amplification, expresses his power as a man of war by his holiness, the determinator that defeats all the facts of the world. Holy war is the semantic war of holiness upon the world of pagan and secular reference—a war of mutually exclusive legitimacies.[3] In this sense, the "holy people" (e.g., Deut. 7:6, 26:19, 28:9) contradict, by the logic of their transcendental legitimacy, all the nations of the world. By that same logic, the Book of which the holy people are custodians disqualifies the legitimacy and changes the meaning of all other books. The warfare of Scripture as holy text on all other texts takes the form of dispossession of reference, as the warfare of the holy people in Joshua takes the form of the dispossession of peoples by reason of prior right—holiness, the power of priority. Reciprocally, the absolute prior legitimacy of holiness by which the holy people are empowered to dispossess requires, by the reflexive implication of the severe logic of holiness, that the holy people also be dispossessed, alienated from God as wanderers whose home is always elsewhere. *Hence, we may say that holiness is the uninterpretable a priori literal fact of being,* the source of interpretation (precisely as the Holy One is the source of the world) in which interpretation, as the trace of autonomous human purpose, seeks to extinguish itself. In this sense, holiness makes war against culture—the making or imaging of anything that is not itself; and the Holy One, the Lord of Hosts, makes war as a matter of a priori dispensation, the sacred order of existence absolutely self-canonizing, intolerant of "discontent," that produces the one real world as its only artifact.

However, when God made the world, as Genesis reports, he did not call it *holy*—he called it *good*. The word *good* is as characteristic of Genesis, in which the transaction of holiness is invoked on the single occasion of the institution of the Sabbath, as the word *holy* is characteristic of Exodus. The rabbis accordingly derive only three of the 613 actions of holiness (*mizvot*) from Genesis. The culture of holiness begins (with the single exception noted) in the precinct of the burning bush—"the place on which you stand is holy ground" (Ex. 3:5)—which is the occasion of the commissioning of Moses and the annunciation of the tetragrammaton *(yhvh)*, the name of God as a form of the verb *to be (h-y-h)*. The transactions of holiness in Exodus mark the beginning of religion, by contrast to the heroic relation to God prior to religion that is the principle of transaction in Genesis. The historical moment of the alienation of humankind from unmediated relationship to reality—the Egyptian servitude and consequent multiplication of the people—requires the reconstruction of that relationship within a system of mediation toward a God whose name is being itself. That system is the culture of holiness, including cult and the later displacement of cult to language and prayer.

The bush *(ha-sneh)* that burns but does not burn up manifests the repeal of natural causality in the same way that the liberation from Egypt accomplishes escape from the domination of immanent generative process, the autonomy of the world not holy. In Genesis the threat to human generativity came from God, and the power of generativity, the continuity of life through time, was supplied by him directly. In the Egyptian servitude to nature's laws, the tribe multiplied, but without the principle of order that refers the meaning and therefore the life of all things immediately to their source in God. That principle of order is supplied by the flame and precinct of the bush at the commissioning of the master of the new culture of holiness, which will function like a language with only one word—the sacred name—into which must be translated all the terms of experience. The wanderings in the wilderness under the guidance of Moses' God enact, once again, the necessary concession of autonomy by the human community to the one creative will, and the turning of the transcendental imperative of Torah, the text received on Sinai, that supersedes the countertext of nature, against the totality of merely human interests represented by the calf of gold.

In Genesis the Sabbath was announced by the voice of God, blessed, and sanctified *(vayekadesh oto)*. It was not called *good*. In the repose of God, the autonomy of the world was displayed, not as a consequence of its inherent structure, but of its identity with source. The root *k-d-sh* introduced at the institution of the Sabbath in Genesis reappears at Horeb, where it defines the precinct of the burning bush. The Jew invokes the power of *k-d-sh* weekly as a privilege of the human will (the two texts joined) in the creational announcement of the kiddush, which memorializes both the creation of the world and the liberation from Egypt. As God, not nature, produces the bread and the wine, so God creates the freedom *(yeziat mizraim,* the liberation from Egypt) that the culture of holiness indicates, not in the *goodness* of immediacy, but in the rigorous transactions of distance that history compels.

By contrast to the Genesis relationship to God experienced in hearing and wrestling and dreaming, the Exodus relationship to God is presented as sacred writing (*kodesh* as the sign of absence); the priest Aaron bears on his forehead "the engraving of a signet: holiness to God *[kodesh le-yhvh]* that he may bear the iniquity of holy things *[avon ha-kedoshim]*" (Ex. 29:36, 38). The iniquity of holy things is thus managed by the perpetual restatement, as in writing, of the principle of difference by which the world is created and in the light of which it must be maintained. The decline of the world from the goodness ascribed to it at the moment after creation is the chief event of history, indeed the process of history itself insofar as history entails captivity to the logic of narrative, which by its nature contradicts the nonnarratable freedom of God as source. Just as the function of the code of holiness is to extinguish history by subsuming its narrative within the sacred story of obedience to legislation, so too the work addressed by the prayers of holiness—the *kedusha* and the Kaddish—is nothing less than the repair of the creation under the sign of absence, the reconstruction of goodness as holiness after the loss of holiness as the primordial goodness of oneness with source.

The Talmud attests the world-maintaining function of prayer and study: "Since the destruction of the Temple, every day is more cursed than the preceding one; and the existence of the world is assured only by the *kedusha* . . . and the words spoken after the study of Torah."[4] Since the *kedusha* incorporates the salute to God by the angels in Isaiah 3 ("Holy, holy, holy is the Lord of hosts"), the repetition of the *Kedushah* became equivalent to Torah study enjoined on every Jew as a daily obligation (the eleventh mitzvah of Maimonides' *Sefer ha-Mizvot*): and Torah study was equivalent to the sanctification of the name—*kiddush ha-Shem*—by which language about the world is restored to its true reference in God whose name, as announced in Exodus 3, subsumes the name of all things and thereby secures their reality. Thus the *kedusha* performs the continuous exchange of experience for holiness by which the world is maintained: the voluntary concession of the meaning of the world to its source obligatory upon the Jew, as the transactive reciprocation of the creation and as responsive to the free act of God by which the Jew was "chosen from among the peoples." The performance of this exchange—the symbolic repetition of the *akedah*, the binding of Isaac—constitutes the *culture of holiness, which conserves the value of the person and his world precisely at the point of the disavowal of autonomous right.*

In prayer, as in Torah study, the Jew acts out a relationship to all source and therefore to his own reality. The structure of this performance constitutes the rationality of the Jewish religion. But the narrative of Jewish history in the Bible and beyond is an account of the failure of this culture of holiness. The right functioning of the culture of holiness as in the *akedah,* its mighty archetype, returns the world it wills to be slain back to the worshiper in the scale of human use and enjoyment—an exchange of all claims by humanity to autonomous continuity in return for the appropriate, and therefore holy, part. But the severity of the claims of the culture of holiness—experienced as the appalling moment between the sacrificing of all and the return of the human part—exacts a confrontation with the horror of loss (in effect, the experience of history) greater than the terms of exchange can be imagined to compensate in the world of prayer, the empty realm of language that is the last temple of sacrifice. By its nature the culture of holiness—addressed to the world of fact it founds—is inimical to the partial exchanges and ethical rationalities that are the consolations of interpretation, as the Book of Job compels us to recognize. Hence, death, which is a negative restatement of holiness as absolute loss—insofar as death is a crisis of consolatory rationality—is the primal antagonist of the culture of holiness, and the chief source of pollution in Judaism. It is for this reason that Joseph Soloveitchik remarks that "death and holiness constitute two contradictory verses, as it were, and the third harmonizing verse has yet to make its appearance."[5]

The mourners' Kaddish, which begins, "Magnified and sanctified be his great name in the world which he has created according to his will," repeats as an act of the congregational person God's paradigmatic self-reference in Ezekiel 38:23; "I will magnify and sanctify myself . . ." (cf. Ezek. 36:23), and thereby affirms God's knowledge of himself in the language in which he states it. As a marker of the division of the service and as a song that both defines and negotiates the space, as it were, between God and his knowledge of himself, the Kaddish functions to effect the restoration of the created world after its diminishing by death by reestablishing and also overcoming the difference between God and the man as in the creation. But the *kaddish* also aggregates death to the severe rationality of the sanctification of the name ("sanctified be his great name") that is at once holiness—the right order of the world—and martyrdom, the gathering of all being into the one sign, the name, which is the shadow of his wings.

The *kaddish,* as also the *Kedushah,* is an act of ridding the pollution of death from the world of the living. In this context, the pollution of death is understood to be the disease of a will that can no longer praise the Name, that can no longer by words of sanctification on its own behalf return the world to its maker. "What is to be gained from my death, from my descent into the pit? Can the dust praise You? Can it declare Your faithfulness?" (Ps. 30:9). The intention accomplished by these central doxological prayers is the alignment of all wills with the one will, which is existence itself *(yhvh)* and of which death would otherwise be a diminishment. The peace that is prayed for at the end of the Kaddish ("May the maker of peace above also make peace among us") is the order of the world restored, as in the moment before creation, to its original unity, of which holiness is the sign.

All cultures function to produce the human world—space, time, objects, and persons—by negotiating differences within and against the background of primary fact. The success of this negotiation—economic in character, as are covenants in general—is the order of the world experienced as at peace. But the nature of the Hebrew culture of holiness—in accord with the strict monotheism that founds it—is peculiarly severe, admitting, as in the Kaddish, no affirmation less than total even in the face of death. The refusal of the will to accept God's description of the one world is the refusal of being. There is no space, as in Greek culture, for example, for the valorization of the oppositional self, and therefore, in the modern sense of things, no space for the self. Again, it may be said that all systems of order, all cultures, are both constructive and destructive. The culture of holiness, however, being legitimated by an absolute conception of order—creation as the radical difference between nothing and something—is in its central nature absolutely destructive of the long and precious inventory of human concerns that are not itself. Such, for example, are the Amalekites, whom it is a mitzvah to abolish. As we have noted, only insofar as the laws of relationship between man and God are ethical can the culture of holiness be called ethical. But the nature of God affirmed in the acts of holiness demands that the difference between man and God (obedient to the paradigm of the creation) be maintained as absolute, at the same time that the good of both, an inference from the nature not of man but of God, is asserted to be identical. Insofar as Judaism as a religion is characterized by the requirements of holiness, the problem of holiness structures the problem of religion for the Jews.

On the other hand, holiness is an aspect of the divine nature, appropriation of which is commanded by God—a tree of life given and not withheld. The injunction to sanctify the name of God (Maimonides' ninth positive commandment, perhaps the highest in Israel) implies the obligation and also the privilege of expressing the totality of things as one word, the name of the Other and the destiny of each self. This injunction is inferred from Leviticus 22:32–33, where the transaction between God and man mediated by holiness—the praxis of covenant—is associated with the liberation from Egypt, exemption from nature as cause, the re-creation of the world by God: "You shall not profane My holy name, that I may be sanctified in the midst of the Israelite people. I the Lord who sanctify you [mekadshkhem], I who brought you out of the land of Egypt to be your God [yhvh], I the Lord." The substance of the liberation accomplished by the Holy One of Israel, of which the culture of holiness is the trace—a liberation that validates the honor of all the facts of the world in themselves—is expressed concretely in Maimonides' eighth principle of faith:

> [We are to believe] that the Torah has been received from heaven.... Thus no distinction is to be made between such verses as, *And the sons of Ham: Cush and Mizraim, And his wife's name was Mehetabel, And Timna was concubine*, and such verses as, *I am the Lord thy God* and *Hear, O Israel*—all equally having been received from the almighty, and all alike constituting the Law of the Lord, which is perfect, pure, sacred, and true.

Just as there is no trivial writing of God, so holiness gives us the authenticity of the facts of the world, including ourselves and all persons, without distinction. Both "And Timna was concubine" and "Hear, O Israel" are "perfect, pure, sacred, and true." We are inexchangeable to any other thing, uninterpretable except in the light of holiness in which we find our place in the order of the one world, if we are to find our place at all. Holiness, then, presents us with our freedom as an inference from our existence, not as an enigma (there is no mystery) but as a problem—the inaugural problem of culture altogether. It neither consoles nor promises, but sets the terms of the work.

NOTES

1. Philo, *On the Allegories of the Sacred Laws,* I, 7.

2. For these and other examples, see Kaufmann Kohler, *The Jewish Encyclopedia,* s.v. "Kiddush ha-Shem." Kohler cites Mekh., Yitro 6, and Mid. Teh. to Ps. 12:5.

3. Cf. the phrase *kadshu milhama* ("consecrate for battle") in Jer. 6:4 and Joel 3:9.

4. BT Sot. 49a, cited in Elie Munk, *The World of Prayer* 1 (New York: Philipp Feldheim, 1961), p. 182.

5. Joseph B. Soloveitchik, *Halakhic Man* (Philadelphia: Jewish Publication Society, 1983), p. 36.

Fragment of an Autumn Conversation between Allen Grossman and Daniel Morris on the Question of Another Logic

We began with a poem by James Wright before us, and with the essays in *The Long Schoolroom* in mind. I had just read, at Daniel's suggestion, the published letters exchanged between Leslie Marmon Silko and James Wright shortly before his death. Here is the Wright poem we were talking about:

The Language of the Present Moment

Off the shore of Gargnano the mountains in this
summer mist look barren. Tall and short mountains stand
still beside me as I drift past on Lake Garda. They throw
their own flowers on the water. It is warmer than the
oldest olive.

A few miles up the lake a town called Limone long ago
gave up hope of surviving. The lemons of Sicily, quicker
and more numerous, banish the town I will see, back to
its own shadow that lies in the Garda water like a garland.

Limone, wreath of the Garda mountains, the stone villa
of Catullus still stands down at the far southern end of
the lake. I hope you are in blossom when his ghost comes
home.

Gargnano

DM Your essay on Allen Ginsberg was first published in 1962, the year I was born. It's strange that in 1995 (in Indiana) we still need to discuss issues you were concerned with three decades ago. Apparently the "problem of writing" is hard, important, and not going away.

AG Well, then, what from your point of view is the problem?

DM From your point of view it's "representation." In James Wright's poetry you see an instance, as you charmlessly put it, of "the bitter logic of representation in the West." By "bitter logic" I believe you mean that the poetry of James Wright is fundamentally a part of an elegaic tradition. Visibility of the person in the poem is contingent upon the loss of some other, more vital, form of personal presence. Endurance beyond death costs precisely the perishable body itself.

In James Wright's elegy for Catullus ["The Language of the Present Moment"] for example, which Leslie Marmon Silko discusses in one of her letters, disciplined representation of the human state of affairs is meant to compensate somehow for a presence that is assumed to be always lost.

AG Is there any other way?—Are you going to claim, Daniel, that the work of Leslie Marmon Silko, which she emphatically does not identify with the culture of the white West, offers an alternative, a nontragic model of "presence"?

DM OK. We are looking at a brilliant, loving exchange of letters between James Wright, poet and student of the novel, and Leslie Marmon Silko, a Native American poet, novelist, and, in her largest work (*Almanac of the Dead*, 1991), a theorist of ethnicity and apocalyptic historian of the West. The Silko and Wright exchange took place between 1978 and Wright's death from cancer in 1980. It was collected and published in 1986 by his second wife, Anne, as *The Delicacy and Strength of Lace.* The book consists of about one hundred pages of letters, some of them profound and, dare I say, beautiful. Silko included her own poetry from time to time, and she also included prose stories that Wright received from her as a kind of gift.

I showed you these letters, Allen, because I want to talk with you about the nature of that gift.

Although James Wright and Leslie Marmon Silko understand what you call "representation" in different ways—and maybe that is a serious matter—nonetheless throughout their correspondence they most certainly do express a common experience of the hardness of life. In any case, a shared sentiment of grief, and a common understanding about how persons get along with one another in the world or do not, and of bodily pain. And also of the value of storytelling and poetry as mediations of interpersonal crises and even the crisis of the death of the body. In this substantial sense "representation" is a help, a benefit. The world is tragic, not the text.

I agree with you that Leslie Marmon Silko has something different and (culturally) new to teach James Wright; but, at the same time, I want to assert that James Wright's openness to difference—part of the logic of his civilization—allowed Leslie Marmon Silko to appear before him as a messenger.

AG Maybe. But the cultural weight, the arguability, and the generalizability of Leslie Marmon Silko's claim to otherness is of particular importance to me. I do not deny that these letters are profoundly loving, and that there is a reciprocal willingness in these two persons to supplement the need each of the other. But my view is that the possibility, for these two artists, of the unmistakeable love that grew up between them was the result— insofar as they perceived one another—of a logical difference, not expressible as common pain or sympathetic reciprocity. The result, in effect, of not understanding one another at all.

As the more powerful of the two, Leslie Marmon Silko, the younger but also the "older" (being a *mestiza,* being of "the first people"), proceeds to contribute this difference and to define it as something that is of cultural significance—a general, abstract, systemic otherness that, I insist, exceeds the importance of the love that was exchanged between them and also expresses it.

When James Wright first addresses Leslie Silko (it is he who initiated the relationship in his letter of August 28, 1978), he appraises her work as high "art." But, in fact, Wright constructs his letter within a trope, not merely of modesty, but of inadequacy—his inability to find the right words for the particular kind of supplement that she has contributed to his experience. He says, any number of times, in reference to Silko's first novel, *Ceremony*, that he cannot say what he *means* about it.

Now what I wish to suggest is that, in fact, *he cannot say what he means* about it.

Notice that when Silko replies to this fan letter, in September of the same year, she insists that what attracts her to him is "some sheer tenacity" in his poems, no "frills of 'style.' " She insists also that she feels very profoundly like an outsider. Outsider to what?

Now, in my view, James Wright belongs to a tradition, in which "style" constitutes and refers to successful mimesis of the speech of a singular person. James Wright's great claim as a poet, or the claim that a critic must make on his behalf, is the brilliance with which he does two things. The first is to produce the effect of the presence of a person speaking with sincerity. The second is to conceal or mystify the constructedness of that effect. In the Western lyric tradition, in which James Wright is a master, great success in the practice of style consists of the construction of the brilliant mimesis of unconstructed personal presence that constitutes style.

Silko's disposition to declare (she does it many ways) that she does not, on her own behalf, perceive or practice style, but perceives and practices (and values) some sheer tenacity of will instead, contradicts, or quite deliberately refuses to refer to, the particular tradition in which Wright is a master, the particular kind of accomplishment for which he is, I think correctly, valued.

DM OK. But let's go back to that very first sentence James Wright addresses to Leslie Silko in that "fan letter" (August 1978) to which you made reference before you started on your usual business about style.

He begins that first letter by saying, "I trust you won't mind hearing from a stranger." I think Wright's assertion of *his own strangeness* is an invitation to Leslie Marmon Silko to feel at ease—an invitation to respond to himself (the elder artist) with confidence. His registration of his own sentiment of estrangement enables her to feel comfortable enough to disclose such elements of her experience as she believes Wright may be able, as a self-described stranger like herself, to acknowledge. An outsider to what she calls the "mainstream poetic style," she seeks to develop an exchange with a stranger from another community who as a stranger could share and, therefore, in Wright's word, "understand" her pain.

In Silko's first letter to Wright, she infers from Wright's poetic practice—that is, from the "no-frills" style she asserts is Wright's *way* in poetry—information about his personal sensibility. Indeed, everywhere in the correspondence, Silko translates literary terms—"no frills of style"—toward descriptions of Wright's personality, his character as a man in the world. By knowing his writing—the "low" tradition of style expressive of his willingness to address an audience outside the academy—she is able to establish her connection to him as a person.

My point, Allen, is this: for both James Wright and Leslie Marmon Silko the *use-function* of poetry and story has to do with how texts translate voice, body, and the personality of the writer into artifacts. And that from Silko's point of view, artifactual appearance (what else is there?) is the residence of personal identity. Her project in this correspondence, her gift to Wright, is a way to articulate his visibility within her Laguna [Navaho] tradition of stories—an alternative narrative reality that exists prior to, and contains within it the personal experiences of, all members of the Laguna people, and maybe somehow all persons. A narrative reality—storytelling—that is not subject to the tragic logics of "Western" lyric discourse.

In the course of the correspondence, Leslie Marmon Silko will situate Wright's story in the living, storytelling tradition of the Laguna people by identifying his spirit with the spirit of her great-grandfather, Robert Marmon, who, I should add, Silko realizes midway through the correspondence, was known to her only artifactually, through photographs and stories told about him by her Aunt Susie.

AG   OK, Dan. But what's in all that?—You are right. My interest in Leslie Marmon Silko's writing does lie in her proposition that what she offers is an account of experience mediated by storytelling, and that storytelling is a kind of representation that incorporates and addresses but does not reproduce a tragic state of affairs.

Leslie Marmon Silko has entered James Wright's life at the

moment before his death. Her strange privilege will be, in fact, to write him a letter designed to console him for the death that both she and he know will be soon, painful, and without alternative. Will that letter be an elegiac story about the predation of one kind of presence upon another, or a story of another kind? And if the latter, can he (or you, or, for that matter, I) make sense of it?

DM Talk about how Leslie Marmon Silko's idea of story is different from the fundamentally tragic "logic of representation" that you attribute to James Wright's lyricism!

AG Let me say something, then, about the "tragic model." In my view, the tragic model depends entirely upon the finitude of alternatives among which we choose when we act, upon the constrained character of the judgments in the making of which the human will can become actual. In a tragic construction of things, the hero, as in Sophocles, has always just two choices, both of which are bad. He must, for example, kill his mother or kill his father! In the same way, the tradition of style stemming from and reproducing this tragic state of affairs, depends entirely upon the constraint of the mind *by the very operation of its impulse toward actualization* to a set of particular and unexchangeable possibilities, all of which produce two things. One is the representation of the person, his actualization in a social and cosmic universe. The second is the death of the person—our common abjection within the scarce economies of representation.

But if there were another way, we could be done with this "bitter logic" business.

DM This tragic model, which I now remember you used to go on about in your lectures, concerns an economy of exchange that compels a kind of zero-sum game. The exchange is unqualified and irreversible: being for meaning, life for lines. I think about Achilleus' terrible choice either to reenter the battlefield and die or not to do so and cease to be Achilleus. Or in the *Gospels,* Jesus' exchange of the sensuality of being—the body bathed in oil—for existence of another kind. This exchange is what you refer to as the tragic model of representation, and it is the exchange that I think Silko does offer Wright a way to defer.

AG Sometimes she speaks of it rather formally (does she not?) as a difference of fundamental or originary story (which may be precisely what ethnicity means). From the point of view of the other originary place of standing and honoring that ethnic story affords, she attempts to supply an alternative account of what it might be like to live in human scale. One of the peculiar characteristics of the tragic model is that it *repudiates human scale for the purpose of recovering it by sacrificial means.* But Leslie Marmon Silko proposes to us that there is an account of storytelling that produces life directly (no mediate sacrificial exchange) in the scale in which it is lived. Thus she speaks directly to a fundamental *scandal* in the Western modeling of possible accounts.

DM I agree that she represents persons in her life in a way that doesn't distort their actual social form. She also does not discriminate when deciding who or what is worthy of representation (or for that matter of love). But I'm also thinking about how Silko imagines the next world in the Laguna tradition—as "Cliff House." When she talks about her ancient legend-laden Aunt Susie, the storyteller who is 106 years old, going over to Cliff House, the place of the dead, it is as if Aunt Susie is just traveling to another town down the way, another pueblo, in Arizona or New Mexico. Blurring of the line between the living Laguna Pueblo community and the place of the dead, Cliff House, speaks to a sense of no-difference, or a difference that is equivocal, blurred, or hazy, between life and death. No bright *eschatological* line.

The consolatory story Silko tells Wright toward the end of the correspondence (when she knows he is dying), about the indestructible Hugh Crooks, concerns a character who endures against all odds in a way that nonetheless maintains, somehow, his presence as actual life, even though his survivability as story is unaccountable from the Western point of view—because Hugh Crooks, as you say, *makes no choices, and is therefore not really actual.*

AG There is in this view no eschaton, then, no demarcation of absolute difference and as a result no economy of scarcity. And this assertion is repeated on many different sites of discourse in Leslie Marmon Silko's account of language. She is, for example, quite clear that whatever "story" may consist of, it does not consist of the words themselves. What I am calling "style," by contrast, is dependent upon the unexchangeability of the particular words that characterize the material specificity of the particular body by registering the resistance of its materials to the intentional will, and in doing so contribute the effect of actuality to the voice of a specific speaker. And it's that unexchangeability that produces the mark of character; and it is that mark of character that is also the mark of the death.

In other words, Leslie Marmon Silko proposes to write an infinitely translatable discourse, for the viability of which she has evidence. Her people, having addressed the world first in their indigenous language, and then in Spanish, and subsequently in English, without ceasing to be a people with powers, exemplifies the superior survivability of a discourse that is infinitely commutable or that in any case baffles the very premise of translation: the unexchangeability of marks.

DM Let's stay on the theme of translation for awhile, because Silko's notion of translation is something that is very curious to me. I also believe you have something very different in mind than I do when you talk about how aspects of *representational technique* are related to questions of the translatability of experience.

Leslie Marmon Silko perceives storytelling in this correspondence and in the lecture she gave to the English Institute at Harvard in 1979 as a third space, a third topos, different from a natural setting and its discourse of ordinary being. But also not a theological space. Certainly not a discourse concerned with eschatological mysteries unrelated to what happens here and now. For Silko, narrative space is as I have said to you the residence of persons. Narrative for her is, however, not merely the space of display for (paradigmatic) aristocratic figures as in Shakespeare and Homer. Stories are a place for the residence of all persons in a community.

Further, the storyteller's task in our time, as Silko understands it, seems to be precisely a technical exploit: the bringing of the practice of story effectively to life in new cultural contexts that require new forms of mediation such as film that offer new possibilities of audience. Silko does not view specific storytelling forms, such as the Laguna *oral* tradition, as sacred. She does, however, conceive of their ultimate use-function (the preservation of the story of the person in community) as residing without alternative in *the maintenance of storytelling as an idealist abstraction*. She perceives herself as a narrative technician who bridges the experience of more than one interpretive community by devising ways to share stories across cultural boundaries through new media forms.

Language in the sense of an unexchangeable set of terms, a fixed text, was indeed beside the point.

AG   OK. But there is also, Daniel, a sense in which life is degraded by the storytelling of which she speaks.

From her point of view, the business of the poet (not precisely a shaman but the master of the words that compose the world) is to *gather in* the separated individual who continuously threatens to fall out of the intelligibility of the universe (identical with the forms of life of the community) into an abyss of storylessness or more precisely nonnarratability. The recognition mediated by the storyteller, whereby persons are gathered into story and thus rescued from the social death of nonnarratability, consists of discovery that the life lived by the singular individual is not a singular life, but is rather already written in the narratives of the People or, more generally, in valid existing stories about persons.

Even Leslie Marmon Silko's disreputable rooster, of which she writes in her letters and which she so deeply loves, becomes valid for her only when, in fact, she remembers that there was another prior rooster and that there are stories about Rooster and that what is occurring in the world around her is an intelligible *repetition,* an intelligibility made possible by repetition. That is, made possible by the fact that experience is seen to be a repetition of narratives about experience that are the common possession of everyone.

Now, I want to stress the likely entailment of all that: Tragedy is to be overcome by a communalization of mind. But that is a death indeed. A death of the individual as the individual. In compensation of which death, the self (considered as infinitely commutable) is gathered up and consoled by the rediscovery of the sameness of its experience with experience as it is already written. Thus, in fact, Leslie Marmon Silko's third-order account of things, alien, strange, perhaps racialized, in any case fundamentally alternative, also involves a profound *but a non-tragic* catastrophe inside it. It is, any way, what the West so deeply fears. And it is this catastrophe that Leslie Marmon Silko narrates in her vast novelization of the end of the white world in *Almanac of the Dead.*

DM In other words, Silko's storytelling supplement (as you want me to understand it) will erase the identity figured as value and truth in James Wright's kind of writing. Talk to me, Allen, about your sense of poetry as a quasi-religious discourse, but also as a fundamentally different kind of discourse than theological discourse. I want to know whether the difference between poetry and sacred discourse is related to poetry's resistance to that absolute at-one-ment that is the catastrophe Silko is attempting, in your account, to draw us toward.

AG From my point of view, Leslie Marmon Silko represents a practice in fact closer to the traditional contribution of poetry in this civilization, by contrast to religion, than does James Wright. James Wright is fundamentally a religious writer, and Leslie Marmon Silko is fundamentally a poetic writer in the Western sense. Wright depends upon transformation, upon bursting into bloom. His happiness seems to be the result of the nonregistration of violence. His peculiar way of dealing with his life, allowing it to bleed into poetic discourse, seems to me an unearned neutralization of the dialectical cost of his practice of representation.

But let me say something about Leslie Marmon Silko as the poet of the two. In my view, the Judeo-Christian-Islamic religious tradition specifies the highest value of the person as absolute value, which becomes possible to write or realize only as a consequence of the (religious) maintenance of nonnegotiable difference between divinity and divinity's creation. By contrast, in what I am calling Silko's (poetic) point of view, our humanity consists of an *endlessly negotiable* relationship, not to marks of difference, but in context of the fundamental similarity, the seamless continuity, not only of all persons but of persons and the world. For, in her sense of things, mind runs all through world, and her preferred Navajo creation stories are about continuity between mind and world.

My view is that poetry is always the Other of religion. Poetry always insists upon a multifariousness of positions, and accordingly upon the endless unfolding and reconstruction of its objects. Poetry's blessing to humanity consists, not in its indetermination, but in its continuous, abundant building-over-again of the always determinate human position such that after one valid poem the only true thing is the next one.

James Wright speaks of Leslie Marmon Silko as "abundant"; and that seems to me an intuition of precisely what ensues when her account of the self, this continuing negotiation between the individual and the collective in which the individual becomes valid and the collective is intact, is projected hypothetically as a world. Logically, "abundance" must ensue.

But whether this is the implication of Leslie Marmon Silko's project or any *actual* poetic project may be seriously doubted. Lets look at one poem by Leslie Marmon Silko. My interest in these matters does not, after all, lie in the question whether there is a theoretical way out of representation, but in whether there is another valid account of representation.

DM   Can I ask you one more question about this and then we will move on. A little while ago, I used the term speech-act and you said that there needed to be social conditions, a context, in which the speech-act can be valid. "Act" requires "world."

In our conversations, you have talked about different notions of translation than what might ordinarily be thought of as translation. You are, I see, sensitive to Silko's understanding of translation. One type of translation she works at is, as I have pointed out, the attempt to turn Laguna stories into film. She discusses with Wright the idea of using film to create a context for her stories, to create a visual account of the landscape in which they come to pass, so these stories could be realized by an audience larger than and different from those who could have gathered around Aunt Susie's storytelling circle. Do you see her purpose, in translating Laguna traditional stories to film as the construction of a context (the "felicity conditions" in Austin's language) for the speech-act, the effective saying which characterizes the difference of her project?

AG I do. But I doubt it can be done that way. In addition, I don't think translation is the appropriate word here. She wishes to supplement the discourse of language by the discourse of image, for the purpose of supplying a universally accessible context. Her continuously avowed need of a supplement speaks to an anxiety that the fundamental truth of her writing depends upon a shared world which is lost.

Wright continuously distinguishes Silko's way with language from literary language. The workability of nonliterary language, including shamanic language, depends upon precisely those conditions not verbal that make "language" effective. Language without responsibility to world becomes ipso facto literary, "aesthetic" in the privative sense. So that the result, which Leslie Marmon Silko most profoundly ought to fear, namely acceptance of her language and loss or refusal of its context, ensues. That is precisely the museological destiny of "other" culture as mere artifact she represents as desperately wrong in *The Almanac*. But that slide into the literary does in fact occur and constitutes, paradoxically, the principal disseminative effectiveness of her work.

Let's look at the poem:

Skeleton Fixer's Story

What happened here?
she asked
Some kind of accident?
Words like bones.
Scattered all over the place . . .

Old Badger Man traveled
from place to place
searching for skeleton bones.
There was something
only he could do with them.

On the smooth sand
Old Badger Man started laying out the bones.
It was a great puzzle for him.
He started with the toes.
He loved their curve
like a new moon,
like a white whisker hair.

Without thinking
he knew their direction,
laying each toe bone
to walk east.

"I know,
it must have been this way.
Yes,"
he talked to himself while he worked.

He strung the spine bones
as beautiful as any shell necklace.

The leg bones were running
so fast
dust from the ankle joints
surrounded the wind.

"Oh poor dear one who left your bones here
I wonder who you are?"
Old Skeleton Fixer spoke to the bones
because things don't die—
they fall to pieces maybe,
get scattered or separate,
but Old Badger Man can tell
how they once fit together.

Though he didn't recognize the bones
he could not stop;
he loved them anyway.

He took great care with the ribs
marveling at the structure
which had contained the lungs and heart.
Skeleton Fixer had never heard of
such things as souls.
He was certain
only of bones.

But where a heart once beat
there was only sand
"Oh I will find you one—
somewhere around here!"

And a yellow butterfly
flew up from the grass at his feet.

"Ah I know how your breath left you—
like butterflies over an edge,
not falling but fluttering
their wings rainbow colors.
Wherever they are
your heart will be."

He worked all day
He was so careful with this one—
it felt like the most special of all.
Old Badger Man didn't stop
until the last spine bone
was arranged at the base of the tail.

"A'moo'ooh, my dear one
these words are your bones,"
he repeated this
four times

    "pa pa pa pa!
    pa pa pa pa!
    pa pa pa pa!
    pa pa pa pa!"

Old Coyote Woman jumped up
and took off running.
She never even said "thanks."

Skeleton Fixer
shook his head slowly.

"It is surprising sometimes,"
he said,
"how these things turn out."

But he never has stopped fixing
the poor scattered bones he finds.

DM   You said that Silko overcomes what you call "style" in her
writing. In this poem Silko questions or maybe even reimagines
authorship itself as different from the idea of original composi-

tion. In *The Delicacy and Strength of Lace,* a note tells readers that "Skeleton Fixer's Story" is actually from a version told by Simon J. Ortiz. So right away we must put an asterisk beside the idea of it being "Silko's poem." We must think about it as something other than Silko's poem, something that is more like a translation, something that is a composition by authors both named and unnamed. No "style."

This poem and another one are contained within the packet that Silko sent to Wright as part of her second letter. Both poems are narratives concerned with the reparation or the reconstruction of the destroyed human image. Both poems suggest that this recovery of the human figure is in part the work of a shamanic figure who is like a poet in some ways but also unlike a poet in ways that we've already specified. In the "Skeleton Fixer" poem the shamanic figure, a worker with words, performs ceremonies with a special linguistic knowledge. His knowledge is a kind of anthropogenetic structuring power designed to revive and literally put back together again dead matter, bones that have been "scattered all over the place." The shaman figure who performs his work through storytelling, the "Old Badger Man," cares for the disarticulated skeleton of the human body in a way that resuscitates the dead bones, makes them live once again.

AG   Well enough. But what is the *real* in Silko? The person is made out of language. Language is not the speech of an individual but the general possession of many. We learn from Silko's preferred account of how the world was made that it was *thought,* from Thought Woman, that produced it. There seems no real, no fundamental bottom to this apparitional world. *All* is words or, dare I suggest, all is representation. The peculiar third orderness, the Otherness of representation in Silko, does not derive from the notion that representation is a trivial relationship to an overwhelmingly apparent reality, but rather that representation and its bitter logic is simply all there is. And that, therefore, when allowed to be all there is, and when centered in consciousness, without any competing claims from a *real* of another sort, becomes itself something else. Is it her meaning that representation changes its character when there is no competition with a real that has an ontology independent of language?

DM Yes, I think that's really to the point. And I think it's why Silko does consistently reinscribe Wright's poetry as a living embodiment of the character of Wright himself. I mean, the way she speaks about his lyrics as possessing "guts and heart." Here in this poem, there's even a kind of rhyme with her statement that his poetry registers his "true guts and heart." In the poem it says the Skeleton Fixer "took great care with the ribs / marveling at the structure / which had contained the lungs and heart." Throughout the correspondence, Silko reads Wright's poetry as the embodiment of his true visibility, his true meaning. For her, representation and textual knowledge of other persons is (as I have already suggested) the only meaningful residence of persons. And I think that her fundamental instruction to Wright, as he faces the death of his body, is to renew his vision of himself as a thoroughly textualized presence.

AG Now, the question of shamanic reenactment is one that your own account, in these conversations, has raised. Let me just call attention to the obvious fact that working with bones is a shamanic technique of divination. But here bones are to be understood as words. Bones are a similitude by which the nature of words is understood.

So this is divination with words rather than divination with bones. And this divination with words seems a reconstruction of the notion of divination consistent with Leslie Marmon Silko's sense of the world, her skeptical ontology, which declares that the recognizability of the human image depends upon the management of words, that the countenance is very much like a veracious story. And the act of divination, the act of language, is not a form of shamanic divination. The case is in fact the reverse: it is just simply that scenes of shamanic divination are a way of talking about the sovereign power that has been transferred to or that has been arrogated to—in any case, conferred residually upon—words in the constructed domain that she calls her world.

DM The Skeleton Fixer's ability to revive the woman in the poem seems to be related to a prior story of transformation that Silko would have known about through her aunt's storytelling. The Old Badger Man's construction of persons out of words is enabled by his knowledge of a reservoir of stories in which there is a transformation of loss into, in this case, a metamorphic beauty.

AG Note that what is built here by this quasi-shamanic working with bones is the restored body of the personified principle or muse of Silko's story-poems in general. A'moo'ooh is a name for Aunt Susie. She is the person whom we see named by the Skeleton Fixer as brought back to life in the form of the words of which she was the master.

She is the Old Coyote Woman. What do you make, Daniel, of the fact that the Old Coyote Woman, having been reconstituted by the Badger Man's skill with language, jumps up, runs away, *and never says thanks?*

DM I think it's a wonderful moment in the poem. It is a comic moment, both plain funny and also nontragic. I think Skeleton Fixer's response of shaking his head slowly in bewilderment, certainly not in anger or remorse, speaks to the humor in the poem. But the end of the poem suggests, also, *the possibility of representation without the need for possession of the world.* No thanks offered and none required.

AG I completely agree. Gestures of gratitude or avowals of obligation are entirely irrelevant here. The Skeleton Fixer is the story process that continuously reconstructs the human form of the old woman, A'moo'ooh, who is the principle of story. Story is scarcely a reciprocal act at all. The story process that is the world process, insofar as the world process is human, is exhibited as maintaining humanity without need of subjective reciprocity.

It is in that region, it seems to me, that there is a fundamental novelty consistent with Leslie Marmon Silko's management of her relationship to James Wright.

DM How, then, do you account for Old Badger's Man's impulse to make these structures at all? The poem ends with a suggestion that the old man's project is an ongoing process. He has never stopped fixing the poor scattered bones, or words, he finds. His act is described earlier in the poem as intuitive, and almost compulsive: "Without thinking / he knew their direction," and "Though he did not recognize the bones / he could not stop; / he loved them anyway." So there's a kind of affection for the act of working with language in a way that will benefit other persons without his recognizing in himself any source of his peculiar affection for those he is helping. He is "so careful with this one," and he sees *this* one as particularly "special," and yet he doesn't say why. There is the impulse to continue to make visible constructions of persons without even understanding what impelled the action or being able to recognize its reason.

AG Some part of the depth of Silko's way of writing lies in her intuition of the relentless and inherently justified self-insistence of the life-process. In this poem, one finds it exhibited as a benign state of affairs. Comedy seems to be here a way of indexing that benignity. This is not a comedy that refuses the human image. It's one that invites it. Nor is it a comedy that insists upon subjectivity; it allows subjectivity but it does not, by any means, assert its primacy.

It is characteristic of Leslie Marmon Silko's earlier work, already darkly qualified in such early stories as "The Storyteller," that the life-process, often figured as genital sexuality, is benign. It can never be guilty because it has no personal identity. But it can never be innocent, because innocence too is a predicate of identity—identity being moral because individual, and therefore committed to choice and susceptible of judgment. In the *Almanac,* the "relentless process of world maintenance" communicates directly to the imagination of desolation, the wars at the end of time. . . .

So there's some urgency for us to settle the question with which we began, namely whether we are here reading two different accounts of the world: on the one hand, a fundamentally atavistic one, that is to say, Wright's—characterized by his mystified lyric-elegiac sublimation of what is fundamentally a tragic text; and, on the other, Silko's alternative sense of the world, not tragic, not elegaic, but associated with story that knows neither of those categories. Or just one account, in which case it must be the tragic—the only *possible* way.

Does Wright read Silko correctly?

DM Well, Wright sees these impersonal and communal "translations"—Silko's stories—as messages that contain information in a displaced form about the authorial Silko's own experience. He also relates her poems to his own personal life. However impersonal the poems may be in fact, Wright tries to connect them to his sense of crises in Silko's personal and private life, such as her divorce, a custody struggle, etc. He believes she is attempting to recuperate losses through the poetry. And that she wants to share, and in this way to console, these losses by communicating her struggle to Wright through the stories, poems and, more generally, the correspondence as a whole.

AG Surely, that's Wright's misreading of Silko's poetry. In fact, it seems to me to be a misreading of poetry in general.

DM But would you not say, Allen, that from Wright's point of view or in fact your own, there are aspects of personal experience that really are also illustrations of general human states of affairs? And that this is a generic effect of poetic language? I think that the issue of divorce is of primary concern for both Silko and Wright because each of them places such faith in the efficacy of speech. Divorce is a disavowal of a prior contractual speech-act. And the breach of such a contract suggests an inadequacy of language to the reality of relationship between persons.

AG. Yes indeed. In fact, the writing of Leslie Marmon Silko, as a whole, is constructed to revise the civil notion of contract or vow. Her central interest—from "The Storyteller" to the *Almanac of the Dead*—is the bringing to mind of the difference between the earth-referenced, communal, native sense of what might constitute a contract, and, by contrast, the Western colonial notion of contract, which specifies the individual as an unexchangeable term. This purpose Wright does not see, except as a supplement, an "abundance" that he does not understand.

DM However, it strikes me that the notion of "the individual as an unexchangeable center" is not precisely the basis for Wright's identity in relationship to Silko. There is to my mind a difference between the private disclosures about divorce that do feel individuated according to the Western rule of contract that you're describing, and a more fluid sense in Wright of valid sentiment that both authors suggest is transpersonal and "translatable" across widely diverse subject positions.

Remember that Silko's assertion of Wright's "gentleness" provides the link between him and a founding member of her own family. Registering Wright's actual temperament becomes a way for Silko to inscribe Wright in the Laguna story tradition. Discovering shared aspects of feeling, rather than negotiating individuated domains in a contractual sense, allows Silko to lift Wright's significance out of the fatal quotidian of mere accident and enter it into an undying story tradition.

AG   In the November 1 letter, Leslie Marmon Silko declares that she wishes she knew Plato better. Plato, she thinks, understands central value-bearing reality as nonidentical with any particular manifestation (the latter being the stock-in-trade of Western legality). On the contrary, "the idea or memory or feeling [of the destructable facts of the world] . . . is more powerful and important than any damage or destruction humans may commit upon them." In this matter, we see Leslie Marmon Silko rereading the Western tradition in such a way as to declare—and we discussed this at the beginning of our conversations—that whatever the truth of language may be, it does not lie in its specifying codes. That is to say, truth (and also property) lies in a general domain not diacritically marked, either by the style of an individual person, or by the characteristics of an individual language.

DM   The issue of recuperating identity, sociality, and territory on the level of spirit, or feeling for a place, by contrast to ownership of it, is especially pressing for a writer such as Silko, who is representing the experience of a community of persons who have been for centuries removed from their land and their sacred places by the United States government. The story that precipitates Silko's discussion of Plato concerns an Army Corps of Engineers that has flooded a sacred Indian shrine in order to build a dam. That's the specific historical context that compels the Laguna storyteller to replace the scarce material reality of homeland with, as she says, ideas or memories or feelings about a place. What you, Allen, would call an economy of infinite resource.

AG But, in this matter, Leslie Silko is profoundly conflicted. The dam that drowns the sacred places of her people, the dam of the Colorado River, she dismisses in the November 1 letter by the simple immaterialist consideration that whatever the particular earth may be, which is invested with significance by her people or by any people, the significance thus invested in the earth is independent of the earth. By contrast, however, in the *Almanac of the Dead,* there is an extensive exposition exonerative of the "necessary" catastrophes whereby that very same dam in the Colorado must be destroyed so that the river can be restored to its initial and particular material condition.

Likewise, there are, in Silko, two contradictory senses of time. One is apocalyptic, and therefore, in your language, "diachronic," that is to say it flows in a single direction from an earlier to a later state and has the characteristic of a fatal arrow that flies in only one direction. In this diachronic time, catastrophe if not tragedy is in the end inevitable. By contrast, there is what you call "synchronic" time, that is to say, the all-at-onceness of things, *in which the whole rationality of the West is literally exploded.* Her reluctance—I call it reluctance and therefore voluntary because I think she's powerful enough to do whatever she wants in fiction—to resolve this contradictoriness is striking.

DM On January 3, 1980, Leslie Marmon Silko responds to news in a Wright letter dated December 18. In that letter he says, "I have some bad news about myself." The news is his cancer. In response Leslie Marmon Silko tells James Wright the story of a man named Hugh Crooks . . .

AG And she introduces that story with the following words:— Wright has said that whatever happens he is going to lose the function of his voice, and she replies consistent with the logic of her account of representation: "You will manage the part about your voice because voice never was sound alone." This, of course, returns us with consolatory recognition to our initial consideration of Silko's difference in the matter of language. It makes me realize with shocking immediacy why it is important and loving to assert that translatability is infinite. Why it might be good that style be defeated and the tragic vividness that style gives rise to by its assertion of unexchangeable individuality be overcome.

She goes on, "Which doesn't mean that you won't feel angry sometimes—Grandpa did, but then he learned his own new language." Now, as I hope I've made clear, I'm fundamentally interested, Daniel, in what this third-order culture might contain, in what can be uttered in this "own new language." And that is figured in the person of Hugh Crooks.

Hugh Crooks is said to have come to Laguna in the 1920s, from "somewhere," but it is not clear where, either the East or the Middle West. And I think his indefiniteness of origin has something to do with the strange qualified mystery of Hugh Crooks. But what is the mystery of Hugh Crooks?

DM   Well, he's mostly unremarkable from the point of view of conventional Western notions of heroism and representational significance. He's also not a remarkable man in any of the ways that are often valued in mainstream American society. He didn't have much money, he never did great things in the world of business, politics, or culture. He never even married. There was a kind of indistinguishability about him that I associate with Whitman's poetics.

Crooks was more or less indistinguishable from everyone else except for one thing. A man who never engaged in heroic acts, his primary distinction was that he seemed to have an ability to survive unsurvivable personal accidents. He might be called a man who kept falling down and who kept being able to get up, to the great bewilderment of everyone who knew him. He survived a car wreck. He survived terrible illnesses. He even got shot in a bar that he owned during a robbery. And nothing, including being shot with a thirty-eight in the chest, was able to finally kill Hugh Crooks. So he's the man who won't die, and his recognizability, his memorability, is related to the fact that he is someone who can't enter, or leave, the world of visibility.

AG   So Hugh Crooks is nontragic, and he's antiheroic—heros, tragic or otherwise, must die—and he's also, as is clear, not heterosexual. In context of this argument we are having about the implications of diacriticality, heterosexuality is the love of difference and, therefore, the continuous rewriting by desire of difference. Hugh Crooks's unmarked destiny, unmarked even by death, precludes logically his ever marrying. It is love of the same that marks Hugh Crooks most distinctly from the others and indeed makes impossible for him that continual reconstruction by desire of difference which marriage and divorce specifies, as well as style, as well as colonialism, as well as (one might add) the racialist motive to repress difference.

For if there is no difference, there must be then an antiheroic world—a world in which the commodity of identity is not scarce because it is not claimed. There must be also a world in which difference-based linguisticity is not the site of meaning.

It's amazing what happened to Hugh Crooks, right? He survives TB, he survives a car wreck, he survives a shooting in the chest, he survives cancer, and *at the telling of the tale he's still alive.* Hugh Crooks is almost eighty now; that is to say, he is living, from a human point of view, beyond all of those who are better and more distinctly marked, indeed beyond all. He may be as old as the world.

The figure of Hugh Crooks is archetypal. Hugh Crooks belongs to a literature older and other than the gentile and also the Christian literature of the West. And that literature which is older than heroic literature is a folk literature. The early versions, for example, of the Gilgamesh epic do not contain the city-generated metropolitan sense of subjective difference that, finally, is narrated in the West as an Achillean sort of heroism, the heroism that requires death in order to produce significance. In effect, Hugh Crooks is a man without significance, and therefore without also a death—timeless, inconsequential.

From your point of view, how are we going to understand this story? Is it not that in the moment when Leslie Marmon Silko's good will is most necessary to her friend, she summons storytelling; and it gives her its gift, which she can give again, the right gift, to her friend?

DM Well, Hugh Crooks is one of many ordinary, undifferentiated, unheroic, characters who are made knowable to others in Silko's work only as they become a part of the repertoire of living stories that belongs to the Laguna community. Like the ornery rooster, like great-grandfather Marmon, like Aunt Susie, and like James Wright, Crooks has entered into the heart, into the imagination, into the memory, and, therefore, into the storytelling tradition of Leslie Marmon Silko.

AG One of the benefits that she seems to derive and that moved me deeply and that seals my sense of the deep love between herself and James Wright is the conviction that we see in many different forms throughout her prose writing that there is an omnipotence of thought, not the foolish and destructive omnipotence of thought that Freud refers to, but a sense of thought as powerfully human in a way that is not destructible as bodies are destructible. She sends a last letter, as you know, to James Wright, one that he could not have read because he died before it was received, or, in fact, on the same day that it was written, March 24, 1980.

In this letter, she speaks of messages that are not written messages. They are messages that express her love in a fashion that is fundamental to her love, rather than digressive from it, as the written message must be. And she enjoins James Wright to trust the messages that move between them, which are, in effect, not written messages, but messages in the *substance* of love, messages, as she puts it,"of the heart."

Toward the end, but by no means at the end, of this last letter that she sends to her friend, who will never receive it, she speaks of the place where she is, and speaks about place as if it were a place in which linear temporality did not exist, a place where "there never has been a time when you and I were not together" (105). She goes on to say, "I cannot explain this. Maybe it is the continuing or on-going of the telling, the telling in poetry and stories." In this last unreceivable letter, she is rereading Wright as one who is a storyteller, a storyteller who becomes identical with the very process of storytelling and, as in "Skeleton Fixer," its theme.

She goes on in the same letter to make reference to a great owl that she's seen, that has landed on a tall saguaro cactus close to her and to the people among whom she lives. This owl is virtually indistinguishable from the world in which it dwells, and her sense of it is so large that it was like largest things. It appears to be a figuration of death, a powerful sense of the savage, that feeds upon animals, that feeds also upon persons. This owl seems to me a profoundly alien presence whose meaning is precisely the otherness we are in search of.

It is not the owl of wisdom, it is the predatory owl. It is, as it were, *death in itself*. Not a symbol that repudiates corporeal fact, but the one signifier that is continuous with fact and includes it.

DM After the passage about the owl, Silko shifts back toward an understanding of writing as loss-based. It is as if she presses against the limits of her own hopes. Perhaps this is the chilling message that she learns from Wright's style. She says, "It is so overwhelming to see your writing on the postcard and to feel how much I miss your letters. There is no getting around this present time and place even when I feel you and I share this other present time and place" (105).

AG. What I've learned is that radical or alternative accounts of the world *never quite appear* (as the great owl never quite appears) because they *cannot* appear, except as articulations from the state of affairs that is at hand and is of the same nature. And that Silko's nonmystical confidence in the force, perhaps unregulatable, of earth-referenced, woman-referenced, and sentiment-referenced counterrealities to the realities that centralize style, patriarchy, masculinity and writing nonetheless draws her back into the doubleness of one who is born into a world in which she must produce her sense of things, her meaning, *as manifest in the one world,* even though that meaning is pitted chaotically against the same world.

Hence, this breaking of actuality in the interest of its reconstruction, in the interest of the already written story, is the theme of the *Almanac of the Dead.* But *Almanac of the Dead* is a parody of a story always known in the west as "the wars before the end of time." In Leslie Marmon Silko's hands such a story can truthfully only display the bitter logic of a world that is finally only manifest, always in time, subject to scarcity, abject to possession, and open to all who are incapable of illusion, capable therefore of the violent transgression of conscious life.

Such is the logic of the poetic principle. Nothing new.

UNDER DISCUSSION
David Lehman, General Editor
Donald Hall, Founding Editor

Volumes in the Under Discussion series collect reviews and essays about individual poets. The series is concerned with contemporary American and English poets about whom the consensus has not yet been formed and the final vote has not been taken. Titles in the series include:

Charles Simic
  edited by Bruce Weigl
On Gwendolyn Brooks
  edited by Stephen Caldwell Wright
On William Stafford
  edited by Tom Andrews
Denise Levertov
  edited with an Introduction by Albert Gelpi
The Poetry of W. D. Snodgrass
  edited by Stephen Haven
On the Poetry of Philip Levine
  edited by Christopher Buckley
Frank O'Hara
  edited by Jim Elledge
James Wright
  edited by Peter Stitt and Frank Graziano
Anne Sexton
  edited by Steven E. Colburn
On Louis Simpson
  edited by Hank Lazer
On the Poetry of Galway Kinnell
  edited by Howard Nelson
Robert Creeley's Life and Work
  edited by John Wilson
Robert Bly: When Sleepers Awake
  edited by Joyce Peseroff
On the Poetry of Allen Ginsberg
  edited by Lewis Hyde
Reading Adrienne Rich
  edited by Jane Roberta Cooper
Richard Wilbur's Creation
  edited and with an Introduction by Wendy Salinger
Elizabeth Bishop and Her Art
  edited by Lloyd Schwartz and Sybil P. Estess